the Mariner's Catalog

Volume 6

Edited by
George Putz
and
Peter Spectre

Bosun and friend by Darrell McClure

International Marine
Publishing Company

PREFACE

Almost always, prefaces are the last items to be written for a book. But when we saw this fine little essay (or should it rather be called a witness?), we knew that we had our preface long before the book neared completion. It first appeared as an editorial in the August 1962 issue of *Woodworker* magazine, and was reprinted in the October 1976 issue of that same publication, published by Model and Allied Publications of Hemel Hempstead, Herts., England. (It is reprinted here courtesy of Model and Allied Publications through the good offices of Polly Curds, assistant editor of *Woodworker*.) Though the essay speaks of cabinetry and furniture making, no manifest or would-be boatbuilder will have the slightest difficulty understanding this message to the very soul.

George Putz
Peter H. Spectre

It seems likely that we are entering upon a new era of craftsmanship, which may develop into something equally as fine as any of the great ages of the past. But this one will be confined to the craftsmanship of the home, which is becoming one of the features of our time. This of itself is an age-old thing, based upon the need of men to provide with the skill of their own hands first the primitive necessities, later the more comfortable amenities of rural homes. Industrialisation and the growth of towns changed all that, but now in the rapid developments of modern times the need is once more being felt for a new, domesticated craftsmanship, which bids fair to take the place of a popular art.

The visual arts of painting and sculpture as they exist today have few or no links with the lives of ordinary men and women. One gets the sense of a loss of direction, a bewilderment and confusion caused by the rapid changes in thought and development which artists are struggling to express in a way which breaks with all reality. The crafts, on the other hand, are tied to reality, particularly such crafts as woodwork, pottery and metalwork, which are linked with the home. To make a chair to a design so impractical that we prefer to sit on the floor rather than use it would soon get us longing for the functional. But if this means furniture looking too severely utilitarian, we are again set longing for something kinder in appearance. We want elements of decoration, in short, we want beauty in our surroundings. And it is by striving to produce such beauty that the home craftsman will gradually increase his skill until his craft becomes an art.

The start is so often almost an accident, the complete amateur thinking one day: "I believe I could do that," and

starting rather hesitantly to work on a simple fitment; or a trade carpenter, ripping his way expertly through a piece of timber, thinking not for the first time how much more interesting it would be to do some finer work and that one day he'd like to get going on a really nice sideboard for the wife.

The trouble is that these fleeting thoughts so often lead nowhere. Most of us are subject to them at intervals throughout our lives, the things we would like to do and don't really ever expect to do, because one life would not be sufficient to hold them all. But there are just a few which recur in a nagging, persistent kind of way, among them the urge to try our skill on something creative. We would like to be able to make things and can imagine the kind of satisfaction it would bring, but the small nagging voice is easily suppressed.

Then one day something jerks us into action and we make some kind of start. The result can be surprising. It had been such such a still, small voice, nothing to warn us that here was a hidden urge of our nature clamouring for an outlet. It had not, in fact, clamoured at all. But once released, it becomes the strong voice of pent-up longing seeking fulfilment. It could easily have been missed altogether and very nearly was, but now, with a marvellous release of energy and satisfaction, it brings new riches, new colour, into our lives.

This kind of experience brings with it the desire to make something really good, an ambition to produce really fine work. At one time, for men who lacked the day-to-day training of the cabinet maker's workshop, it might have been difficult to keep the flame of enthusiasm alight. But today we are much more mobile, especially at holiday time, and going about the country, there are often opportunities for seeing the work of first-class craftsmen displayed in their proper setting, of forming shrewd, observant judgments and gathering a host of new ideas.

Some of the furniture items may be displayed, large-scale, in rich, large-scale surroundings, but any which especially attract us may be broken down mentally to the elements in their design and so simplified and with suitable proportions be adapted to our own needs, bringing the freshness of a new-old beauty into a modern setting. Even to become acquainted with the best work is stimulating. One cannot then be easily satisfied with one's own.

There are occasions, when preparing to start on a new and ambitious piece of work, one's heart can sometimes fail one. Not perhaps because of any doubts of skill, which may already be proven, but just because we are able to foresee the long weeks, perhaps months of work entailed, as one stage unfolds after another, each needing careful, patient handling. It will be a long time before we come to the final stages, when our beautiful piece will begin to beam upon the eye and we can look forward to every moment of bringing it to its finished perfection.

But if such a dismal mood occurs, we are forgetting all the small hidden things which star the path of every good craftsman: the moments of intense pleasure when the work is going well and, even more, the moment when a difficult problem has been solved and we can murmur: "That's it," as the obstinate piece slips easily into place.

THAT IS PURE JOY.

CONTENTS

THE COVER

The art for the cover was painted by Darrell McClure, marine artist, of Talmage, California. Readers of *Yachting* magazine back in the 1950s and of the Sunday funnies during the same era probably remember his fine boating cartoons and his syndicated comic strip, "Little Annie Rooney." We're proud to put his painting on the cover of our book. We also offer him our thanks for once again allowing us to reprint a few of his cartoons here and there as appropriate.

THE BOOKS

Many of the titles reviewed in this Catalog are published or distributed by International Marine Publishing Company, 21 Elm Street, Camden, Maine 04843. IM's booklist is revised monthly and contains hundreds of marine books and prints. It's yours free for the asking.

LEST WE FORGET

You can tell by the cover that this is the sixth volume of *The Mariner's Catalog.* Since we go out of our way to avoid repeating ourselves—primarily to keep a sane outlook on our subject—there are books, items, services, and other sources discussed in past volumes that are not discussed again. And among all of those reviews and references are some mighty fine things. For instance, back in the first volume we reviewed *Cruising Under Sail* by Eric Hiscock, which is one of the finest works on the subject ever written. We haven't said a word about it since, but the book is still in print and it is still most worthy of your consideration. What we are trying to say, then, is that *The Mariner's Catalog* is a multi-volume encyclopedia of sorts, and if you are in any way serious about the sea, please don't take a single volume of the *Catalog* as the only word.

Consider this note as an avaricious plug for the previous five volumes of *The Mariner's Catalog,* or consider it as a helpful hint. But do consider it.

DEDICATION

This volume of *The Mariner's Catalog* is dedicated to the memory of R.D. "Pete" Culler, boatbuilder, boat designer, author, sailor, adviser, and friend. Pete was with us from the beginning, and we like to think that his contributions always formed the core of our Catalog. We will remember him always.

Photograph of Pete Culler by Robert G. Bergeron.

COMMUNICATIONS

Our mail is our sustenance, so if you have something to offer in the form of advice, opinion, contribution, or whatever, we want to hear from you. You can get in touch with us at any one of three places. Take your choice:

George Putz
Box 543
Vinalhaven, Maine 04863

Peter H. Spectre
Pleasant Ridge Road
Camden, Maine 04843

The Mariner's Catalog
21 Elm Street
Camden, Maine 04843

THE PRICES

Buying a head of lettuce this week reminded us again that, along with the price of a good cigar, everything is leaping along in fine form. Don't shoot us; we're just the messengers. We only want to remind you that only the price of admission to this catalog is stable—everything inside is subject to the vagaries of the marketplace. Last year we thought inflation was caused by the Democrats or the Republicans. A year's worth of experience tells us that's not the case: neither group is clever enough.

OUR THANKS

We offer our thanks to all the people who have helped us put together this new volume of *The Mariner's Catalog.* Without them, the contents would be thin indeed. We also would like to extend special thanks to Julia Littleton for her index, Kathleen Brandes for her editorial advice, and Katy Campbell for her production expertise.

Interesting Boats

Few objects, in this mechanized modern world, instill in their owners as much concern and love as their boats.

—Gilbert Klingel

It was silly to think—as we once did—that a civilization of a quarter of a billion people had few builders of interesting boats; it was something of a conceit perched atop a persecuted vanity. Oh yes, there are lots and lots of interesting boats. This section could go on forever.

Of Wood

Paul Schweiss is a fascinating and intense young builder, certainly among the best of the new breed. Trained in Scandinavian practice, he's at his best with lapstrake construction. Size doesn't seem to be a limitation. Last year he built a 30-foot, five-station gig. His flexibility is perhaps best expressed by this letter we received recently:

Dear Editors:
   . . . I am still building one at a time here; it has been fun delivering boats all over the place, and the variety has been gratifying, only a little scary at bid time! I just put a 24-

foot outboard launch, Chesapeake style, by Pete Culler, on the barge to Petersburg, Alaska. I have Danish skiffs now to build before traveling to Bath for a Norwegian boatbuilding session of 4 to 6 weeks at the Apprenticeshop. Next comes a 20-foot faering having oak planking, square-sail, and side steering rudder/oar; followed by an 18-foot Danish pram that boasts a main, stays'l, flying jib, and tops'l. And I almost have a deposit on a "snekka," a typical small Norwegian motorboat—lapstrake, double-ended, Sabb diesel, beamy, seaworthy, cheap to build, run, maintain, etc., etc. . . .

—Paul Schweiss

Clinker Boatworks
8905½ 35th West
Tacoma, Wash. 98466

The sweet lines of some of them all but took my breath away when I saw them for the first time in all their naked elegance. I revelled in their good looks and desired them as much for their beauty as for their use.

—John Gardner
We think it only fair to tell you he was speaking about dories.—Eds.

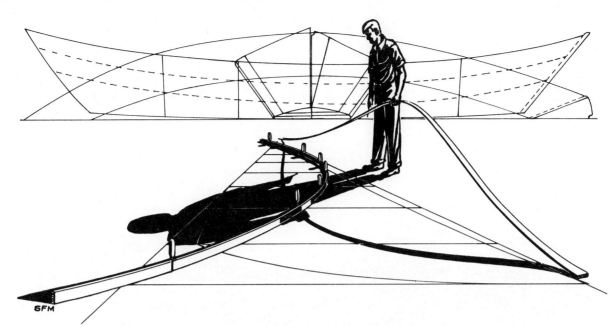

Illustration by Sam Manning from The Dory Book.

The Dory Book, by John Gardner
Illus. by Samuel F. Manning
International Marine Publishing Company
Camden, Maine
272 pages, illus., index, 1978, $20

The dory, in all its variations, revealed. History, lore, how to build, and 22 dory designs with full construction details.

Dear Editors:
. . . Providence Bay Boat Works is a one-man boat shop which will custom build in wood any kind of boat from six to thirty-six feet. As I have over 1,000 designs on file, I can come fairly close to what a customer might want. Construction ranges from "workboat" to "yacht finish" depending on the customer's needs and purse. A standard model (between orders) is a 15-foot pleasure rowing dory, I do carry a few esoteric items such as Stockholm Tar, which I will be glad to ship to any reader who might be interested.

Joseph K. Hall

How about a Strawbery Banke Dory? 14-feet ($565). They also build Banks Dories, and rowing flat-bottomed utility skiffs. Strawbery Banke, by the way, is a terrific place to visit—a genuine refurbished 18th-century community in the tradition of Williamsburg and Sturbridge Village. The boatshop is also a boatbuilding school.

Strawbery Banke
Boat Shop
Portsmouth, N.H.

Providence Bay Boat Works
Providence Bay, Ontario
Canada

Strawbery Banke Dory, 14'. Adapted from an older round-sided dory with slight but practical alterations, this graceful boat combines fine lines with great stability and rowing ease. One of the finest small wooden boats obtainable.

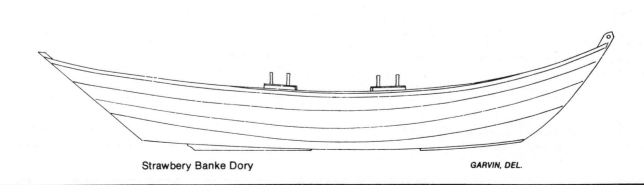

Strawbery Banke Dory   *GARVIN, DEL.*

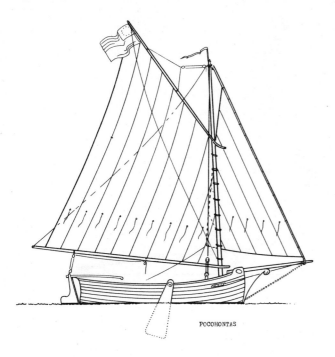

POCOHONTAS

Nakomis builds a 17-foot gaff sloop, designed by William Atkin, for $5,500 and a cunning cutter for $15,117, ready to cruise.

Nakomis Boat Works
Route 105
Washington, Me. 04574

Left: The Atkin Pocohontas *by Nakomis Boat Works.*

Any reader of Chapelle's *American Small Sailing Craft* will recall stopping to consider the merits of the Hampton lobster smacks. The reasons why are self-evident. The Hamptons are available again, as powerboats, thanks to the building efforts of Dick Pulsifer. $8,600 with a 16-hp diesel, pump, lights, instruments, and controls.

Richard S. Pulsifer
RFD3, Mere Point Road
Brunswick, Maine 04011
Brochure is $2.00

In selecting a boat to build, care and attention is given in historical research to retain authenticity and the general character of the boat. Yet, even as these boats were constantly evolving—some going through rapid changes of design based on usage and experimentation—so, we feel, must today's boats undergo some changes from their predecessors. By evaluating the performance in retrospect and by taking into account new information, as well as making use of new materials (epoxy glues, wood preservatives, Dacron sails), we can select and use the best features of a design and incorporate improvements when possible. This is done without sacrificing the primary qualities of the boat to meet the mass market demands. But, whether a change be as major as a modification in the hull or as minor as a change in a lamp bracket, the dictum of "form follows function" is adhered to, and inevitably the result reflects an honesty of purpose as well as being esthetically pleasing. We take pleasure in the fact that every piece of Cedar, Oak, Spruce and Fir which goes into our boats was personally selected from the standing trees here and cut and seasoned by us for the best possible stock. Most of the fittings are custom cast in manganese bronze from our own patterns.

—Nakomis Boat Works

The Hampton Lobster Smack from Richard Pulsifer. Illustration by Sam Manning.

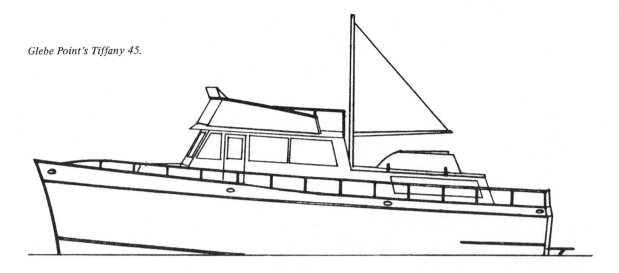

Glebe Point's Tiffany 45.

We have found two firms that still manufacture power cruisers and sportfishermen in Good Ole Wood (GOW). May all nymphs and nereids bless their houses.

Hankins, in business since 1912, makes a couple of Sea Bright surf dory (skiff) models, and open sea skiffs in 22-, 24-, 26-, and 28-foot models (shades of the rumrunners), but their *tour de force* is the cabin sea skiff in lengths from 22 feet to 40 feet.

Glebe Point, at it since the 1930s, uses the following four types of construction:

1. Double planked with inner planking diagonal mahogany, outer planking carvel-planked mahogany. Epoxy used as glue.
2. A sandwich of diagonal plywood inner planking, then glass with epoxy resin, and cross-diagonal plywood outer planking covered with glass.
3. A sandwich of diagonal plywood inner planking, then glass with epoxy resin, and carvel-planked mahogany outer planking.
4. Chesapeake Bay single-planked deadrise.

Glebe's primary line is the famous "Tiffany" series of luxury sport cruisers and fishermen in the 37- to 60-foot range. We're a little taken by the Tiffany 45-footer.

Charles Hankins
504 Grand Central, Box 7
Lavallette, N.J. 08735

Glebe Point Boat Co.
Glebe Point, Box 133
Burgess, Va. 22432

Hankins's 24-foot hard-top sea skiff.

Shanty Boats

If a man's home is his castle, his houseboat's his heaven. The material luxury of an elegant yacht can never match the luxury of soul one can find on and in a houseboat tied up to the shady bank of some oxbow lake off the main stream of the river. They are snug and warm in the winter, and make good bases for hunting excursions into the swamps. In the summer they are open and airy with the cool, clean (we hope) river at your door.

A shanty boat is within the reach of anyone old enough and responsible enough to be allowed to run at large. Down here (Alabama), though, we don't call them shanty boats. We calls them houseboats.

The best way to get your houseboat is to buy one from someone who's built it—or build your own. If you can build a box, you can likely build a houseboat. Just make your box with raked ends like a barge; you're going to want to tow it somewhere sometime, and the raked ends made this easy.

(Continued on next page)

(Continued from previous page)

It can be as large or as small as you want. The one in the picture, which belongs to Clark Harris, is about eleven by twenty feet inside. The front and back porches (for God's sake, don't call them decks) are about four by eleven. The walls and roof are framed out of two by twos and two by fours (for the roof) and covered with plywood. It's a good idea to fill the hull (box) with some kind of foam. We have a certain type of citizen down here that (we don't refer to this type as "who") likes to shoot holes in your boat with rifles. The foam discourages this because the boat won't sink. It is also a good idea in case a snag coming down on a rise punches a hole in your heavenly haven. Paint the hull well, and if you want to go first class, fiberglass it.

You can make the hull out of wood, steel, or any other suitable material. Be careful, though, and avoid things like surplus wing tanks and old drums. They just ain't stout enough.

When the boat is finished, furnish her with an apartment-size range with a butane tank, a couple of double-decker bunkbeds, good food, good drink (coffee?), and good friends. A couple of weeks later your wife may wonder where the hell you went.

—**Warren Norville**

Clark Harris sitting on the front porch of his houseboat in Lower Dead Run, an oxbow lake formed by an old meander of the Alabama River about six miles below Dixie Landing.

Inside Clark's houseboat. There may be no place like home, but there sure isn't any place like a houseboat. That's Clark and George waiting for the sausage to cook.

It was while working on the first *Mariner's Catalog*—a period of nautical despair for those who liked traditional boats made of traditional materials—that we first encountered the design works of J. Benford Associates. We could not believe it, a firm devoted almost exclusively to boats so salty that they made our eyes rust. So, like the girl who dreamed away childhood over knights on white chargers and screamed rape when one finally showed up, we didn't list them. Peculiar, the human mind . . . .

Here are a couple hundred designs in all sizes, all power modes, all materials, for which all options and services are offered. For starters, send them $3.25 for their book *Cruising Designs*.

J.R. Benford and Assoc., Inc.
P.O. Box 399
Friday Harbor, Wash. 98250

Psychologically, one of the most important considerations in selecting a boat is, "Is she beautiful?" If she is, and that beauty is classical in nature, then she will never go out of style with the passing fads, and will still be thought beautiful years from now. This will keep her master attentive to her needs, giving her lasting value and serving to protect her as an investment. If she generates pride in her crew, they will get more pleasure out of every aspect of her—and that's what it's all about—a yacht is a pleasure boat and should be fun!

—from *The Benford 30*

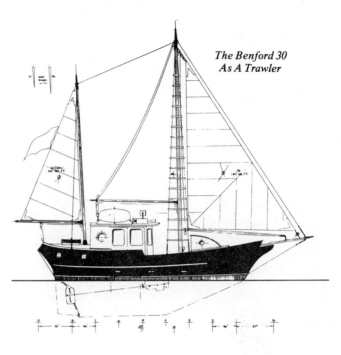

*The Benford 30
As A Trawler*

The Classic Boat
by the Editors of Time-Life Books
Time-Life Books, Alexandria, Va.
176 pages, illus., glossary, index, 1977, $10.95

We won't bore you with a long, erudite criticism of the Time-Life Library of Boating. Suffice to say that we find it deficient because of its amorphous, characterless, over-digested superficiality. So why are we recommending *The Classic Boat*, one of the volumes in the Library? Because of its photography and diagrams. There are some beautiful color photographs here, and the drawings, especially those of lines and construction details, are meticulously done. The boats shown are truly classics—dories, Whitehalls, steam launches, electric boats, guideboats, skipjacks, runabouts, Friendships, and Chesapeake log canoes.

We have found two more firms that specialize in classic boat restoration:

A and D Woodcraft
Box 610
Old Lyme, Conn. 06371

Baker Boat Works
26 Drift Road
Westport, Mass. 02790

Of Glass and Plastic

Traditional small boats in fiberglass are *not* two a penny. But very likely you no longer have to leave the shores of your own state to find one offered.

A 16-foot Swampscott dory, $1,290 rowing, $2,650 sailing, from:

>**Roger Crawford**
>**1240 Ferry Street**
>**Box 1041**
>**Marshfield, Mass. 02050**

Each geographical area has evolved its own local dory design. This "Swampscott" dory (considered by many to be the most eye appealing of the many different styles) not only rows and motors easily, but with its round sides can be set up to sail smartly. Its designer, Jon Blanchard, modelled it similar to a Swampscott built around the turn of the century and added a bit of beam throughout and particularly across the bottom to increase performance under power. The lovely roundness of her lines and salty profile easily distinguishes her from today's "production" boats.

—**Roger Crawford**

Roger Crawford's fiberglass Swampscott. Note the motor well in the transom.

The glass West Coast Whitehall is 13'6" overall and base priced at $1,200, from:

>**Thomas Wylie Design Group**
>**1924 Willow Street**
>**Alameda, Cal. 94501**

There is a 16'6" fiberglass St. Lawrence Skiff now in rowing, sailing, and square-stern configurations, from:

>**Grumco**
>**(Division of L.S. Phillips and Sons, Ltd.)**
>**Lansdowne, Ontario**
>**Canada**

Grumco's St. Lawrence skiff.

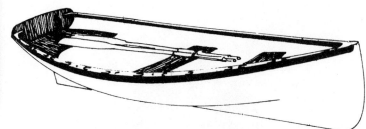

The West Coast Whitehall.

And a 16-foot Rangeley in vinyl/ABS/foam, from:

Old Town Canoe Company
Old Town, Maine 04468

If you like the funky and the pugnacious, not to mention the on-the-cheap, there is the Stump Knocker, an 11-foot, $180 (FOB plant) bundle of love, from:

Stump Knocker Boats
P.O. Box 26
Headland, Alabama 36345

Old Town's ABS Rangeley.

The Proper Yacht, Second Edition
by Arthur Beiser
International Marine Publishing Company
Camden, Maine
376 pages, illus., index, 1978, $25

An expert, who knows a proper yacht when he sees one, analyzes the latest developments in boats, hulls, rigs, accommodations, and engines. This is a complete revision of the first edition.

Tubing, by Whit Perry
Greatlakes Living Press
Matteson, Illinois
192 pages, illus., index, 1977, paperbound, $6.95

That's right, tubing—inner tubes—the art of using a tube for floating, rafting, fishing, drifting, racing, swimming, what have you. It seems that the Cult of the Inner Tube has reached manic proportions in some parts of the country (such as the Apple River in Wisconsin, billed as "The Tubing Capital of the World"). And why not? A tube is the cheapest quick and dirty boat to be had today and is certainly versatile.

The joys of the tube. From Tubing.

"All we have to do is fix it up a little bit, and . . ."

Building to the designs of Benford, listed previously, Bryken offers the 8-foot Portland Yawlboat and the 11-foot Oregon Peapod.

Bryken Boat Builders
1431 S.E. 202nd Ave.
Portland, Oregon 97233

Yawlboats of old had sweet shapes, and were commonly carried on stern davits of larger working vessels. Our modern version, the Portland Yawlboat, is likewise designed as a tender for a larger boat, but she's also fun to sail for kids of all ages. She's lighter in both relative displacement and material than her older sisters, and at 8 feet, considerably smaller in size. Much shallower in draft, yet still typically beamy, our Portland Yawlboat offers more stability than the older types.

—**Bryken Boat Builders**

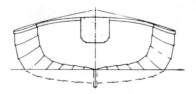

Above and right: Bryken's Portland Yawlboat, designed by Benford.

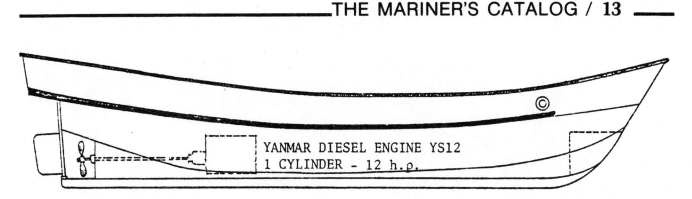

YANMAR DIESEL ENGINE YS12
1 CYLINDER - 12 h.p.

Fiberglass sampan from Sea Gate Yachts.

Just try and tell us you aren't intrigued by the idea of a 24'9" fiberglass sampan powered by a 12-hp Yanmar diesel. See, not a peep! From:

Sea Gate Yachts, Inc.
1322 Airlie Road
P.O. Box 524
Wrightsville Beach, N.C. 28480

While doing some consulting work for a yacht builder in Taiwan, I came across a fiberglass sampan that was produced for commercial fishermen. After doing some research on these vessels and understanding more about the design, I decided that an economical, light weight, low powered vessel of this type would fit the needs of many.
—Sea Gate Yachts

Direct descendants of the flattie, sharpie, skipjack, bugeye, Chesapeake-model power workboats in fiberglass, 24 to 40 feet, are offered by:

Chesapeake Work Boat Co.
Route 1, Box 108
Hayes, Va. 23072

English friends have told us of the 16-foot Devon yawl, from:

Devon Craft Ltd.
Shadycombe Creek
Salcombe, Devon TQ8 8DP
England

Above: The Devon Yawl.
Left: 40-foot stern trawler from Chesapeake Work Boat.

Above: The Wasque from Vineyard Yachts.
Below: Boxed quote from The Dream Boats.

As do all local waters, those around Martha's Vineyard float their own distinctive type. The Wasque 26 and 32 are archtypical examples. The 26-footer is available in all states of construction, from $4,750 for base hull to $19,750 complete, ready for power. From:

> **Vineyard Yachts, Inc.**
> **Beach Rd., Box 1046**
> **Vineyard Haven, Mass. 02568**

Her fine entry turns into a flat run aft, providing a full keel semi-displacement hull capable of good speed but with no flat lifting surfaces to produce pounding. You can run this boat all day in heavy seas without returning bone-weary from the brain-jarring ride of typical planing hulls. She is a maneuverable, agile, no-nonsense boat with off-shore capability.

—Vineyard Yachts

The Dream Boats
by Nancy Holmes
Prentice-Hall, Englewood Cliffs, N.J.
191 pages, illus., 1976, $9.95

Subtitled "The Beautiful People on Their Beautiful Yachts." Indeed.

The quality that set Onassis apart from most men, and from all other Greeks, was impact. You *sensed* him. He had star quality, animal magnetism, authority and presence, to everyone who met or knew him, in large ineluctable doses. If you analyzed his looks, feature by feature, particularly in the latter years, you came up with a droop-eyed, rumple-suited, beak-nosed little fellow. The secret of *his* impact was yours. If you warranted his total attention, his eyes and voice alone made him irresistible. When he wanted something.

He always wanted something. The best of everything. *Christina* was, and remains, a shining example of Ari's tasteful wants. There are, have been, and will be bigger yachts, more beautiful yachts, faster yachts, and more expensive yachts. But when *Christina* was launched in 1954, she immediately became the ultimate status symbol yacht to the haves and the have-nots alike.

Canny Mr. Onassis knew how to spend money, when to spend it, and when not to. With *Christina*, he ricocheted from one end of the pole to the other. He bought a war surplus Canadian frigate in 1952 from John Shapiro, who was then a Baltimore scrap dealer. Shapiro owned a number of vessels which he planned to break up for scrap. Somehow, he sold one of them, the *Stormont*, to Onassis for $35,000 and he has been sorry about it ever since . . . but not very, since he does not even pretend to be a yachtsman.

Small Is Fast

Despite what most people think, it is possible to go fast on water with relatively low power. It is possible to troll all day long at low speed, throw in a few quick runs between the best fishing spots, and then make a swift haul back to the dock—two persons in a big 14' skiff—all on less than three gallons of gas.

And there's no magic involved; the answer lies in just about any community with a boat dealer and a nearby lake where you can test out your rig. Testing is important, too, for when you are seeking speed *and* economy, the line between satisfaction and dismay is a thin one.

We discovered years ago the beauties of a "tin" skiff and an outboard motor. If utility, low upkeep, and long life are what you're looking for in a small boat, an open aluminum skiff and a low-horsepower outboard motor can't be beat. Careful shopping and a friendly dealer who wants you to have what you want and not what he wants to sell you, should provide a boat that will surprise you with its performance, especially if you've been sold on the idea that only a boat with loads of power is "safe."

We like to fish, any kind of fishing, but especially for landlocked salmon in the spring in Maine's big northern lakes. Those magnificent fish thrive in conditions worthy of their fighting ability—clear, cold waters, preferably those smashing against windswept granite boulders where swirling currents and heaving waves keep baitfish moving. We call such broken water a "salmon chop," and it takes a good

(Continued on next page)

(Continued from previous page)

boat and reliable power to fish it with comfort and safety. For years I used an old 14' Duratech which a friend of mine had paid $50 for back in the early '60s, for which I paid him $50 in 1966 and which I sold to another friend a couple of weeks ago for $50.

The Duratech was adequate if somewhat cramped when two men and their camping gear were headed up the lake. She also had an irritating leak amidships that we never could find; it was only a trickle but it sure could wet the bottom of a pack. For power, I first used a 9.8 h.p. Mercury outboard, bought new in 1964. This gas-stingy motor did a fine job for nine years until I replaced it with a 7.5 h.p. Merc in 1974.

Now 7½ horses is really thinning the herd when it comes to pushing a heavy 14' skiff, camping gear, and two persons. Any 7½ will drive such a boat at hull speed, say 4 or 5 m.p.h., but plane it? Not all motors. But the Merc did, every bit as well as the old 9.8, as nearly as I could see, and at a considerable saving in gas. (It should be noted that the difference between the Merc 7.5 and the 9.8 is mainly in numbers and a little internal gadgetry. The two look like twins, weigh almost exactly the same, and even sound alike. But my 7.5 had a three-bladed propeller against the old 9.8's two-bladed wheel.)

Late last summer I found the replacement boat I had been looking for. It was a deep-bodied, beamy Starcraft Seafarer, a 14' model I had admired for a long time. This one sat on a trailer on a lawn in mint condition and the $350 price for boat and trailer wasn't something one is likely to quibble over in these inflationary times. The sale hinged on a test run to see if the boat would plane with the little Merc—the owner had no objection to a tryout, but he was openly skeptical, since he had never been able to plane the boat with his 10 h.p. Chrysler outboard.

The boat seemed huge after the narrow Duratech as my wife and I pushed off from the launching ramp on a test run. I fired up the Merc, cruised along at a quarter throttle while getting the feel of the boat, and then gave her a jab. The big Starcraft lifted her nose a bit and then dropped onto an easy plane, skimming down the bay at a pleasing clip. Even at half throttle the water broke cleanly from beneath the transom. I'd seen enough.

A few weeks later my son and I pointed her out across Moosehead Lake's sprawling Lily Bay for a late-season go at salmon and trout. We hadn't been choosy about our gear, bringing tent, stove, firewood, fishing gear, clothes, ice cooler, lantern, and other necessities for roughing it in the wilds. The boat took it all in with plenty of room to spare. And the little Merc? It shoved the boat, two men and all the rest up on top, and away we went. We covered miles and miles that weekend, fast and slow, and when it was all over, we had used about 5 gallons of gas.

Oh yes, we had a fine salmon chop, caught a few fish, and came away from a memorable weekend more than happy with our fast-stepping, low-powered rig.

—Dave Getchell

Junk

Dear Editors:

A short note on a package that might interest your readers:

Design Your Own Chinese Rig by J. K. McLeod, Hawk Hill, Rosemarkie, By Fortrose, Ross-Shire, Scotland. A three-part set showing how to design a Chinese (junk?) rig of the type developed by H. G. Hasler (of *Jester* fame) and J. K. McLeod (owner of *Rón Glas*).

Part I: An 11-page pamphlet covering the history, advantages, disadvantages, and suitable hull forms for the Chinese rig. Cost: $3.00.

Part II: 17 pages, 7 charts and graphs, and 3 blueprints covering the drawing of the sail plan, its positioning, and structural modifications necessary for using the rig on existing hulls. Cost: $35.00.

Part III: 52 pages, 14 charts and graphs, and 11 blueprints plus two pamphlets on setting up and using the Chinese rig. Detailed design of the masts, sails, battens, spars, and deck layout are covered in this section. Cost: $70.00.

R.L. Watkins
Topeka, Kansas

The Western seaman, on being confronted with the Chinese rig for the first time, is liable to see at a glance half a dozen ways in which this archaic lash-up could be made more modern and efficient. In our experience any one of these "improvements" is usually enough to ruin the rig, but there is great benefit in the judicious use of modern materials.

—J.K. McLeod

Inflatables

Having listed about half the inflatable companies that exist to date, we thought that we would fill the gap and round up the others. Room does not permit a full, and therefore fair, description of all the models offered. All of these companies produce numerous sizes, grades, and specialties. Those we show here, as usual, tend toward the most unusual.

Having started business in 1896 making inflated airships, Zodiac is the oldest and most distinguished factor in the business. Cousteau and all that . . .

> **Zodiac of North America**
> **11 Lee Street**
> **Annapolis, Md. 21401**

Among the usual, Bonair offers the unique Seasled, a pointy-pontooned answer to the tunnel-of-love boat, designed to be towed.

> **Bonair Boats**
> **15501 W. 109th**
> **Lenexa, Kansas 66219**

An ordinary line offering good value is:

> **Achilles Corporation**
> **25 Branca Road**
> **East Rutherford, N.J. 07073**

Camp-Ways's full line includes *Apache,* featuring an extra inflated gunnel.

> **Camp-Ways**
> **12915 S. Spring St.**
> **Los Angeles, Cal. 90061**

Anyone interested in sheer variety of inflatables really must have the Callegari catalog. They've the usuals plus everything from floating beds to ferryboats.

> **Callegari**
> **c/o Beaver Boats of N.A.**
> **Barrington Commercial Center**
> **3695 Barrington St.**
> **Halifax, N.S. B3K 2Y3**
> **Canada**

The Grand Raid from Zodiac.

Two sailing rigs for inflatables are currently offered. Those with a Redcrest can get a kit from:

Sailing Cradles, Inc.
15631 Ventura Blvd.
Encino, Cal. 91316

And Metzeler, one of the most respected names in the business, offers their own Markart S. In the U.S., it's available via:

GIL, Inc.
1919 Hadley Rd.
Fort Wayne, Indiana 46804

Above: Sailing rig for the Redcrest from Sailing Cradles.
Left: Bonair Boat's Seasled.
Below: Callegari's Bikini, the only way to go.

Knowing Rowing: An Illustrated Introduction to
Rowing and Sculling
by Ronnie Howard with Nigel Hunt
A.S. Barnes, New York
95 pages, illus., 1977, $12

Written by one of Britain's most successful rowing coaches, this book should be a great help to those cross-country skiers or joggers who are seeking a new way to flog their bodies. Not a book of narrative, rather it uses a step-by-step approach through photographs. As near as we can tell, it's a fine beginner's guide.

Safe position

Although a racing boat is narrow and unstable on its own it becomes stable when considered together with the oars or sculls. Provided that the blades are kept flat on the water and the handles are firmly held, the boat behaves as though it was nearly six metres wide.

The narrowest boat, a single, becomes perfectly stable with the blades flat on the water and the handles held together. You should be taught this safe position. It is quite possible to stand or move about in a boat with the sculls or oars held firmly in this way.

Boats, Oars, and Rowing, by R.D. Culler
International Marine Publishing Company
Camden, Maine
160 pages, illus., 1978, $10.95

Our own Pete Culler provides advice on choosing rowing craft, making oars, selecting oarlocks, and learning how to row correctly.

Above: Boxed material from Knowing Rowing.
Below: Spoon oar plans from Boats, Oars, and Rowing.

Two Last Shots

You've dreamed of a one-man submarine? Someone the military trusts will make one for you. The K-250 sub is 11' 8" overall, $12,000. Optional are trailer, u/w telephone, bottom floodlight, and mechanical claw. From:

**Kittredge Industries, Inc.
Warren, Maine 04864**

"We gotta go 'round the horn—they've never even HEARD of the Diner's Club!"

GO FAST. 9' 6" to 14' class runabouts and hydros, power packages offered. From:

**De Silva Boats
P.O. Box 394
Sebastopol, Cal. 95472**

*Left: The Kittredge one-man sub.
Below: Hydro from De Silva.*

Canoes and Kayaks

There are canoes—and there are canoes.
—C. Bowyer Vaux

This isn't a cop-out, you understand, but our coverage of canoes and kayaks has been upstaged just a tad by our new sister publication, *The Canoeist's Catalog*. We continue with our own review of the scene here, but you'll find much, much more in:

The Canoeist's Catalog
edited by Bill and Fern Stearns
International Marine Publishing Company
Camden, Maine
192 pages, illus., 1978, paperbound, $7.95

Boxed quote from The Canoeist's Catalog.

Bagging a Canoe

Recently, kayaks and canoes have been constructed using the bag-molding or vacuum-bagging method. With this method, all of the reinforcement is laid into the mold and all of the resin required is poured atop the reinforcement. A thin, tough film or "bag" is then laid over the top of the laminate and sealed to the flange of the mold with a plastic sealant. The bag covers the entire laminate and the two perforated "bleeder tubes," which run the length of the mold along either edge of the reinforcement. The bleeder tubes are connected to a resin trap, which in turn is connected to a vacuum pump. The pump evacuates the space between the bag and the mold. As a vacuum is formed, the resin is forced throughout the part, forming an almost void-free laminate. The fabricator now uses squeegees over the bag to remove excess resin from the part until the desired resin content is reached. The structural advantage of a bagged part comes from the uniform application of atmospheric pressure on the bag. This pressure compacts the reinforcement and overcomes the surface tension of the resin, allowing thinner parts containing less resin.

— W. A. Clark and Associates

Bart, Again

We find ourselves forced to re-list Bart Hauthaway. We don't do this usually, but look at his new Greenland-model kayak. No getting around it, the fellow and his boats have class.

Bart Hauthaway
640 Boston Post Road
Weston, Mass. 02193

Right: Bart Hauthaway's Greenland model and friend. By the way, no Hauthaway boat goes on the market until Bart has caught a fish in one.

Some Reflections on Small Canoes

by Bart Hauthaway

Canoes have been called the poor man's yacht. If this is true, then the average canoe buyer should consider carefully which model might be best for his use. No one canoe is best for everyone.

Fifty years ago Nessmuk championed the ultralight double-paddle canoe. A frail wraith of a man addicted to lone wilderness travel, his rig, including canoe and two days rations, weighed twenty-six pounds. Such an outfit might be a bit Spartan for most, but a fifteen-hundred-mile trek through the Adirondacks in his super lightweight convinced Nessmuk most paddlers used boats that were at least twice as heavy as needed.

"Go light," he advised, "the lighter the better." Modern canoe catalogs advise buying the largest canoe you can conceive of ever using. Who is right? Well, neither is right for everyone, but while Nessmuk based his advice on personal paddling preferences, the advice of the canoe sellers might be based on profit motive alone.

Indians built an incredible variety of canoes in all shapes and sizes according to materials available and intended use. These ranged from tiny one-man craft to huge cargo carriers capable of hauling a ton or more. The design of bark canoes was a highly developed primitive art, little changed by its adoption into civilized society, and even the worst of modern factory canoes still retain the basic lines of their primitive origin.

The larger Indian canoes were beautifully crafted and finished. Although built primarily for performance, they were also status symbols, built to be proud of, built to last, often intricately decorated. But the boats the Indians used most—their everyday hunting and fishing canoes—were often crudely built. Singlehanders of from nine to twelve feet, known as woods or pack canoes, they were often so crude they were considered expendable, and might be left at some distant watercourse for possible future use. Obviously, we didn't invent littering the countryside with disposables, we just perfected it; bark canoes are more biodegradable than beer cans. But when we copied the Indian craft, we paid small attention to the little singlehanders, and the myth persists today that a canoe isn't a good canoe unless it's a big canoe.

"Buy the largest canoe you can ever conceive of using." I think for most people this is terrible advice. Much publicity is given to "classic" canoe trips in "real canoe country," the once-a-year trip, or once-a-lifetime. For this we are told the large canoe is faster, carries a heavier load, and is more seaworthy. Maybe so. It's also a beast to handle alone and without a load, and there's a world of difference between a canoe you can handle and one that handles you.

Too little is said about finding one's sport close to home. Remote wilderness areas are beginning to suffer overuse; when you have to line up and take a number to launch at a remote area, local suburban wilderness becomes more and more attractive. It's nearby, it's available, and often it's so overlooked it becomes more private and remote than the "real canoe country." Here is where the singlehander shines; it goes wherever a muskrat swims, and with discretion it's equally at home in remote waters. I find no fault paddling with others, just as long as each of us is in his own canoe.

I do not favor using an outboard motor on a canoe. If you plan on hauling out a moose in a Grand Laker, or hunting beluga in a Hudson Bay Boat, that's another matter. But when you hang an outboard on a canoe, you no longer have a canoe; you have a motorboat. In our overcrowded existence, it is increasingly difficult to enjoy oneself without infringing upon someone else's enjoyment, but canoeing is essentially a quiet and private exercise, and should not invade the privacy of others. Mounting a motor on a canoe violates the whole concept.

Even the color should be quiet. I'm sure the almighty Coast Guard would like all small craft covered with blaze orange for greater visibility, but I prefer not to be seen. The color should blend, not swear. Canoes in psychedelic colors and beer-can patterns are an insult.

If your small canoe is decked, so much the better. Decking adds some weight, but the advantages are many. Adaptable to use with either single or double blades, such a boat is at home either in constricted passages of rivers and swamps or in open water. A canoe of twenty-nine inches beam will use a double paddle of about one hundred inches; for each additional inch of beam up to a maximum of about thirty-three inches, you can add an inch or so to the paddle. Take-apart paddles are advisable, since one-piece shafts in these lengths are a bit awkward to transport, and a T-grip handle can be fashioned to fit the female ferrule to convert half of the double blade to a single.

An enclosed deck and a cockpit coaming effectively increase freeboard, reducing the risk of swamping when

(Continued on next page)

(Continued from previous page)

heeled, and make the double-paddle canoe particularly suitable to sail. Sailing rigs should have a low center of effort, should be ridiculously small and equally simple. Just a few square feet will move the boat smartly. Perhaps the most practical design is the old dory spritsail, loose footed with no boom, so nothing but cloth can hit you in the face. If the sail is cut with squared sides and fitted with grommets at all corners, it will also serve as a ground cloth or tarpaulin. Clamp-on leeboards and rudders are a nuisance; either the double-blade or single-blade paddle works fine

for steering, and the deck provides support for a single, offset daggerboard well if needed. If you have no sailing rig, don't neglect to carry an umbrella; it will serve not only its intended purpose, but will also sail a small canoe surprisingly well in a fair wind. And if kept handy, the crooked handle is useful for retrieving gear stowed under the decks.

Travelling light makes just as much sense today as it did for Nessmuk. Go light, go alone, and go quietly. A double-paddle canoe will do it all, and for my money it's one of the greatest values in small craft. Of course that's just my opinion, and I admit to some prejudice.

Wood and Canvas

The deathknell of the wood-and-canvas canoe was a mistaken signal. We've found still more new sources and have been told by several builders that they get many requests for reconstruction and repair work on veteran craft. The reasons are clear—wood and canvas canoes are more than a vehicle of sport and transport. They are statements about being, of who one is or wants to be.

Ugo models, 16 feet long, 34½ inches beam, 11¼ inches depth, 51 pounds, from:

The Kirkstone Company
1205 Washington
Leavenworth, Kansas 66048

Fortunately, sawmills have been located which supply clear spruce and elm for planking and ribs. Spruce is light in weight and has excellent strength due to its long fibers. Elm has beauty, strength, and is the premier bending wood, especially when quarter sawed. Gunwales are of white ash and/or Honduras mahogany depending on availability in long lengths. Stems are laminated spruce which are light in weight yet exceptionally strong due to the waterproof glue layers. Seats are hand caned and thwarts are hand carved. Both are made of either Honduras mahogany or white ash. Fastenings are copper nails with special points for easy clinching, and brass screws where nails cannot be used. Canvas is best grade available, fastened with copper tacks and is filled, sealed, waterproofed, and colored by the application of 7 or more coats of nitrate dope.

—The Kirkstone Canoe Company

Fully a dozen models of cedar-strip and canvas canoes are offered by Langford; from a 12' Trapper ($499) to a 25' War Canoe ($2,590).

Langford Canoe
R.R. #1
Gravenhurst, Ontario
Canada

The Langford 14-footer. Some canoe models are available with a Dura-lite vinyl-type covering over the wood.

E.M. White is forever part of the hagiology (study of saints—think of that next time you argue with the lady) of canoeing in the Northeast, especially Maine. His forms went unused for some years until Clint Tuttle, a well-respected Maine craftsman, resurrected and began construction of these superb canoes under the banner of the Island Falls Canoe Company. Now retired, Clint has sold the business to a couple of graduates of the boatbuilding school at Lubec, Maine, and a great tradition lives on.

Island Falls Canoe Company
RFD #3
Dover-Foxcroft, Maine 04426

In addition to the 16', 18' 6", and 20' canvas-covered Whites originally offered by Clint Tuttle, we now sell a 14' pack canoe, a 16' featherweight version, 18' 6" and 20' decked sailing canoes, and a modified version of Rushton's Nomad sailing canoe. Our canoes come covered with either No. 8 cotton duck canvas, or marine fiberglass cloth and polyester resin. In addition we do minor and extensive rebuilding, recanvassing, and general repair on any make of wooden canoe; and we sell materials to people who wish to repair their own.

—*Jerry Stelmok, Island Falls*

Bill Thomas, also of Dover-Foxcroft, builds and repairs canoes. His oak-leaf finish, described below, beats the hell out of the infamous Budweiser beer-can canoe.

Thomas Canoe
RFD #2
Dover-Foxcroft, Maine 04426

I am retired and build and repair canoes as a hobby. I build only a 12-footer. It weighs 50 pounds. I use native clear cedar for ribs and planking. Clear timber spruce for rails. Decks and middle thwart are of black cherry. Seats are slatted oak on white ash. Canoe is about 40 inches wide with quite a flat bottom for stability. Form was built by E.A. Levenseller 30 years ago at Frost Pond. I cover canoe with fiberglass cloth and polyester resin. Last year I built one canoe resined with clear resin, and I put dried-out oak leaves in a pattern under the fiberglass.

—*Willis Thomas, Thomas Canoe*

Island Falls's 18-foot 6-inch White guide canoe on an upstream passage.

Improved Double-Paddle?

We get some *most* interesting correspondence from Norman Benedict. Here's a taste:

Dear Editors:

. . . I believe I noted a photo of one of you paddling a Hauthaway 10½' Rob-Roy—and wonder if you'd think or experiment with an idea I can't shake. My 14' wherry got sold, and for sure I'm still interested in rowing and the likes.

The point is better transfer of the human energy to the boat. As is, by rowing and paddling said "transfer" occurs mostly through the buttocks and foot wedges. One's pants can get tired, and I imagine you think about back pains also.

By contrast, the Chinese yuloh actually transfers a great deal of the energy by the lanyard that runs from the sweep handgrip to the bottom planking. Incidentally, I used to be a helicopter engineering pilot biggie—said yuloh "under-slung" blade and cyclic feathering is quite like "discoveries" that made helicopters possible.

Anyway again—in paddling the energy transfer is by tension through the paddler's body. Question: could/should this be via a lanyard from the paddle to the boat? One thought would be a single lanyard possibly running from the paddle center down to possibly a location near the paddler's crotch. Another thought would be a bridle from the gunwale underneath the armpits to a midpoint on the paddle. In any event, it seems simple dog-leash type snaps should suffice at first with emphasis on sliding, as the paddle midsection movement is considerable. Sort of aerial zig-zagging.

A third idea I can't shake is a type of Barney Post between the paddler's legs. If it had a yoke atop it, it would bear the weight of the paddle also—or the "yoke" shape could be that of an hourglass when viewed vertically down-ward.

Norman Benedict
Lomita, California

How to Build an Indian Canoe
adapted by George S. Fichter
David McKay Co., New York
90 pages, illus., index, 1977, $6.95

An interesting industry has developed lately—you reprint government publications, which are copyright-free, and sell them to the public at a greater price than that charged by the government. This book is a case in point. The "adapter" took a very small portion of *The Bark Canoes and Skin Boats of North America,* by Edwin Tappan Adney and Howard I. Chapelle, published by the Government Printing Office at $6.75, 20 cents less, and made it into his book. Neat trick.

We don't condemn this; after all, private enterprise deserves to make a buck. But we do think you are better served by purchasing the real thing, not an adaptation—you'll get probably five times as much—many more pages, with many more illustrations, with plans, historical background, and bibliographic references:

The Bark Canoes and Skin Boats of North America
by Edwin Tappan Adney and Howard I. Chapelle
Superintendent of Documents
Government Printing Office
Washington, D.C. 20402
242 pages, $6.75

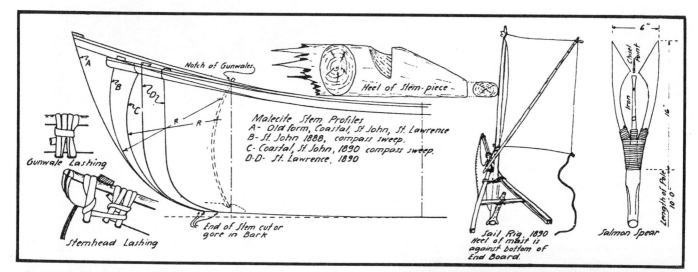

Above: From The Bark Canoes and Skin Boats of North America.
Right: From Building a Chippewa Indian Birch-Bark Canoe.

Building a Chippewa
Indian Birch-Bark Canoe
by Robert E. Ritzenthaler
Milwaukee Public Museum
1950-1972, Milwaukee, Wisconsin
$4.25 including postage

Considering what there is on the subject, if you don't have this concise illustrated manual on native practice, you're out of a significant percentage of the literature.

Canoe Books

Grumman promotes books as well as canoes. Their annotated list, "The Book Rack," describes 80 publications and includes the names and addresses of the publishers. It's available free, from:

Mr. Ed Nelson
Grumman Boats
Marathon, N.Y. 13803

Bent Paddles, Bent Canoes

Primarily a factor of paddles ("300 in stock," they say) and especially "bent" paddles, Camp Woodworking also offers an 18½-foot cedar-strip canoe laminated inside and out with 6-ounce fiberglass. Very light (37 to 40 pounds) and of peculiar model, it is an item for one's "check it out" list. Very interesting is this line in their literature: "Resin, cloth, cedar boards and many other canoe-related items available on request."

Camp Woodworking
9 Averill St.
Otego, N.Y. 13825

Blow-up

Metzeler, a German manufacturer of superior inflatables, also produces an excellent line of top-grade inflatable kayaks, rigid kayaks, and 3 models of *folding* kayaks. They should be an arrow in your quiver.

Metzeler
GIL Inc.
1919 Hadley Road
Fort Wayne, Indiana 46804

Above: Camp Woodworking's 18½-foot bent canoe.
Below: The Spezi-Duo inflatable from Metzeler.

The Acquisition and Documentation
of an Artifact
by David Zimmerly
National Museum of Man
Ottawa, Canada
34 pages, paperbound

Dave Zimmerly continues his life's project of meticulously recording every phase of native kayak construction. This particular document deals with his field work with Dick Bunyan, a native builder at Hooper Bay. Without equivocation, Zimmerly's work is of the best that contemporary ethnography offers—professionally sound, plainly written, beautifully illustrated, his work is complete enough for you and me to go to the beach and begin our own.

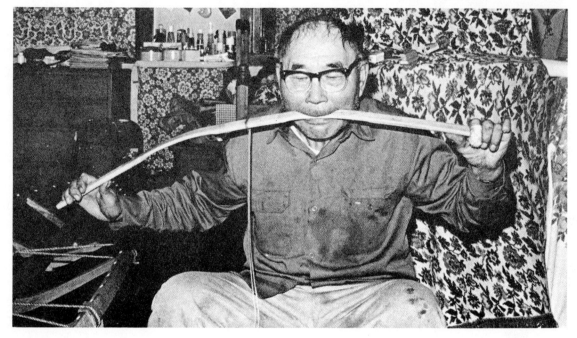

Above: Dick Bunyan bending a kayak rib without steaming it.
Below: Boxed quote from The Acquisition and Documentation of an Artifact.

My plan was to go to Sheldon Point, a small Yukon community my contact said had kayak builders, and find a man able and willing to construct a kayak. During the building I would completely document the process as well as gather supplementary information on the use of the kayak. When my project was approved I had to plan in detail what equipment and supplies were necessary.

What I consider complete documentation of an artifact includes the following:

I Written Documentation

1. Complete written log of all work performed giving date, time, persons involved, the tasks they performed and other pertinent data on their background such as how they are all related, previous experience, type and amount of payments received, if any, etc.

2. Descriptions of all tools used with notes on the names and methods of manufacture of the tools themselves if locally made.

3. Descriptions and drawings of all processes involved such as methods of alignment and measurement. This should include drawings with measurements of all pieces at various steps during the process of manufacture. Finished pieces should be traced full size if possible and also measured in detail before their incorporation into the finished whole.

II Audiovisual Documentation

Black and white and colour still photographs should be taken of each different step in the processes of manufacture including views that show closeups of the artifact, medium shots of craftsmen at work and wider views that include the social context of the work. A log should be kept giving date, time, place, film, camera and names of people involved along with short descriptions of what is taking place.

I use a Nikon F for black and white (usually Kodak Plus-X film) and a Nikkormat EL, which is automatic, for colour (normally Kodachrome 25 slide film). Having two cameras with interchangeable lenses, such as the ones above, helps cut down on the number of lenses and peripheral equipment carried. It is also insurance against being put out of business by having a camera fail halfway through the work.

TOOLS

The tool does not really have a mind of its own. It simply triggers a response in the mind of the user.
—Michael Dunbar

A very complete set of caulking tools found for sale in 1977 at Schneider's Antiques, 120 Water Street, Hallowell, Maine.

'Tis odd to think that a nautical publication such as this has now accumulated some sixty-odd pages on tools, their sources, books, and whatall. Offhand, we can't think of a *shop* publication that has done this, other than two industrial registers in common use, Thomas's and MacRae's.

And that brings up a point. When confronted with a tooling problem in boatbuilding, shop, railway, wharf, float, or dock construction, it is as important to draw upon one's mental resources as it is to depend on specific sources you have relied on in the past. Very often an unusual building problem (and all construction harbors some surprises) will create some need that the "obvious" outlet cannot meet. In such cases it's often useful to think of some entirely different industry that confronts your difficult situation regularly and has the required tools on hand as a matter of course. How about the railroads? Telephone companies? Steeplejacks?

Our Kind of Place

Dear Editors:

In MC-5, page 33, you mentioned that, to your knowledge, Hall Hardware in Maine is the only store to have a catalog with a caulking mallet in it. I'm happy to report that I have been dealing with a place that not only has mallets, but also caulking irons, oakum (bales of it), bench hooks for sail work, marlinspikes, fids—just about everything traditional and practical that you can think of.

Their catalog is very large and thorough, not to mention interesting:

**Elisha Webb
136 South Front Street
Philadelphia, Penn.**

Michael Smyjewski

Sarver, listed in the last volume, now has a catalog available, and there are some delightful surprises in it—for instance, they have four adzes and two clinker tools, a roving and bucking iron and a rivet-maker's anvil, all in the to-hell-with-the-budget department.

Sarver Smithing and Tool Co.
3030 17th Ave. W.
Seattle, Wash. 98119

A selection of adzes from Sarver. (a) The carpenters' plain adze, (b) The gouge adze, popular for log cabin building, (c) The shipwrights' lipped adze with nail punch, (d) The small lipped adze for small boat work, uses a short handle of 16 to 20 inches. Available in plain or gouged, also. It can be had with nail punch on special order.

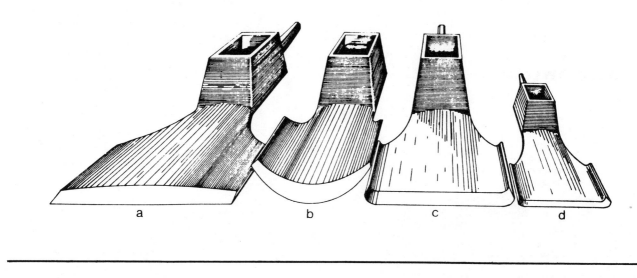

a   b   c   d

Drafting Tools

by Pete Culler

Many boatbuilders, both pro and amateur, try their hand at design, and I think this is very good. Drafting tools, especially a full set for marine drafting, can be quite expensive. However, there are simple ways around this, and you don't need as much as you might think.

I pass on some ways, methods, and tools I've found most useful; many of the tools can be made, often working better than bought stuff. First let it be said that I don't call myself an N.A.; I'm entirely self-taught, so no doubt have missed much that formal training would have given. On the other hand, I did not learn other people's bad habits, only my own. Most of what I know was learned the hard way—not a bad way, though wasteful of time.

The first tool you must have is the drawing board; how big this should be is often a matter of space available as well as the maximum scale you may want to use and the fact that tracing paper or drafting film has limits as to available size. Your actual prints will no doubt be professionally done—some Diazo print machines can do large sizes in theory; in practice there are reasons why you don't get good rendering all over on a very large print.

I work to these scales only: Very small boats and canoes, 1-1/2" to the foot; craft a little bigger, 1" scale; 3/4" for modest size craft—builders much like this scale, as 1/16" on a standard rule is an inch. I use 1/2" scale in the 45' range, 3/8" for craft somewhat larger, and for big craft, 1/4".

Sometimes you can use a larger scale for the hull, but have to use the next smaller scale for the rig. Due to space limitations, I've split my scales more than once, but don't like to.

My own drawing board is dry white pine, heavily cleated together. It has worked well. The board is a knock-down affair, and it does come and go somewhat as the seasons pass, but not enough to be a bother. Whatever your board is made of, be sure the stock is soft enough to readily take thumbtacks, though sometimes it's convenient to use tape instead of tacks. I like a couple of thicknesses of well-stretched stout paper on the board before I put any drawing paper on. This underlayment must be renewed once in a while. With prolonged service without protection, a drawing board will have to be re-surfaced.

The next tool you must have is paper for the roughing out, or original drawing. Unwrinkled and uncreased discarded chart backs are fine. Charts are printed on good paper, but if you don't have any to spare, paper just for the purpose can be bought. I use various types of paper, which depend on what's available, since I have a source of free sheets: I use the backs of large photostats that don't quite make the grade in professional printing. This is new, clean stuff, paper of excellent grade that is fairly stable, and that can take a lot of erasing. The only drawback to this paper is that it comes in odd sizes and has to be spliced up. This I do by careful layout on the board, accurate trimming of the joints, and taping—not the best way to arrive at a sheet of drafting paper, but for the price quite worth it.

Tracing paper: I'm no shakes at inking, and as I got going seriously in design about the time Mylar tracing film

(Continued on next page)

Another outfit for your files is Peck. They have the fine Kunz-brand planes, including a circular ship's plane, and the Garantie-brand scrapers, chisels, and plane irons.

The Peck Clamp-Tool Company
1170 Broadway
New York, N.Y. 10001

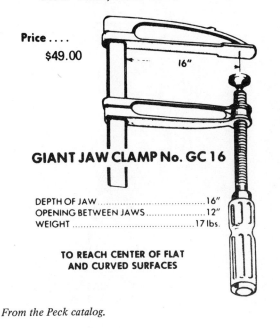

Price....
$49.00

16″

GIANT JAW CLAMP No. GC 16

DEPTH OF JAW .... 16″
OPENING BETWEEN JAWS .... 12″
WEIGHT .... 17 lbs.

TO REACH CENTER OF FLAT
AND CURVED SURFACES

From the Peck catalog.

From Sporty's Tool Shop catalog.

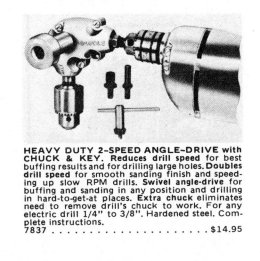

HEAVY DUTY 2-SPEED ANGLE-DRIVE with CHUCK & KEY. Reduces drill speed for best buffing results and for drilling large holes. **Doubles drill speed** for smooth sanding finish and speeding up slow RPM drills. **Swivel angle-drive** for buffing and sanding in any position and drilling in hard-to-get-at places. **Extra chuck** eliminates need to remove drill's chuck to work. For any electric drill 1/4″ to 3/8″. Hardened steel. Complete instructions.
7837 .... $14.95

We found this reasonably priced 2-speed angle-drive attachment at Sporty's, which, by the way, has a good general catalog in the Brookstone tradition.

Sporty's Tool Shop
Clermont County Airport
Batavia, Ohio 45103

(Continued from previous page)

came out, saw no point in inking. Mylar is so far ahead of tracing paper, tracing cloth, and other tracing mediums, I see no point in considering any other. Its advantages are: You get good Diazo prints from it simply by using pencils or leads and erasers made just for it. It's near wrinkle-proof, waterproof, is difficult to smudge, ages slowly, won't tear, and is not subject to changes in humidity. Mylar can stand any amount of erasing, even radical altering of a cabin plan, and in a reprint you can't see any sign of an alteration. It wears well, but at any time all or parts of the drawing can be retouched if wear dims it. Mylar's matte surface (one side only) is very abrasive—it takes ink very well, but must be hell on the pens. You must continuously sharpen your pencils and rotate the lead in drawing a line, good practice on any surface. I like #4 or #5 leads; try various out and see what suits you best. For shading boot tops and such, I use a softer lead.

Pencil sharpeners made just for drafting can be bought. I still use a sharp knife and a sandpaper block. Take your choice. I buy the Mylar leads in tubes, and use a couple of cheap lead holders. The Mylar erasers seem to go forever.

For holding battens in place on your board, you must have ducks, whales, or whatever you want to call them. I cast these in lead. I've tried the whale shape, making a wood pattern with a "draw," then a split plaster mold, and so on. It's not worth it, though the shape is attractive. I find it simpler to use the English shape—rectangular with a pointed nose—using quickly made wood molds. I have these in a couple sizes, and they are stable. The "fingers" for holding the batten are simply pieces of 9-gauge fence wire,

with one end flattened and sharp, the other threaded and self-tapping into a hole in the lead. The weights are smoothed up, given a couple of coats of black enamel, and a common cork auto gasket is cemented to the bottom; some designers use billiard cloth. After much use of both, I think the whale shape, popular in this country, is not all that good.

Battens: I make these, too, having tried various woods. I like white pine best, Port Orford cedar next, and occasionally local cedar. Mahogany is a bad last, as it's grainy and brittle. Make your battens plenty long; excess can always be cut off. Planing these fair on a true piece of board, with a very sharp block plane, is a matter of practice. I've tried all the batten shapes given in books, and find square or rectangular shapes are all I use. I have tapered battens and find I seldom use them. Softwood battens—in fact, all battens—are easily damaged by the fingers of the ducks. Take care, and when too many nicks develop, re-plane the batten and use it for sharper bends.

Some make much of "a fair line by batten." This is fine up to a point, but I do not let a batten design my boats; I make the batten take a shape I like. If you let the battens do the thinking, often a spindle-shaped craft, of which we see many, is the result.

Next to battens come ship curves and sweeps. You can spend a bundle here on store-bought items. I simply copy shapes from a book or catalog and reproduce them in pine, cedar, or mahogany. The number and shapes of curves are fascinating, but start out moderately. Many of the curves are only suitable for big-ship work, or types of craft you

(Continued on next page)

Jensen, listed a couple of volumes ago for their pneumatic line, also has a very extensive line of precision tools; in fact, 3,000 of them in a catalog 152 pages long! Especially interesting are their made-up tool kits, such as the trouble-shooter's roll-pouch.

Jensen Tools and Alloys
1230 S. Priest Dr.
Tempe, Ariz. 85281

The JTK-84 Troubleshooter's Roll Pouch kit from the Jensen Tools and Alloys catalog.

INCLUDES THESE FINE TOOLS

Hammer, 4-oz. ball pein
Hex key set
Knife
Nutdriver, self-adjusting, 1/4 to 7/16"
Plier, chain nose with cutter, 6-1/2"
Plier, diagonal cutter, 4-1/8"
Plier, groove joint, 6"
Punch, center, 3/32"
Punch, pin, 1/8"
Punch, pin, 1/16"
Rule, 6"
Screwdriver, 4-in-1
Screwdriver, pocket, Phillips
Screwdriver, pocket, slotted
Solder aid
Solder brush
Soldering iron
Solder sample
Solder wick sample
Spline key set
Tweezers, cross locking
Wire stripper
Wrench, adjustable, 4"
Wrench, adjustable, 6"
Roll pouch, 12 x 21"

25 essential tools

A handy vinyl-coated roll pouch containing a select complement of tools for troubleshooting, servicing, repairing most electronic-electrical equipment. Includes pliers, screwdrivers, nutdrivers, tweezers, wrenches, hex and spline keys, soldering iron, hammer and more. See complete listing at left. All tools fit snugly in 12 x 21" roll pouch. A Triplett 310 VOM test meter is an optional accessory. A good looking kit at an attractive price.

JTK-84 WITHOUT METER **$75.00**
(In lots of 5-19, $65.00 each, 20-49, $57.00 each.)
JTK-84 WITH TRIPLETT 310 VOM METER **$128.00**
(In lots of 5-19, $115.00 each, 20-49, $104.00 each.)

(Continued from previous page)

may not be working with. Doing designs based on classic craft only, I find 5 or 6 ship curves the most used, and about that many sweeps. I have a drawer full of curves I seldom use.

Doing the type of craft I'm interested in, I find that one particular body curve, helped out by a couple of very small sweeps, handles the sections of almost any craft, from a yawlboat to a schooner. Changing scale has a lot to do with it. This is an offshoot of the ancient method of whole moulding, but using modern fairing methods, it works well and gives a handsome hull, scientific or not. For practice, and to learn what went on, I designed by whole moulding and built a half model of the result. A handsome craft can be turned out, but you do have to use some judgment in fairing in the ends. If this is delving into the long-buried past of naval architecture, so be it, because you learn something from it. I've always learned something from investigating how other designers worked, be they ancient or modern. I've been in the workrooms of some of the great designers—L. Francis Herreshoff, Murray G. Peterson, Ralph H. Wiley, to name just a few. Their equipment was modest, their ability with it was something else again. As in many things, stay simple.

Straightedges are easily made of pine or other stable wood. Have plenty on hand—long, short, light, and heavy. Check them occasionally and true them up if needed. Sometimes a store-bought rule of some kind does well for one size. I like the thin little transparent plastic rules for cabin layout. The open, clear design with the markings showing through is very handy, as you can line up parallel to other lines with little fuss; the scales have some use, especially if you are using 1" or 1/2" scale.

Other measuring devices: I use the common, triangular, white molded architect's scale, plus one marked in tenths, as it's handy for some calculations. Use the decimal system instead of getting involved with fractions. Sometimes a very long rule is nice to have; these are not usually triangular, so a set of several scales becomes expensive—I don't have any. I do have a set, to all scales I use, of short (about 6") homemade rules. They are very handy for cabin layout; they save constant flopping of a long triangular rule about. You can buy these, with 2 scales on each side. The way they are beveled, plus the four scales, makes them awkward, though they make handy pocket rules. My scales are each to its own and beveled on one side, of Port Orford cedar. They look like boxwood when varnished. Where to get them? Simply make them. Making small rules seems unheard of, yet with a bit of patience it can be done. I've found that these little rules save a lot of time and fumbling, and they are little more trouble to make than the drawn scale seen on many older plans. You may well find other measuring devices that suit some particular work. I like to use a yardstick and a two-foot rule in imagining how some part of the design will look full size. Table heights, locker heights, and many other things you find follow a pattern, but it's good to fool with the yardstick and rule to be sure if things will work.

Drawing instruments: I've had a nice German silver Dietzen drawing set for some 50 years. Recently I was given a similar, much heavier set of the same make. These are the best, as I don't ink, I don't use the pens. Less expensive sets

(Continued on next page)

We've finally found another factor of non-sparking, non-magnetic, corrosion-resistant tools in Ampco. In addition to the usuals, they have farmer's and bricklayer's tools.

**Ampco Metal
Box 2004
Milwaukee, Wisc. 53201**

An impressive array of special-alloy tools from the Ampco Metal catalog.

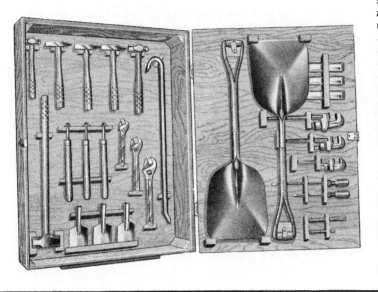

TOOL KIT M-50

Contains the following standard Ampco tools in a sturdy wood case approximately 50″ long, 36″ wide and 11″ deep. (Case can be locked when not in use.).............................. Wt. Lbs. 148.000

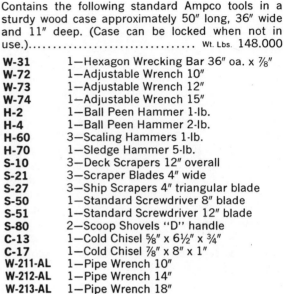

W-31	1—Hexagon Wrecking Bar 36″ oa. x ⅞″
W-72	1—Adjustable Wrench 10″
W-73	1—Adjustable Wrench 12″
W-74	1—Adjustable Wrench 15″
H-2	1—Ball Peen Hammer 1-lb.
H-4	1—Ball Peen Hammer 2-lb.
H-60	3—Scaling Hammers 1-lb.
H-70	1—Sledge Hammer 5-lb.
S-10	3—Deck Scrapers 12″ overall
S-21	3—Scraper Blades 4″ wide
S-27	3—Ship Scrapers 4″ triangular blade
S-50	1—Standard Screwdriver 8″ blade
S-51	1—Standard Screwdriver 12″ blade
S-80	2—Scoop Shovels "D" handle
C-13	1—Cold Chisel ⅝″ x 6½″ x ¾″
C-17	1—Cold Chisel ⅞″ x 8″ x 1″
W-211-AL	1—Pipe Wrench 10″
W-212-AL	1—Pipe Wrench 14″
W-213-AL	1—Pipe Wrench 18″

(Continued from previous page)

do about as well, though there is no question the heavy Dietzen has a great feeling of stability about it. Along with these, I was given a huge, bronze, Dietzen rolling parallel rule by a person who did not know what it was—if I could name it, I could have it. It's a wonderful instrument. I thought this would be very handy—in some cases it is—but it does not get the use I expected. In some cases it's awkward and not quite accurate, which is not the fault of the instrument, but of the surface it works on. It's more suited to the charthouse of a Flying "P" nitrate clipper than to a drafting board.

We now come to that badge of the N.A., the planimeter. I don't own one, which confounds many people. A planimeter is nice to have, but they are now quite expensive. I simply use the old builder's method—the square paper method—of figuring areas. No matter how you do it, it's tedious, but it works. And I often go one better, using the great shipbuilder Griffiths' method (1850?). I nearly always make a half-model of a new craft. The lifts are to scale, of course, and include the buttocks, also, though these are glued up and can't be taken apart. Buttocks aid you later in other ways. The lifts are dowelled together in the usual way; sheer, profile, and half-breadth are cut closely on a bandsaw, and the waste is saved. Once the model is shaped and finished to my satisfaction, using templates from the original draft, though I sometimes alter this until I'm happy with the model, I separate the model at the waterline and put it on a "justice scale" of my own make. This scale is accurate to 15 pounds at 1/2″ scale. The scrap I've saved in bandsawing out the model is, of course, in lifts. Say the waterlines are 1′ apart in a scale of 1/2″. These are carefully

squared up with a scriber and square in cubic feet. I get as many cubic feet out of the bigger chunks as I can; this helps accurate work. These pieces are carefully sawn, and sometimes trued on a sanding disk, using calipers. The pieces are marked with the cubic content. As I work the smaller scrap, I have a few tens, a couple of fives and twos, and a one. Simply put these blocks on the scale until they balance the model. You have weighed volume, not pounds, and only one half the vessel. Double the volume and multiply it by 64 pounds for salt water, and you have the displacement, less that of the appendages, which in classics are more or less rectangular in section and easy to figure.

Designing to the inside of the plank, which is what builders are interested in, using Griffiths again, I add 1/18 of the total displacement with the plank off, to get the displacement with the plank on. This formula changes with the size of a vessel somewhat, but as I don't design big clippers or wooden warships, the 1/18 rule is suited to most of my cruising craft.

If you work displacement out by areas and construct a curve of areas, and do it to the inside of plank, Chapelle gives a formula for adding the plank in his *Yacht Designing and Planning* (W.W. Norton, N.Y.). When using the paper methods, I don't use Simpson's Rule, because I draw to mold stations for a sprung-frame craft or to sawn-frame stations in bigger craft. Using the above rule, I would have to strike in false ordinates, which is a waste of time. I use the builder's or trapezoidal method, which, along with the squared paper and lack of planimeter, seems to work just as well. When you think about it, all these paper formulas must be in some error—some say as much as 5 percent in

(Continued on next page)

Antique Woodworking Tools, by Michael Dunbar
Hastings House, New York
192 pages, illus., index, 1977, $12.50

Subtitled "A guide to the purchase, restoration, and use of old tools for today's shop," this is essentially a tract by a craftsman who believes that to do period reproductions, you must use period tools. His argument is well thought out and reasonable, and his advice on what tools to buy and what to pass up is worth the price of admission.

What the author has to say about today's so-called master craftsmen is worth repeating: "Today, the word 'master' is attached with ease and there are currently more master cabinetmakers and master carvers than ever existed back when the word had meaning. Both terms, craftsman and master, are so abused that many talented woodworkers worthy of being called by either one, or both, avoid them. They are afraid they will be judged guilty by their association with those who are less demanding of the definition."

Our criticism of this book is threefold: (1) there is too much discussion of planes at the expense of other tools; (2) there aren't enough illustrations; (3) the author talks continually of craftsmanship, yet the book itself lacks it—the editor let the author and the reader down by failing to root out an incredible number of typographical errors. Despite this, the book is must reading for those contemplating the use of antique hand tools.

SPAR MAKERS' PLANE.

SMOOTH PLANE.

TOOTH PLANE.

(Continued from previous page)

some designs—simply because they must be based on straight lines somewhere, with assumptions to allow for this. I wonder if Griffiths' method is so very out-dated!

There are other methods to figure displacement based on measuring volume, such as the spill method with water, said to be used by Capt. Nat Herreshoff in his early years; anyhow, I have a description as to how he was said to have done it. Scotty Gannet, the famous but long-gone builder of small sloops and schooners at Scituate, is said to have used a spill method using sand—from one beach only, Plum Island. I really don't know, but his little craft were works of art. If sand helps produce a good boat, why not use it?.

Other simple tools are probably best bought, as they are not costly. Triangles, protractors, plastic things with various size holes or ellipses, all come in handy and are time savers. I do have a big wooden, home-built "gallows square" on the English design that is sometimes handy. I also like to have a big plastic triangle around, besides the usual smaller ones.

The drafting machine seen on the boards of many house designers and engineers, I don't have. It has not been popular with any marine designers of my acquaintance, for just what reason I don't know.

A while back I mentioned altering the lines of a model from the original draft. To get these lines on paper, I simply create another grid; the original will be pretty shabby by then anyhow. When the model is half apart for weighing, I first balance the underwater part on a sharp edge. This gives the center of buoyancy, volume again, not pounds. This is most accurate, so mark it on the new grid. I take the model totally apart and use the mid frame or mold scribed on

back to locate each piece in its place on the grid. I *spot,* not trace, around these pieces; tracing does not work out too well. Glued-in buttocks come in here; I square down with a fine little standing square and spot these on the sheer plan. The half-breadth at the sheer is taken by a tick strip from the assembled model. All these spots are faired in by batten, as it's most difficult in a flat-run craft to trace around what become feather edges in a dis-assembled model. From the sheer and half-breadth plan I create a new body plan, adding the diagonals there, then putting them in the half-breadth plan. If carefully done, there is very little adjustment to make in the lines.

This might be a backward way, but many a big, fine sailing ship was designed just this way, and at least I know how my hull will look in the round. A half-model is always a big thing with a client who often can't interpret plans too well. If the client builds the boat, he gets the model; it's all part of the design fee. I find these models are of much interest to most builders. They are mounted on a nice backboard, appendages added, often the masts and bowsprit in stump form, with the proper rakes, sometimes the centerboard partly down, if there is one, trailboards if a clipper head. Bulwarks, if any, are usually painted in, though the rest is semi-dull varnish. Thick strakes, if any, are indicated, and the stations marked in with a very flexible rule. All in all, a half-model is a very attractive thing. Once I assemble a model for the last time, I glue the lifts for stability and to hold feather edges, then the model is carefully fine-sanded so the above finishes can be applied. Sounds like a lot of work, but not as much as you might think.

(Continued on next page)

	Bit Diameter	Length	
07P01-BP	1/4"	24"	$9.75 ppd.
07P02-BP	1/4"	30"	$12.60 ppd.
07P03-BP	5/16"	24"	$9.75 ppd.
07P04-BP	5/16"	30"	$12.60 ppd.
07P06-BP	3/8"	30"	$12.60 ppd.
07P07-BP	7/16"	24"	$9.75 ppd.
07P08-BP	7/16"	30"	$12.60 ppd.
07P09-BP	1/2"	30"	$12.60 ppd.

LAMP STANDARD SHELL AUGERS

This special purpose tool for end grain boring will cut straight and true with a minimum of wander. Preferred by wind instrument makers and turners, and used most effectively with our Hollow Boring Guide (04N41-D), plus the appropriate bushing. The tang is tapered and shaped to fit perpendicular, into the handle, in the same manner as our gimlets.

Here's something a little extraordinary from Woodcraft's ever-growing catalog. How we could have used these shell augers a time or two!

Woodcraft Supply Corp.
313 Montvale Ave.
Woburn, Mass. 01801

Top: Lamp Standard Shell Augers from the Woodcraft catalog. Below, right: The Klemmsia Quick-Grip clamp from Champion (Bromley Boats) Ltd.

Some readers have written in to knock our recommendation of quick-action or guitar clamps some volumes back. So we went back to the shop a few hundred times to check out the complaints of unsteadiness and softness. Phooey! They are just super, and here we have found a place that makes them in lengths up to 4 feet. Made by A. W. Champion Ltd., in Surrey, they are distributed by our old friends:

Champion (Bromley Boats) Ltd.
109-123 Southlands Roads
Bromley, Kent
England

(Peck, listed on page 29, also has them.)

(Continued from previous page)

Here are some things I've found out the hard way.

• As mentioned before, some drawing paper is much affected by humidity; find something you can work with.

• Keep your design work simple, especially for small craft; there seems to be no scientific method of designing these.

• Calculations are fine, often necessary, and just plain helpful, but don't make these a way of life; you can get carried away by them and not see the woods for the trees.

• A boat or vessel, sail or power, that steers poorly is an unhappy craft—seldom do corrective measures do very much good; the mistake was made in the beginning.

• Take care in using the raking midsection in designs—sometimes you must use it to some extent, but it can get you into trouble.

• A planing powerboat that needs trim tabs is either overloaded or defective in design.

• Most boats, especially powerboats, now are too short, and usually overpowered.

• Simplicity never hurt any design.

END

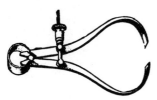

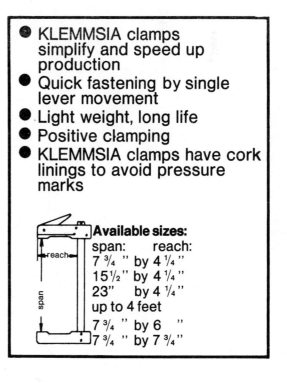

• **KLEMMSIA clamps simplify and speed up production**

• **Quick fastening by single lever movement**

• **Light weight, long life**

• **Positive clamping**

• **KLEMMSIA clamps have cork linings to avoid pressure marks**

Available sizes:

span:	reach:
7 3/4 "	by 4 1/4 "
15 1/2"	by 4 1/4 "
23"	by 4 1/4 "
up to 4 feet	
7 3/4 "	by 6 "
7 3/4 "	by 7 3/4 "

No-Twist Clamps

Dear Editors:

I would like to recommend a relatively new clamp that we use extensively in our machine shop. They are made by various companies and are available from most machine shop supply companies, one such being:

Enco Manufacturing Co.
4520 West Fullerton Ave.
Chicago, Ill. 60639

The Enco No-Twist Clamps are greatly superior to C-clamps, being much stronger, unbreakable, and having deeper throats. Built-in "V" clamping blocks allow the clamping of angular surfaces. They are not too cheap, but they will outlast a C-clamp.

H. Talboys
Emerson, N.J.

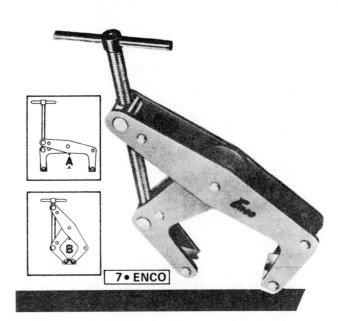

Right, top: The Enco No-Twist clamp.
Right, bottom: Boxed material on the Cutawl from the Foredom catalog.

Neat Cutter

Got a nice note from Jack Spangler of the Foredom Electric Company about his Cutawl:

The Cutawl is the only portable sawing machine of its kind. It is commonly used by signmakers and by display makers. I have always thought that the Cutawl would be valuable to boat building people who do intricate cutout work in sheet materials, ordinarily plywood, in making cabinet work for cabin interiors and the like. It can also be used for decorative scroll cutout work such as might be found on a transom, trailboards, or bowsprit.

The Foredom Electric Co.
Bethel, Conn. 06801

Mr. Spangler also had a few words to say about saw blades:

The Olson Saw Company division manufactures woodcutting saw blades for band saws, coping saws and the like. We acquired this company, moving it from Brooklyn, New York, in 1976. So far we have published new price sheets under our new logo, for scroll saws and coping saws. We would like your readers to know that they can purchase directly from The Olson Saw Company spring temper, set, and filed, woodcutting band saw blades, the kind of saw blade preferred by true woodworking master craftsmen.

The Olson Saw Company
Bethel, Conn. 06801

Cut Sheet Materials

Better and Faster

Into Any Shape or

Design You Want

The Cutawl power tool is designed for cutting sheet materials into shapes and patterns impossible to make with any other type of cutting tool. It is unmatched for speed, precision and ease of operation. Completely portable, the Cutawl power tool is easier to use than a jig saw or saber saw. It glides effortlessly over the surface of the work, following any line, because the blade holder swivels 360° in any direction.

There's No Tool Like an Old Tool

As the man said, it takes all kinds. We know a fellow who collects bricks, another who collects marbles, still another who has boxes and boxes of buttons. We even know a fellow who collects common beach stones. We don't know Ken Roberts, but we do know what he collects, or should we say, what he is obsessed with.

Tools. It's not just tools by themselves, but books and catalogs about tools as well. And he's not content to just have them lying around; he reprints them. Looking for the *Stanley Rule and Level Catalog* for 1859? Roberts has a reprint for $2.00. He has the *Alex Mathieson Joiner and Cooper Tools* catalog for $4.00, and the 1890 *Buck Brothers Chisels* catalog for $6.00. There are many more as well. Ken Roberts also has a couple of texts on tools: *Tools for the Trades and Crafts,* with documentary by Ken Roberts himself ($22.70), and *Wooden Planes in 19th Century America,* by you-know-who ($22.50).

If you take *your* tool or tool-book collecting at all seriously, send for Ken Roberts's latest list of publications:

Ken Roberts Publishing Company
Box 151
Fitzwilliam, N.H. 03447

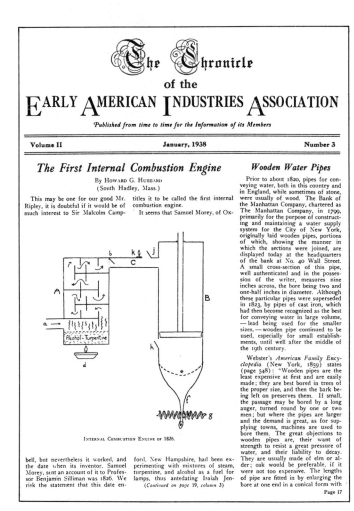

Above: Cooper's tools from Tools for the Trades and Crafts.
Left: A sample page from the EAIA's reprint of the Chronicle.

The Early American Industries Association, described in MC-4 (page 42), has reprinted the first 25 years of its journal, *The Chronicle*. This clothbound book has 1,096 pages and around 1,000 illustrations, and covers the period November 1933 to December 1958. Obviously, much of the material published in *The Chronicle* doesn't have marine application, but plenty does—"The File Maker," "The Cooper," "The Rope Maker," "Some Notes on Axes," "Making Wood Planes," etc. The price of the book is $20 to EAIA members; $48.50 to nonmembers (last we heard, membership was $14—a compelling reason to join if you want the book). Send your order to:

Early American Industries Association
Book Orders
Mrs. P.B. Kebabian
11 Scottsdale Road
South Burlington, Vermont 05401

A cabinetmaker and master carpenter, David Rego has established a tool outlet on the side. $1.00 gets his catalog, the first entry of which describes a 4-in-1 package—a combination molder/planer/jointer/edger.

David Rego
49 Downing St.
Fall River, Mass. 02723

It's easy and fast, and your choice of patterns is virtually unlimited with this low-cost 4-in-1 workhorse* molder, planer, edger, jointer.

Make professional quality frame moldings for a fraction of the cost. Select from stock sets of molding knives or custom knives for any pattern. Quickly change patterns, turn out intricate moldings in minutes.

Framers who've used it say they wouldn't be without this rugged, simple, inexpensive molder-planer.

Above: David Rego's combination molder/planer/jointer/edger.

A Challenge

A local agent for Garrett Wade, a company with whom we have been a little left-handed in the past, says that this company is *planning* to gear up and become the country's leading distributor of specialized boatbuilding tools. Gentlemen, start your engines.

—Eds.

Garrett Wade
302 Fifth Avenue
New York, N.Y. 10001

Dear Editors:

As a boatbuilder, I have urged Gary Chin and Henry Lang, who run Garrett Wade, to find, or have made, tools of the finest quality for the boatbuilder. These tools have heretofore been impossible to buy new. Their response has been entirely enthusiastic, and both are doing research for sources here in the US and in the UK and Europe. Hopefully the results of our efforts will make Garrett Wade the marine-oriented woodworker's source of tools. Anyone who wants a Garrett Wade catalog, thinks a certain tool should be in it, or knows of a tool source of first quality should get in touch with me.

William Cannell, Boatbuilder
Garrett Wade Rep.
Box 911
Camden, Maine 04843

Take a look at this nice upper blade guide mechanism on the 10-inch Inca bandsaw from Garrett Wade.

Black and Decker recently sent over their heavy-duty industrial-grade-tool catalog—the line you're not likely to find in the friendly local. We're impressed. When writing, you'll be wanting a letterhead.

Black and Decker
Towson, Md. 21204

Right: The Black and Decker heavy-duty 12-inch cut-off machine.
Below: The Major CMB 500 Mk II from Coronet Tool.

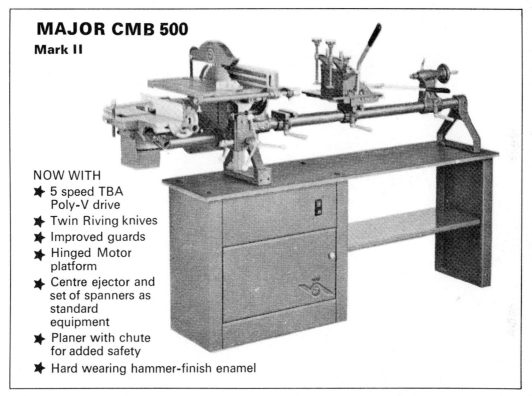

MAJOR CMB 500
Mark II

NOW WITH
* 5 speed TBA Poly-V drive
* Twin Riving knives
* Improved guards
* Hinged Motor platform
* Centre ejector and set of spanners as standard equipment
* Planer with chute for added safety
* Hard wearing hammer-finish enamel

Professional cutting/welding torch.

Real oxygen torch.
Cuts, welds, brazes, solders.
No hoses or filters.
Completely portable.
Professional type for the Do-It-Yourselfer.

Cut, Weld, Braze, solder

* Real oxygen
* Instant on, instant off
* Easy to use
* Built-in check valve
* Single tip operation for both cutting and welding
* Portable—one hand operation
* Includes goggles, spark lighter, oxygen cylinder and welding rods

Propane or Mapp gas not included.

The Shopsmith—the multi-purpose woodworking machine—has formidable competition in the British Coronet line of tools—this their Major CMB500 Mark II. We know of no American distributor but suspect there is one in Canada. For 10p they'll send their catalog, *Wood Working and Wood Turning on Universal and Independent Machines.*

Coronet Tool Co.
Alfreton Road
Derby DE2 4AH
England

Small But Effective

With the cost of custom and repair work being what it is, surely something small is better than nothing at all in the low-budget shop. Bernzomatic helps you make do with a lightweight cutting/welding torch. Your hardware dealer has it, or will soon.

Heed the Saw, Beware the Tree

Dear Editors:

Your remarks in MC-5, page 60, about Zip-Penn, and about fear of chainsaws, are very much to the point. I think, though, that there are a few important points you've overlooked.

In the first place . . . it isn't easy to sharpen chains, particularly with modern high-speed saws (such as my Partner). I'm fairly bright with mechanical things (I've filed my own circular-saw blades for years), but it took me a long time and a lot of trouble to learn to sharpen chainsaw chains properly.

With high-speed saws, a slightly mis-sharpened chain will eat up bars in a few minutes. When roller-nosed bars cost $25-$30, this can be quite painful. One fall, I cut 45 cord of maple firewood, and ran through six bars before I found out what I was doing wrong.

That's why I don't buy from Zip-Penn. I bought my saw from a wonderful local dealer. Through all of my trials in learning how to look after the saw, he gave me as much help as he could in diagnosing my problems and helping me to overcome them. In return, I'm glad to give him a couple of bucks extra whenever I need a new chain. Skilled professional help is invaluable, in my opinion, in learning to look after a chainsaw. Around here, about one adult male in three works in the woods at least part of the year. Every one of them has his own idea how to file a chain. In my opinion, an honest dealer has to know better.

If you ask me, I think that you should tell your readers that the best way to go to the woods is to go with some old-timer who is willing to have them, and to keep eyes and ears wide open.

In addition, I'd like to make one comment on your remarks about fear of chainsaws. You're quite right about saws—but, you neglect to mention trees. Around here, trees are quite stunted with respect to those found west and south of here. Our biggest trees are much smaller than those found in Nova Scotia, southwestern Quebec, or northeastern U.S. Still, our big trees run, I figure, between 3,500 and 5,000 pounds on the hoof.

When you cut down something that big, with a center of gravity twenty-odd feet off the ground, you liberate a hell of a lot of energy. The danger of that makes the danger of a chainsaw seem trivial. It's something that one has to think of when going to the woods.

A friend and neighbor of mine died this afternoon as a result of an injury suffered in the woods in 1961. A tree that he had felled hung-up partway down. The butt struck him in the chest and drove him back a hundred-odd feet from the stump.

The moral is that trees are big, and heavy: if one chooses to kill them, one must do it with great respect, and with great caution.

Ted Wright
Shigawake, Quebec, Canada

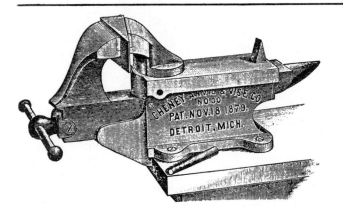

Edge of the Anvil
by Jack Andrews
Rodale Press, Inc.
Emmaus, Penn. 18049
$6.95 (paper), $9.95 (hardbound), 1977

Since the first *Mariner's Catalog*, our enthusiasm for forging has been cherry-red-blue-oil-quenched for the simple reason that some control of iron is another road to independence in the woodworking shop, as well as the garage, garden, etc. Of the several books we've reviewed on the subject, this is the most practically useful. If you've got some books on the subject, add this one. Otherwise, get this one as your first purchase. Blacksmithing for students, start to finish.

Right: Table from Edge of the Anvil.

Resource Information

Expanded Temperature Chart
of Temper Colors

Color	°F	Use
	660	
Steel grey	650	
	640	
Greenish blue	630	Light springs
	620	
Light blue	610	Screwdrivers
	600	Wood saws, punches
Dark blue	590	Springs
	580	Picks, hot chisels
Blue	570	Cold chisels, light work
	560	Knives
Dark purple	550	Cold chisels, steel
Purple	540	Axes, center punch
Light purple	530	Hammers, sledges
Brown with purple spots	520	Surgical instruments
Dark brown	510	Twist drills
Bronze	500	Rock drills
Dark straw	490	Wood chisels
Golden straw	480	Drifts, leather dies
Straw	470	Pen knives
Straw yellow	460	Thread cutting tools
Yellow	450	Planer tools
Light yellow	440	Drills for stone
	430	Paper cutters, lathe tools
Pale yellow	420	Razors
	410	Burnishers
	400	Scrapers

Making Knives

For a growing number of people, making tools has become as important as, and sometimes more important than, using them. You can see this reflected in the publishing industry: Just a few short years ago, you could hardly find a title on amateur toolmaking in print. Now you can walk into almost any reasonably well-stocked bookstore and find a number of titles on the subject (many of them have been reviewed in past *Mariner's Catalogs*). One of the latest is easily the best we've seen yet:

Step-by-Step Knifemaking, by David Boye
Rodale Press, Emmaus, Penn.
270 pages, illus., index, 1977, $7.95

You have to want a handmade knife in the worst way to go through what you must go through to do it right, but you won't make any mistakes because of the lack of instruction. The author's text, in combination with beautiful photographs and clear sketches, takes you from the beginning (choosing your steel) to the end (making a sheath). But it is obvious from this book that it takes a number of big, expensive tools to make your own knives to the author's standards. And that's the rub.

I get a little tense when giving birth to a blade.

Below and above, right: From Step-by-Step Knifemaking.

Cutting the Steel with a Torch

If you use an acetylene torch, draw out a number of shapes on the same piece of flat stock and cut them all out in one operation. If you are using a band saw, it is better to reduce the size of the stock to only slightly larger than the intended knife blade. The acetylene torch is probably faster in cutting out a number of knives from a large piece of steel, but affords less control when it comes to the precise contours of the blade.

Here are some ways to improve the efficiency and precision of the cutting torch performance:

1. Thoroughly clean the steel before cutting.
2. Use a small-size tip; keep it clean.
3. Use an open metal frame to support the stock while cutting.
4. Thoroughly preheat when starting a cut before shooting oxygen or you may "blow away" part of the knife.
5. Do not have the oxygen pressure too high or it will pop.

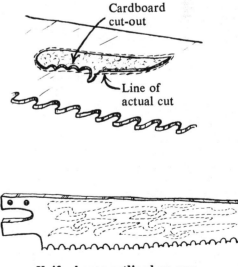

Knife shapes outlined on saw

Handling Knives

Indian Ridge Traders puts out a stainless knife blade made by Sheffield in England. It is called the MM 055 and sells for $11 postpaid. Fair steel—for stainless. It is made as a general-purpose lifeboat knife. A bit too long for me, so I chopped an inch off the end and refiled the proper bevel.

**Indian Ridge Traders
Box 869
Royal Oak, Mich. 48068**

Indian Ridge only sells blades and supplies for finishing them, including rivets. You make your own handles. I epoxied two thin pieces of micarta on the handle section and wrapped with #21 seine twine. Two dips in spar varnish set things up pretty good. A thin handle on a thick (3/16"), super strong blade makes a light, compact knife that can be depended on under almost any circumstances. No slip.

Indian Ridge also sells three other blades fabricated from 440 stainless. Tough stuff and harder to sharpen than carbon steel, but it doesn't rust and will last a long time. Quality is extremely high and service is immediate.

Send for their catalog, which also includes instructions and advice on finishing their blades.

—**Mark White**

Right and below: Steel lesson and illustration from the Indian Ridge catalog.

A Quick & Dirty Knife

For a really quick homemade knife, take an old wornout 12-inch planer blade and grind it in half (don't try hacksawing). Let it in to a piece of stray teak and sharpen it in a sheepsfoot pattern. The blade can be sandwiched between the wood with five-minute epoxy, but be sure to degrease the teak with nail-polish remover (which is acetone with a smellgood added) and roughen the surfaces before gluing. The blade should go almost full length in the handle. This carbon steel from planer blades is eminently sharpenable and seems to hold an edge well. I've made three of these knives and am convinced that all of them are at least as good as any I could go out and buy.

—**Mark Roeyer**

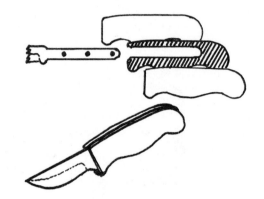

SHEFFIELD CARBON CUTLERY STEEL is essentially a high carbon steel with very small amounts of alloying elements that tend to add toughness to a blade without getting into Tool Steel or Stainless Steel characteristics. This steel will rust and stain so it requires some care, but it hones to a fine edge as easily as a simple High Carbon Steel while being just a little bit tougher and thus more resistant to damage. We think this is a good choice for hunting knives.

SHEFFIELD STAINLESS STEEL has some 12% Chromium added to the melt to produce a stain and rust resistant character. We specify this steel for only one regular blade (MASTER MARINER) where the stainless nature is of value and the much tougher steel combined with a sturdy grind gives us the most rugged blade in our catalog. It is harder to sharpen than any simple High Carbon Steel, but the trade-offs seem desirable in this particular blade pattern.

AMERICAN CARBON STEEL is used in most of our blades made in U.S.A. It is a simple High Carbon Steel which has long been the favorite of cutlery makers (it works easiest of all cutlery steels, hardens simply to a Rockwell C-60 and draws-down simply to any desired hardness). It is also the favorite among knife users because it sharpens much more easily than any other steel and readily comes to a real razor-quality edge. It does rust and stain, so it requires some care and at higher hardness levels it is somewhat brittle (compared to other steels) and is more likely to be damaged by misuse. All in all we think this is the easiest-to-live-with steel for much used knives.

Boatbuilding + Materials

THE KIBITZERS

Wooden boatbuilding takes time because it is almost totally custom work. Some time ago I built a boat for a man who had a service business. He had stock bins with parts for anything his work force needed to do its work. He seemed to think that my crew was extremely slow and even went so far as to say we were dragging our feet. This stunned me for a moment, as we had a pretty good name for being fast, as well as being neat in our work.

I regained my senses soon enough and said to him, "Suppose you didn't have anything in your shop but iron ore and a foundry, and a customer came in and ordered a complicated piece of machinery with many parts. You would have to make patterns to cast these parts, then machine them all, and assemble them to build this piece of machinery.

"Then and only then, my dear man, could your operation compare with boatbuilding."

—Royal Lowell

Leather has its place around the boatshop, both as a boatbuilding material and as a sharpening strop for your edge tools. Pete Culler had a few words about the former:

Leather

I use leather a good deal in making up gear for small boats, mostly for oars, portable masts, at the partners, and, to a lesser extent, other places. I never tack leather on oars or masts, as this makes a fracture point where the most strain is. The question I'm most often asked is, "How do you make that stitch?" It seems a great mystery, and most mutter, and leave it at that, even though I show them. The idea of using a palm and needle somehow seems like a black art to many.

The illustration shows how it goes; naturally a bit of practice does help, but there is nothing difficult. It's simply the herringbone stitch, shown in several works on yachting seamanship. It's only the "baseball stitch" inside out.

(Continued on next page)

(Continued from previous page)

If you are left-handed, start with the knot on the right side, pull each stitch tight, locking the cross stitch with the thumb while taking the next. Some leather takes stitches better than other. If the stuff is a bit weak, take wider stitches; about 3/16" is a norm. Use well-waxed twine, double if it's light, and a sail needle, though a curved needle is also good. Some ask if I soak the leather first—sometimes I do, though leather seems weaker than it used to be and if wet, some stitches can pull out.

Sometimes the leather gets slack and slips down the oar, what then? I simply smear the oar with contact cement, and shove the leather back up. That's what miracle mixes are for—they seem to work.

If you use leather at all, it should be lubricated; plain tallow does just fine. Much used to be made of covering rigging eyes and splices with leather; as a regular practice, I don't like it, just a place for water to lodge. If it must be used on account of chafe, put it over properly parcelled, tarred, served, and tarred again. Leathering is often done on the chafe points of sails, notably at the clews, on the roping, and such.

I use leather pads contact-cemented to the foot and pads of C-clamps; this is most handy, as it saves much fumbling with small pad blocks at times. The leathers get compressed and hard in time, but being scrap are easily replaced. Often I use leather washers under iron washers on machinery that does not give a good seat for the washer—this was common for inside work in colonial times, under nails holding forged hinges on; often the pads were cut in a decorative way. A scalloped leather washer under a stopper knot is a handsome thing. A square of good leather is a must for the final hone of cutting tools. It makes fine washers for many things, including garden hoses and packing glands, but it will not take much real heat. Scraps, useless for much else, can be cut in a spiral, and make passable lacings or stuff to serve with. Leather cuts well, but the knife must be very sharp. Like many other things, leather is being replaced by plastic, but for much work there is nothing quite like it, and it's workable with the simplest tools. Somehow, it's a very pleasant material to work with.

Most have seen leathered gaff jaws, which are supposed to keep the gaff from chafing the mast. More often than not it's not very effective. I show here about how I go about leathering jaws. Copper tacks are used, and as the jaws are hardwood, start the holes with an awl. Use a tough piece of leather; there is plenty of pressure here, and often much movement in a seaway with light winds. I think leather is a waste of time on masts above 8 inches in diameter; the pressure is just too great for most leather to stand with a big sail area.

There are so many places to use leather that the way to go is to acquire some and you will soon find all sorts of things to do with it. And how do you acquire leather? Most towns of any size seem to have a leather worker; visit him and discuss things; sometimes he fixes you right up. Let it be known you use leather. Once in a while someone shows up with a hide; buy it. It's expensive, but what now is not?

—Pete Culler

Right: Illustration from Tan Your Hide!
Above, right: Illustrations by Pete Culler.

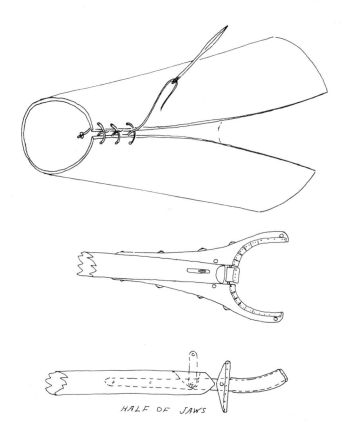

HALF OF JAWS

And if you have a raw hide that needs tanning, you might spend some time with:

Tan Your Hide!
Home Tanning Leathers and Furs
by Phyllis Hobson
Garden Way, Charlotte, Vermont
135 pages, illus., index, paperbound, 1977, $4.95

*Using the beam
to flesh a hide*

Finding Plans

A lot of people have been asking for it, and finally they have it:

The International Boat Plan & Kit Directory
North Island Publishing Co.
Box 399
Eastsound, Washington 98245
$3, plus $1 postage and handling, paperbound, 1978

The printing of this Directory gives the amateur and professional boatbuilder, for the first time, a single publication to look to for boat plans and kits plus the hundreds of other items needed to build and use a boat with a high degree of proficiency. There is absolutely no other publication printed that caters to the do-it-yourself boat builders' needs in the comprehensive manner that this Directory does.

—IBP & KD

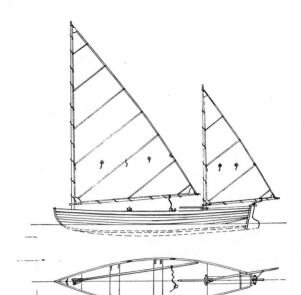

Ready Made

Anyone considering the joinery problem below decks either has talent or cards he ain't showin'. Prefab anything might go against your grain, but consider the various pre-built modules that are available for drawers, cabinets, etc. St. Louis Marine has some pretty good-looking stuff:

> **St. Louis Marine Hardware Co.**
> **Box 2888**
> **St. Louis, Mo. 63111**

Above and right: Prefab units from St. Louis Marine Hardware.

Caning

Several readers have mentioned their frustrations in boat restoration work when they've come to the old caned canoe seats and, in one case, the caned sternsheets of a guideboat. Most craftshops will have at least a chapter in a book to show you caning procedures, but, for 50 cents, there is a fine little pamphlet on the subject that tells and *shows* all. Spectre's already completed one job following it. Putz is waiting for the right moon.

Cane Seats for Chairs
by Ruth B. Comstock
Extension Publication Office
College of Human Ecology
Cornell University, Ithaca, N.Y.
50 cents

Chairs with small holes drilled through the frame around the seat opening should have cane seats. If these seats are carefully woven, they will be strong and wear well.

Cane for chair seating is made from a palm called *rattan*. The plants come from the Indian Archipelago, China, India, Ceylon, and the Malay Peninsula. They grow in dense forests and frequently reach tree height; then they fall over and form a matted undergrowth. The stem, which is covered with beautiful green foliage, grows in length from 100 to 300 feet and is seldom more than 1 inch in diameter. For export, these stems are cut in 10- to 20-foot lengths. The outer bark is stripped in varying widths and packaged in amounts for one or two chairs, or in 1,000 foot hanks for four chairs with medium-sized seats. The cane is cut in pieces, preferably 6-8 feet long.

Seating cane differs from domestic sugar cane and from the cane known as *bamboo*, which grows in the Southern States. Bamboo, which is shorter, straighter, and thicker, is used for furniture, walking sticks, poles, and the like. Neither bamboo nor sugar cane is suitable for chair seating.

Text and photos from Cane Seats for Chairs.

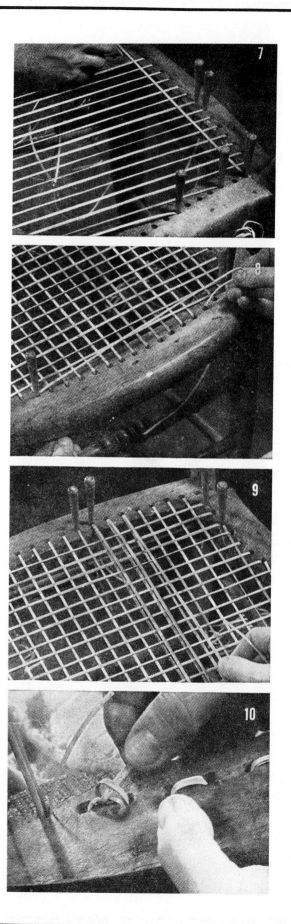

Fastenings

In building Adirondack guide-boats, the laps were fastened by two rows of #2 copper tacks, one driven from the inside, the other from the outside. These small tacks, although only slightly more than 1/4" in length, were still long enough to go through the 3/16" planking and clinch on the opposite side.

Because of a lack of demand for such small tacks, #2 copper tacks have not been manufactured in this country in some years, and are no longer on the market. In consequence, it has seemed that guide-boats could no longer be built in the traditional manner unless a supply of suitable tacks could be found.

But recently friends of the Adirondack Museum arranged to have a quantity of small copper tacks manufactured in Italy. Although these tacks are of a slightly different pattern, two experienced guide-boat builders have tried them and have found them suitable. Should they prove a little hard for easy clinching, they are easily annealed by heating them in a tin pie plate to a red heat over an electric or gas burner and quickly quenching them in cold water, just the opposite from steel.

The supply is limited, but while they last, they can be obtained in small lots approximately at cost from:

Adirondack Museum
Blue Mountain Lake, N.Y. 12812

[As of the Spring, 1978, one pound of tacks (about 5,200) was $8.50 plus $1.75 postage and handling; 4 ounces was $2.25 plus $.50 p&h.]

—John Gardner

Strawbery Banke, whose boatbuilding program is described elsewhere in this catalog, has recently acquired three nail-making machines and related apparatus to produce clench nails. They have a bit of preliminary work to do before production can begin, but expect to be in business at the end of 1978.

Strawbery Banke
Box 300
Portsmouth, N.H. 03801

We've located another source of hot-dip galvanized cut boat nails, from 3d to 60d sizes. The supplier also has cut nails of other patterns: spike, masonry, common, foundry, sheathing, rosehead clinch, floor, common siding, finish, clout, and box. Get them from:

E.K. Spinney Industrial Division
Box 310
Yarmouth, N.S.
Canada

E.K. Spinney is also a first-rate chandlery, with a wide range of products for the traditional boatman.

And then there's the Locked-Recess screw, from:

Lila Robin
620 So. Alaska
Seattle, Wash. 98108

The Locked-Recess screw utilizes a simple principle—the square. A tapered square recess replaces the conventional slot or crossed slot with amazing results. Locked-Recess screws are faster to install, have positive drive. It is impossible for the driver to slip out of the Locked-Recess. They are safer and faster to use, and give longer life to driver bits.

Damage to screw heads is eliminated. The Locked-Recess screw is ideal for repeated maintenance operations. Operator fatigue is drastically reduced due to the positive driver-holding properties.

—Lila Robin

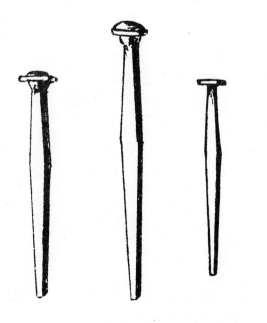

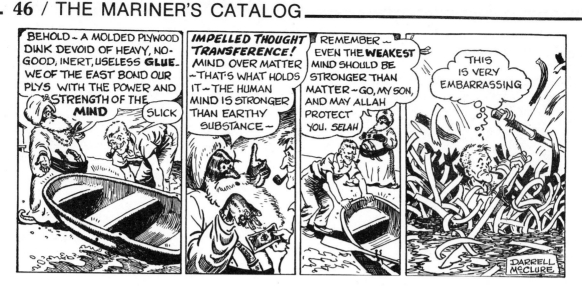

Sheetrock Screws

Do you know about wallboard (sheetrock) screws? Sheetrock guys don't nail anymore, they use screws. I know the screws are only steel—but wait—the design of these things is weird. Since they are made to drive with a power screwdriver in plywood and wood 2 x 4s *without* pilot holes and hold forever, they just might be useful to boatguys. A sheetrocker gave me about three handfuls of them (1¼") about ten years ago, and I'm just running out now. I've used them for all sorts of things and can vouch for the fact that they do not split plywood or wood (soft stuff, though), and they are self-countersinking in softwoods. And they do *hold*. Maybe they are good for fabrication of certain items without the need for tedious predrilling countersinking, etc.—like molds, for instance. Or gluing up various things without 879 clamps or gizmos to hold the wood. The screws come in different lengths and head designs. Get them from your building materials supplier.

—**Mark Roeyer**

Confirmation

Dear Editors:

One aspect of the *Mariner's Catalog* which is so appealing, aside from the obvious sources, information and ideas, is that there is always a thought or premise or quotation which stimulates a reaction because it either confirms or denies some long-held belief or puts into words some vague notion which has been kicking around in the back of your own mind.

For instance, in the first catalog on page 114, a quotation by Gilbert C. Klingel from his book *Boatbuilding with Steel*, "We should believe that when we build, we build forever, and that what we build should be as lovely or as graceful in ten years as it was when it was produced."

From Volume 3, page 48 by David Pye from *The Nature and Art of Workmanship*, "Workmanship can be 'good' or 'bad,' 'precise' or 'rough,' but work that is good doesn't have to be precise, nor does rough work have to be bad." Why didn't I think of that?

And so it goes. Now, in the latest catalog (Volume 5) I have only gotten as far as page 55 and Lowell P. Thomas's article on Boring A Shaft Log and already you've hit home three times with the same provoking topic. The cartoon on page 44 shows the bearded amateur builder standing by his unfinished craft and the caption, "There is nothing an amateur cannot do if he lives long enough." Again, on the next page, "It is probably easier for a fast workman to improve his craftsmanship than it is for the crafty workman to become a fast one."

Lowell P. Thomas, in his article, makes no bones about it—he spells it right out, telling of how much time is spent sitting in a chair puzzling out what has to be done. I have a mate of his chair and I'll bet my work pants have a shinier bottom than his have. Talk about dubious distinction.

But why is it that we must ever plod and plug along, the endless lists, make a template, cut and try? Why must every step be so carefully measured, every move so calculated, every new move so conservatively initiated? Ah hah, have we come down to it, is that the answer? Is the uncertainty on the one hand and the striving for perfection on the other nothing more than the binding of a conservative nature? If so, damn it, tell me, how did we get to be this way?

Ralph J. Ellis
Columbia, Conn.

P.S. Are others with this affliction always early for appointments, too?

Building the Herreshoff Dinghy
by Barry Thomas
Mystic Seaport, Mystic, Conn.
50 pages, illus., foldout plans, 1977,
paperbound, $3.75

A nice little monograph on building an 11½-foot dinghy using the methods practiced by the Herreshoff Manufacturing Co. Basically, the Herreshoff method was to build the boat upside down, with molds set up for each frame and the frames bent over the molds. Such construction requires many more molds than the usual method, but is said to make construction quicker and easier.

Building Classic Small Craft, by John Gardner
International Marine Publishing Company
Camden, Maine
314 pages, illus., index, 1977, $20

The dean of traditional boatbuilding presents a wide variety of boat types—among them dories, flatirons, peapods, wherries, St. Lawrence River skiffs, and Whitehalls—and describes how to build your very own.

Below: Diagram of foundation from Building the Herreshoff Dinghy.
Bottom: Lines of surf dory from Building Classic Small Craft.

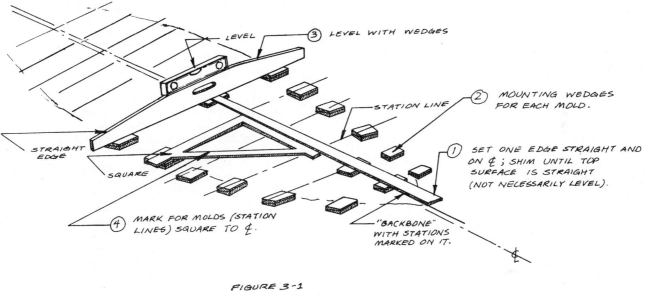

FIGURE 3-1
THE FOUNDATION
TO ACHIEVE A PLANE SURFACE ON WHICH TO SET UP THE BOAT

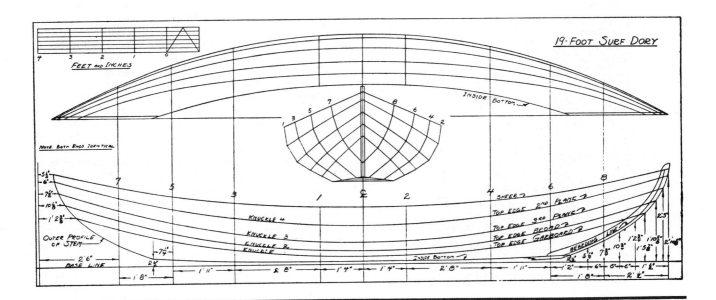

A Scheme for Renewing Plank Fastenings

by Maynard Bray

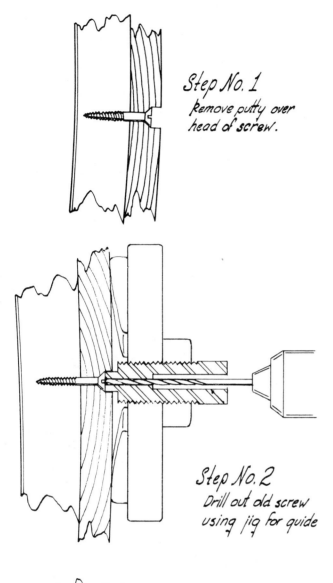

Step No. 1
Remove putty over head of screw.

Step No. 2
Drill out old screw using jig for guide

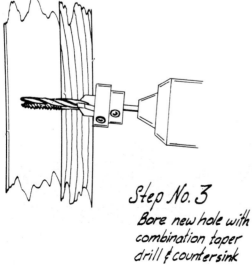

Step No. 3
Bore new hole with combination taper drill & countersink

If bronze or brass screws were used for plank fastenings and the boat is thirty or more years old, chances are that refastening is needed. The test is to try to back several of them out—just as a surveyor does when he goes over a boat. If their heads split and break off or if the screws twist off further down their length, the time has come to take action. Actually, the time has passed when this job could have been easily done by backing out the old screws and driving new ones in their place. Thus, if you want to make use of the same holes through the plank, you are faced with extracting the old screws by some other means.

Doing this is slow and tedious work, no matter what the method, and one sometimes wonders whether boring brand new holes for the new screws isn't about as good. This is what "refastening" means to a professional. His customer is rarely willing to pay extra for fussing around with extractions, so he straightforwardly bores new holes and drives new screws into them.

The dedicated amateur or the boat restorer, on the other hand, just hates to see the planks perforated with more holes. They go through all kinds of agony to utilize the existing ones. This usually involves getting rid of at least enough of the old screws to make it appear all clear for the new ones. I think it is rare to be able to get 100 percent of the old out unless they can be unscrewed.

Drilling a hole down the center of the old screw, then winding it out with a screw extractor (sometimes called an "easyout") should do the job—one would think. This method, or variations of it, is the common one, but the results are rarely as good as hoped for. Sometimes the drill runs off into the surrounding wood before it goes deep enough; sometimes the extractor splits the screw without extracting it; sometimes the entire screw turns to mush the minute the drill hits it. It's not satisfying work even when things go as well as can be expected.

I've seen a lot of boats refastened this way, and have done a number myself. By now, I should have figured out a slick way of doing this job. Although effective in most cases, the method I'm about to describe can hardly be termed slick. It's slow, and it's hard work. It is the outgrowth of what was used in refastening *Alerion* at Mystic Seaport a few years ago, and most recently was applied to a couple of Herreshoff 12½-footers. When the first of these came to the Brooklin Boatyard for restoration, Joel White and I came up with the tool shown in the photographs. It did a good, albeit slow, job of getting rid of the old weakened screws and later was loaned to the Seaport for use in renewing the plank fastenings in that museum's 12½-footer, *Nettle*.

The photos and sketch show how the tool is built. If the threaded piece, which serves to guide the drill, is made from a big Allen screw, it will wear better. We found mild steel wore out quickly in spite of frequent oiling. In operation, one cleans out a somewhat circular hole down to the screw head, either by popping out the bung over it or by carefully digging out the putty. The jig can then be inserted and adjusted until it contacts the screw, after which the locking nut is tightened. (This setting is usually good for all simi-

(Continued on next page)

(Continued from previous page)

larly shaped areas of the boat, provided the screw heads are somewhat evenly countersunk. Adjustment will have to be made in going from convex to concave parts of the hull, however.) With the jig held firmly against the hull with one hand, the next step is to drill into the body of the screw, using the jig as a centering and aligning guide. This works as long as the screw was originally driven square with the surface of the hull, thus matching the attitude of the guide hole in the jig. This works out pretty well, at least until the drill passes through the shank of the screw and into the smaller, weaker, threaded part. Here, the drill often runs out into the surrounding wood where the going is easier. The result at this point is a hole through the upper part of the screw in way of the plank, and the beginnings of a newly bored hole in the frame right up next to the old screw. The hardest part is now over, at least for the 1" #7 screws used in a 12½-footer, and there is no need for the jig from here on.

We found that the correct size Fuller taper drill/countersink/stop collar, used in the above hole, did best at making a hole for the new screws. The old screw's head and some of its shank would spin right out on the taper drill, leaving a correctly shaped hole going through the plank (the old hole dressed up a bit) and into the frame (in most cases alongside the old screw's threaded portion). Our initial concern that the new threads might be dulled or stripped by rubbing against the remaining old ones while being driven was put to rest after we backed out and inspected a few. Apparently the old metal was so softened it lacked the ability to cut into the new.

The new screws were a size larger than the originals; an advisable step, I think, if the planking and frames are large enough to take them.

Boring metal, even when it is weakened, is slow and takes a good bit of push. Even with care, drills are bound to break off and spares have to be figured on. As the hand not pushing on the drill is pushing on the jig to hold it firmly against the hull, it isn't long before one has to rest a bit. Laying the boat over, first on one side then on the other, made things less uncomfortable, we found.

Bigger, stronger screws drill out proportionately harder. Soon it gets to a point where you have to put so much more pressure on the drill than on the jig—the drill takes charge and alignment is lost. In these cases a screw extractor, which needs only a small hole, may work. But it may not, since its success depends upon its jamming tightly inside a pilot hole, and oftentimes the screw shank can't stand this stress. Playing around with different-size holes and extractors sometimes improves things, but if the screw is very weak and quite large, I haven't yet found a way to remove it. One has to bore brand-new holes, far enough away so the old screw doesn't interfere—a perfectly acceptable solution in some cases, and one which is ever so much faster.

A lesson to be learned from all this is that boats should be refastened while the screws can still be backed out, if one doesn't want his planking perforated with new holes and wants to avoid the time and expense of drilling out old fastenings. Take note, you owners of twenty-year-old boats!

Photos on this page are official Mystic Seaport photographs by Peter Vermilya.

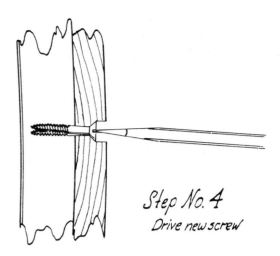

Step No. 4
Drive new screw

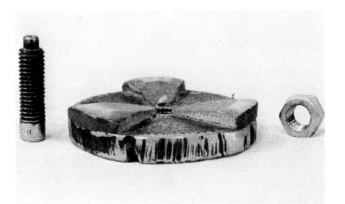

Mylar for Lofting

A reader questioned us recently about a source of 10-mil Mylar to be used as a lofting sheet. It seems that the stuff is ideal for lofting in that it is strong, easy to handle, easy to store, and not subject to the comings and goings caused by humidity changes. The closest we could come to the 10-mil was the 7-mil variety, available from:

**Charrette
31 Olympia Ave.
Woburn, Mass. 01801**

But we're glad we took the time to search, because in reply to our query, we got this most interesting letter from Charrette:

Dear Editors:

You ask for 10-mil Mylar to be used for lofting. I have known of a great deal of 5-mil and 7-mil material used for this purpose, but never 10-mil. I don't even think any 10-mil Mylar is coated for drafting use.

In our latest catalog (1978) we list a product called UC-7 Inking Film. This material is made by Dupont (in fact, all of our polyester films are made from Dupont base) and we stock this material in Woburn. In addition, Technifax Erase/Dure is available in 7-mil rolls at the prices shown below.

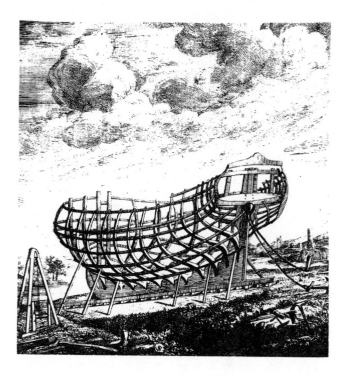

Technifax Brand Drafting Film

	Size	List
Single Matte		
9107	30 yd. x 20 yd.	$ 76.13
	36 yd. x 20 yd.	$ 91.40
	42 yd. x 20 yd.	$106.61
Double Matte		
9207	30 yd. x 20 yd.	$ 79.80
	36 yd. x 20 yd.	$ 95.80
	42 yd. x 20 yd.	$111.75

I would consider the Technifax (made by a division of Scott Paper) superior to the UC-7 in two regards. First, it is cheaper; this is a reflection more of the higher volume of the Technifax than of any implicit quality difference. Second, the surface is probably better suited to general usage than the surface of the UC-7, which is fine for certain types of technical pens, but not much good for pencils or other media.

In our catalog appear several items that might be of interest to your readership. I draw your attention to the imported Spline Weights on page 89, which we bring in from Japan. They are quite handsome—although I wonder what the Japanese phrase "lead alloy" is really a euphemism for—(I think it must be a little like those pieces of hardware you buy which weigh the same as domestic products, which have all the same specifications, which even look the same, but which after a few weeks of usage suddenly dissolve) and because of the cover, which keeps your hands away from the "lead," they are great to use. Of course there are thousands of other "goodies" in the book which might be of interest to you or to your readership. We are not unlike other suppliers of this kind of merchandise. There are a few items that we sell that the others don't. The most important difference is that we maintain over two million dollars in inventory, here in Woburn, which probably makes that the largest inventory of this kind of material in the country.

**Blair Brown
President
Charrette Company**

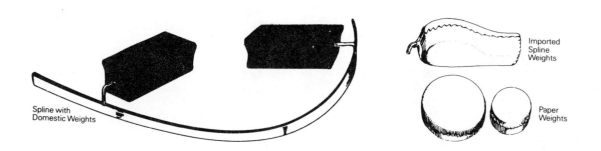

Spline with
Domestic Weights

Imported
Spline
Weights

Paper
Weights

West Coast Chemicals

Dear Editors:

I've been building a cruising sailboat for a few years now, and all my chemical needs have been filled at one place just north of San Francisco. Any quantity of epoxy, epoxy resin, thinner, vinyl paint, antifouling paint, varnish, rubber caulking compounds, etc., are available at very low prices compared to the local yacht chandleries or hardware or paint stores here in the S.F. Bay area. Also lots of good advice on different paint systems, etc.

Morgan's Marine Chemicals
520 Cleveland Lane
Petaluma, Cal. 94952

On an average, I'd say their prices are about 50 percent off what you pay in a store.

John Andersen

Steel Fabrications

Dear Editors:

I have been fabricating stainless steel fittings for my boating projects as there is a fair supply of scrap sheet, rod, and pipe from winery and food processing equipment fabricators. For cutting, I use a radial arm saw (2 hp Dewalt) with abrasive cutoff blades for heavy material, over 1/4" thick, and a toothed friction cutting blade by Simons for lighter stock. A bandsaw is also used. A wavy-set fine-tooth blade is run at wood cutting speed (3,000 fpm) and cuts by friction. The teeth rapidly dull but are not needed when friction cutting.

A standard AC arc welder (Miller 202) and 308-16 rod makes adequate welds. Fittings are wire brushed for a satin luster. After all drilling, welding, wire brushing, etc., has been completed, the part is dipped in acid for 1/2 to 1 hour. I use about a 4:1 dilution of phosphoric acid. This bath is also handy for removing rust from mild steel. A water rinse completes the operation.

James M. Rudholm
Kingsburg, Cal.

Lasting Protection

Steve Lang at the Owl's Head (Maine) Transportation Museum, a place that is heavily involved in metal preservation and protection, told us about a miracle coating that keeps polished metals from tarnishing. We were skeptical, having seen products fail after similar seemingly outrageous claims, but it seems the compound, inspiringly entitled Brass Protective Coating, is as good as the promise. The maker, Jerome Hubert, had this to say: "First experimental piece (a brass carbide generator) has been on the running board of my Model T for 10 years now and still looks like new. Has been exposed to sun and rain." The folks at Owl's Head report similar results.

Brass Protective Coating
Jerome W. Hubert
18714 N.E. Halsey St.
Portland, Oregon 97230
Information and prices on request

Survival of the Craftsman

You've decided to pack it in as an insurance salesman and build spoon-blade oars for a living? How do you go about doing it without going under a week after you start? You'll find plenty of hard-core advice in:

The Craftsman's Survival Manual
by George and Nancy Wettlaufer
Prentice-Hall, Englewood Cliffs, N.J.
94 pages, illus., index, biblio., paperbound,
1974, $2.95

Subtitled "Making a full- or part-time living from your craft." The authors, who know whereof they speak, tell you how to keep records, handle insurance, keep up with taxes, price your goods, sell wholesale and retail, gain publicity, and generally make a go of it in a hostile world. The book is directed toward potters and leatherworkers and their ilk, but practitioners of the nautical crafts can get almost as much benefit from the book.

Seaworthy Dreams, edited by Lawrence M. Mahan
737 Race Lane, RFD 1
Marstons Mills, Mass. 02648
Quarterly newsletter/magazine
$2 per issue, $8 per year

This quarterly is in its formative stages and suffers from the problems most new publishing endeavors suffer from: lack of resources and weak material. The editorial slant of the publication is good, though—the avowed purpose is to publish articles by people who are building their own boats in order to share ideas, problems, sources, and advice. Misery loves company, as it were. With a little luck and some solid contributions by people who know their stuff, this quarterly could go somewhere. We wish it luck.

Boxed material from The Craftsman's Survival Manual.

29

Pricing for Survival

educational levels than average, and have a positive orientation to counter-culture values. Some may look like suburbanites, but they think of themselves as young and "with it." After a few craft fairs, you develop a knack for spotting the types who are more likely to be turned on to crafts.

In some cases, customers find themselves in a similar peer group with the craftsmen—in fact, craftsmen *are* good customers (although they may barter with you instead of paying money, which is fine). This identification with crafts-men gives the customers and additional incentive to buy. They will also tend to feel that their money is supporting something they believe in and not a large impersonal department store. Using money to influence social patterns, such as supporting the efforts of poor people (as in the case of urban and rural co-ops) or starving artists (as in the case of craftsmen at a fair) contains all three of the motivations we have been talking about—economic, psychological and social—to a degree.

WORKSHEET FOR FINANCES

	Sample Figures	Your Figures
I. *To figure your material costs and overhead* (see pp. 20-21)		
1. Your direct material costs per year (raw materials, fuel, etc.).	$ 3,500	
2. Your overhead costs (expenses of operating studio).	$ 2,500	
3. Total of nos. 1 and 2.	$ 6,000	
4. Your total (gross) income per year.	$24,000	
5. Your average material and overhead cost (divide no. 3 by no. 4).	25%	
II. *To figure your hourly wage* (see p. 21)		
1. Number of hours you work in a good week.	120	
2. Amount of ware (full retail value) produced in one week.	$ 1,000	
3. Your material and overhead costs (multiply no. 2 by % figure from Section I, no. 5).	$250	
4. Your cost of selling (take maximum, usually 50%).	$500	
5. Add nos. 3 and 4 and subtract from no. 2 for the amount of money you earn.	$250	
6. Divide the total in no. 5 by your total hours to get your hourly wage.	$2.08/hr	

The Repair of Wooden Boats, by John Lewis
David & Charles, North Pomfret, Vermont
96 pages, illus., 1977, $11.50

Hull Care and Repair, by David Maclean
Tab Books, Blue Ridge Summit, Pa.
151 pages, illus., index, paperbound, 1977, $5.95

All boat repair books suffer from the same problem: there are so many variables to be considered that the books are never big enough to cover everything. Every time I have a repair job to do, I check it out first in every boat repair book I can find. To this day I have yet to find a book that tells me in detail all I need to know to do the job correctly. Sure, they all tell you how to sister a frame, but for some strange reason (could it be fate?), there are always extenuating circumstances surrounding *my* broken frame that make it different from the author's broken frame.

There's no solution, naturally, except to keep on reading and hoping, or perhaps talking to those who have done a lot of boat repair. But when all else fails, the problem is one between you and your corroded keel bolts.

(Maclean's book is no different from all the other repair books, with perhaps one exception—the index is a joke.)

Illustration and caption from The Repair of Wooden Boats.

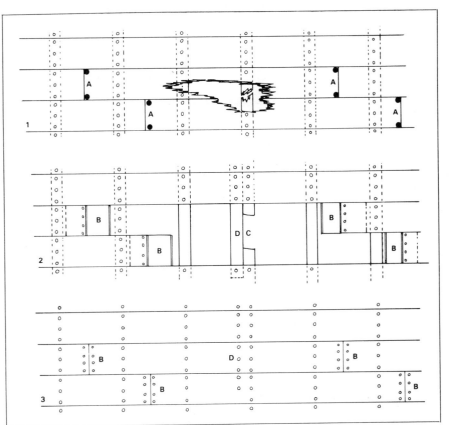

Repairs to carvel planking:
1 Hole extending over two planks with one broken timber
(A) Holes drilled for keyhole saw to cut out damaged planks
2 The two damaged planks are cut out so that butt joints at the ends of the two planks will not come between the same pair of frames
(B) Butt pads in position
(C) Damaged ends of broken timber cut back
(D) Sister frame in position and side-fastened to broken frame
3 Replacement planks in position and fastened
(B) Butt-pad fastening

From a Bare Hull, by Ferenc Maté
Albatross Publishing Co.
Box 69310, Station K
Vancouver, B.C., Canada
534 pages, illus., index, 1975, $19.95

Suffering from chronic bibliomania, I sometimes buy books on impulse, especially if they seem comprehensive and well illustrated, as this one is. After carefully reading it twice, my one-line review is: "A fascinating blend of ignorance and arrogance." Mr. Maté suffers from the problem many young people these days have when they get "into" something: the belief that the first thing they run across in a particular subject is the best (or only) thing that has ever existed on that subject. It distresses me to see putting threads inside a drilled hole described thus: "... simply *tap and die* the steel plates, ..." The italics were the author's.

He used the phrase twice. A review of the book jacket notes and copyright notice leads to the real heart of the matter. The whole book is a shill for the Westsail Company. They hold the original copyright. The naval architect who designed the hull described in the book writes words of warm praise on the dust jacket. The four reputable publications quoted in these notes apparently didn't follow their own advice: "... should be read cover to cover...." My concern is that a lot of beginners to boatbuilding will get a hold of this book, and after memorizing it, get laughed out of machine shops, thrown out of boatyards, and busted for trying to rip off retail stores as per the instructions on pages 173-174. It could turn away a lot of people.

—P.F. Jacobs

Ferrocement

Dear Editors:

Some years ago I purchased your first *Mariner's Catalog* from New Zealand. I remember then how disappointed I was with the coverage of ferrocement. Recently I saw your latest catalog and I am still disappointed. In the hope that you would want to remedy this deficiency, I hope you will mention these facts:

1. Since 1972 a publication devoted to ferrocement construction has been published. This was taken over by the Asian Institute of Technology in 1977. [*Journal of Ferrocement,* quarterly: Asian Institute of Technology, Box 2754, Bangkok, Thailand; subscr. from developing countries $15; from developed countries $25.]
2. Scantling rules for ferrocement fishing vessels are available from:

    Det Norske Veritas
    P.O. Box 6060
    Etterstad, Oslo 6
    NORWAY

    (ask for: *Tentative Rules for the Construction and Classification of Ferrocement Vessels* 1974).
3. Continuing progress is being made in ferrocement construction. This mode of construction is growing despite a decline in amateur construction, particularly in North America. The New Zealand Ministry of Foreign Affairs regularly funds ferrocement vessel construction as part of its aid program. The latest project involves the building of ten 150-ton tuna vessels in the Solomon Islands using indigenous labor. (Honiara Shipyard and Marine has been building vessels in ferrocement since 1970.)

I realize that ferrocement suffers an image problem in the United States. To some extent this is also true in many countries. Over a period of time I hope that sound construction to intelligent designs will eventually change the situation.

G.L. Bowen
Dept. of Engineering
University of Auckland
Auckland, New Zealand

Mr. Bowen also sent us a brochure of stock designs from the New Zealand Ferrocement Services, Box 15-447, Auckland, New Zealand. The designs are worthy of consideration.

An explanation: We haven't published much on ferrocement boats in the *Mariner's Catalog* because neither editor has a particular interest in them. The same holds true about multihulls. We *are not* antagonistic toward them, however, and welcome contributions from our readers who have information to impart on ferrocement technology, multihull development, and any other marine subject we fail to cover in depth. What we are looking for are sources of information in these areas—products, books and publications, people with data to share, etc.

—Eds.

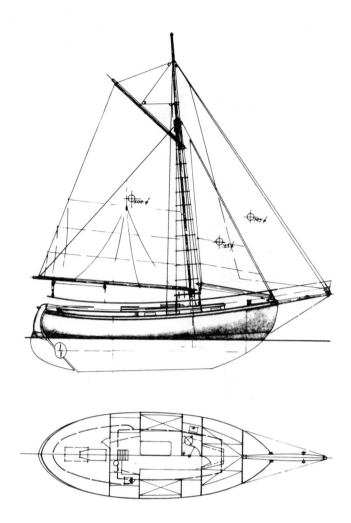

Above: 36-foot Colin Archer-type gaff cutter designed by New Zealand Ferrocement Services (address at left).

Dear Editors:

One enormous (five volumes) source of ferrocement research is the Canadian government. They sent free of charge to many of the builders in this area the results of their extensive testing of panel layups, painting systems under test conditions, and design work. The pubs came from:

Industrial Development Branch
Fisheries Service
Department of the Environment
Ottawa, Canada

Never have I received so much for nothing. Not even shipping.

Kaza
Aptos, Cal.

THE SMALLEST FERRY-BOAT ON RECORD.

Just What *Is* A Quick & Dirty Boat?

Dear Editors:

I'm working on a pithy definition of quick & dirty boats. Also, since this *is* Kansas, I'm going to slap one together soon. There ought to be a class organization—rating rules and everything. See, you guys think that Phil Bolger's Navel Jelly is a quick and dirty, but I think it's entirely too elegant. Ought to make mine a proa of bound-up cornstalks powered by two carefully cut-out shower curtains. Arabol the whole thing and steer with a pair of plywood-covered tennis racquets.

I'll send you a slightly fuzzy, underexposed Polaroid taken from a half mile when it's done.

Mark Roeyer
Lawrence, Kansas

Dear Editors:

Regarding the aluminum welding rods (Lumiweld) in MC-5, page 47. The diagrams you show are for soldering or brazing, not welding. I saw these items at the boat show. Heli arc welding is the only proper way to weld aluminum. Solder or brazing will not have the penetration or strength to do a proper job.

Do not let good boatmen believe that soldering has the *strength* of welding aluminum.

Bill Colish
Harrison, New York

We might add that Alumismiths, maker of Lumiweld, has a new address:

Alumismiths, Inc.
Box 374
215 Commonwealth Ave.
Massapequa, N.Y. 11758

We might also add that David Register of Damariscotta, Maine, came to the same conclusion about Lumiweld as did Mr. Colish.

—Eds.

The Encyclopedia of Wood:
Wood as an Engineering Material
Drake Publishers, New York
375 pages, illus., index, 1974, $17.50

This is a reprint of a book originally published by the Forest Products Laboratory as the *Wood Handbook*. It would serve well the boatbuilder who is interested in knowing more about the technical side of wood—its strength under various conditions, wearability, decay resistance, chemical makeup, gluing characteristics, etc. It should be especially valuable for the legion of craftsmen seeking to marry traditional woodworking methods with modern technology: the WEST System and the various edge-glued planking systems come immediately to mind.

There are nuggets in here: "Wood members after immersion in liquid ammonia or treatment under pressure with ammonia in the gas phase can be readily molded or shaped. As the ammonia evaporates, the wood stiffens and retains its new shape."

This book can also help those who are doing research. Each chapter has a bibliography to lead you to new sources.

Table below from The Encyclopedia of Wood.

Boatstock

Teak. The most over-rated item in the world.
—George Buehler

To add to our list of West Coast boat lumber dealers published in MC-5, page 59, we have:

Richmond Lumber
6815 N. Richmond
Portland, Oregon 97203

We presently have on hand spruce, air dried to approximately 15% moisture content. The sizes range from 1/2" x 1" through 6" x 12" with predominantly 1" x 4" through 2" x 12" sizes. The above sizes are available in 3 to 24 foot lengths based upon our stock on hand.

The price on the above items is $1,400.00 per thousand board feet or $1.40 per board foot. These items are S2S (surface two sides) and FOB per our lumber yard. For lengths longer than 16', there is an additional 20% charge. [Prices are as of January 1978.]

—Richmond Lumber

Table 9–1.—*Classification of various hardwood and softwood species according to gluing properties*

Group 1 (Glue very easily with glues of wide range in properties and under wide range of gluing conditions)	Group 2 (Glue well with glues of fairly wide range in properties under a moderately wide range of gluing conditions)	Group 3 (Glue satisfactorily with good quality glue, under well-controlled gluing conditions)	Group 4 (Require very close control of glue and gluing conditions, or special treatment to obtain best results)
HARDWOODS			

Aspen
Chestnut, American
Cottonwood
Willow, black
Yellow-poplar
	Alder, red
	Basswood [1]
	Butternut [1,2]
	Elm:
	  American [2]
	  Rock [1,2]
	Hackberry
	Magnolia [1,2]
	Mahogany [2]
	Sweetgum [1]
		Ash, white [2]
		Cherry, black [1,2]
		Dogwood [2]
		Maple, soft [1,2]
		Oak:
		  Red [2]
		  White
		Pecan
		Sycamore [1,2]
		Tupelo:
		  Black [1]
		  Water [1,2]
		Walnut, black
			Beech, American
			Birch, sweet and yellow [2]
			Hickory [2]
			Maple, hard
			Osage-orange
			Persimmon

SOFTWOODS			

Baldcypress
Fir:
  White
  Grand
  Noble
  Pacific silver
  California red
Larch, western
Redcedar, western [3]
Redwood
Spruce, Sitka
	Douglas-fir
	Hemlock
	  Western [3]
	Pine:
	  Eastern white [3]
	  Southern [1]
	  Ponderosa
	Redcedar, eastern [2]
		Alaska-cedar [2]	

[1] Species is more subject to starved joints, particularly with animal glue, than the classification would otherwise indicate.

[2] Bonds more easily with resin adhesives than with nonresins.
[3] Bonds more easily with nonresin adhesives than with resin.

Wood Data

I work at a cabinet shop here in the Flatlands. The shop subscribes to a magazine that publishes information perhaps useful to boatguys.

Wood & Wood Products
Vance Publishing Corporation
300 W. Adams
Chicago, Illinois 60606
$12/year

But get this: They put out a *Wood & Wood Products Reference Data/Buying Guide* annually in March that is a goldmine. (It costs $5.00, and can be had separate of a magazine subscription.) Well, maybe not a goldmine, maybe a well-kept tree farm. It has sources of supply in it for materials, machinery, and processes, among other things. Most impressive for me was the rundown on glues. The "Wood Glue Reference Guide" is a six-page listing by manufacturers of glues, giving brand name, type, form, percentage solids, working life, fed and/or milspecs met by products, processing equipment required, uses, and characteristics. Also in this buying guide are lists of manufacturers with addresses, including machinery dealers.

I grant that a lot of this information is high-production oriented, but there's enough there that sly one-off people or small producers could make use of selected stuff.

—Mark Roeyer
Lawrence, Kansas

Wood in Marine Structures
edited by Michael Levi and Jerry Machemehl
UNC Sea Grant, 105 1911 Bldg.
North Carolina State University
Raleigh, N.C. 27607
92 pages, illus., paperbound, 1977, $2.50
(free to residents of North Carolina)

Building a marine structure out of wood? You might want to spend some time with this publication, which is a compilation of papers presented at a seminar held at NC State in 1976. Some of the nine chapters: marine borers and fungi; preservative systems and specifications; fasteners in marine structures; planning, design, and construction of piers and walkways; wharf inspection and maintenance.

Shoreside Designers

The design and construction of modern marinas, boatyards, docks, and marine parks is no easy thing, especially when you consider that there is a genuine labyrinth of government rules and regs to be followed. Doing it up right takes the services of architects and engineers with experience in the field. Find them fast in "Directory of Architects and Engineers," a booklet listing architects and engineers familiar with shoreside construction around the country, available from:

Outboard Boating Club of America
401 North Michigan Avenue
Chicago, Illinois 60611

The following article originally appeared in the Asheville (North Carolina) *Citizen-Times*. It is reprinted here courtesy of Mr. Luther Thigpen, Executive Editor.

They Set a Heap of Store by the Moon

by John Parris

WOLF MOUNTAIN—Most of the wood lore practiced by the old-timers is looked upon as superstition.

Perhaps that's why today's lumber, even with all our modern methods, is so much inferior to that used in the old days.

Maybe that's why it's not uncommon for floors to buck and doors to warp and shingles to curl.

The woodwise old-timers never had to contend with such unless they went "ag'in the moon."

And that was rarely ever.

For they set a heap of store by the moon.

Whether it was trees to be felled and hewed, fence posts to be cut and put in, floors to be laid, shingles rived and coursed, or just firewood to be cut, the oldtimers usually did it "by the moon."

Folks who dismiss such practices as mere superstition would do well to sit down with one of the dwindling clan of practitioners and hear him out.

Such a practitioner is Blye Owens, an 81-year-old mountain man who lets the moon rule his ax.

"When it comes to workin' with wood," he said a couple of days back, "I look to the moon for the right sign. Always have. So did my daddy and my grandpa. They weren't ones for goin' against the moon."

The old man had spent the morning in the woods above his house cutting locust for fence posts.

"You want to cut on the old of the moon," he said. It's right now a good time to cut. Will be through Saturday.

About five more days good time to cut fence posts, handle timber, sled runners, board timber, anything like that.

"Then the moon news the 29th of February. Then you don't want to cut nothin', or set no stakes. After the moon news for three or four weeks, gettin' back down to the old moon, why then you can cut timber and set stakes.

"You don't want to cut on the new moon. I have cut some timber way back yonder and made a few ax handles after the moon had newed, and, pshaw, ever' time you used your ax you'd have to straighten your handle. It'd just crook up in all kinds of shape. You couldn't do nothin' with it.

"You want to set your fence stakes on the old of the moon. Don't never set a stake on the new moon. They'll just get looser and looser.

"If you've got fencin' around you, where you live, and you've got some stakes, just try this. Get out there—right now, for the next two or three days—just set you two or three. And then wait till after the moon news—after the 29th—and then go right out there and set you two or three more.

"Then wait a while and you'll see that them you set after the moon news will be like they'd just come up out of the ground. They'll just be fallin' over, they'll be so loose. And them you set before the moon news—on the old of the moon—they'll get just as solid as a stump.

"Now you try that, and if it don't work, you tell me I told you wrong. I've well-tested it. Had to do a lot of fencin'. Got a lot of fencin' here on my place. I know what I'm talkin' about."

He paused a moment to relight his pipe that had gone out while he talked. He took a couple of puffs and then went on.

"Used to make a lot of boards for roofin' the house and barn and crib. If you laid 'em in the light of the moon they'd just querl up and pull the nail heads right through the boards. That's what'll happen if you cut 'em and put 'em on in the time of the new moon.

"You just wait till you're right on the old moon and make you some boards and put a course on, join' 'em, and they'll lay down just as straight till they rot off.

"Another thing, if you want to get rid of growth so it'll not come back and the stumps come out easy, the best time to cut is when the signs are in the heart in May.

"You watch that calendar, and when the signs are in the heart, go out there and chop on a dogwood or go out there and chop on a grapevine. Watch that grapevine and it'll just start drippin' that water. And stuff'll run out of that dogwood. That dogwood's dead to the roots. It'll never sprout.

"Locust will do the same thing. Hack 'em off and let 'em drop over. Knee-hack 'em. Let the bark hold on 'em. Go back in two years and just take hold of 'em and they'll pull right out of the ground.

"I done that. When I moved here there was the awful awfulest thicket. Oh, my goodness alive! And I cut the biggest part of the locust when the signs was in the heart in May and just let it drop over. That's the way I cleared it.

"Now there ain't a sprout in my field. I've got eight acres here that you can shut your eyes and set on a tractor and go over it without a hitch. Not a locust sprout on the whole place."

He paused, reached down and picked up a piece of wood and put it on the fire.

"Yes, sir," he said, "you've got to look to the moon.

(Continued on next page)

(Continued from previous page)

You can depend on wood cut during the old moon of January or February to stand straight and true.

"The time for hewin' foursided beams is on the old of the moon, particulary in March or May. And because the sap runs best in May, that's a good time for cuttin' poles and splints. The bark comes off easier."

He sat staring into the fire a moment, then shook his head.

"No, sir," the old man said, "it don't pay to go ag'in the moon when it comes to workin' with wood."

The Salt Book, edited by Pamela Wood
Doubleday, New York
430 pages, illus., 1977, $5.95

By now probably everyone has heard of the *Foxfire Books*, a series begun in 1972 by the younger generation in Appalachia to record the fast-vanishing way of doing things of the older generation. The brilliance of the idea, and its fascinating execution, spawned a number of similar projects, and so we have the *Salt Book*—created by the students of Kennebunk High School on the coast of Maine. With tape recorders and cameras in hand, the students beat the bushes and scoured the coast to talk with and *listen to* men and women who have control over their lives. What they learned is published here—how to build a lobster trap, sea moss harvesting, gill netting, trawling, snowshoe making, barn raising, collecting and eating fiddleheads, making cottage cheese. As interesting as the how-to parts are, the pleasure of the book is in meeting a variety of people who are still around but who have been passed by in today's technological society. These people have a lot to say.

156. "Wanna hear a bootleggin' story?" asks Reid Chapman.

Above and below: Photos from The Salt Book.

137. **Rum running vessel pictured in a 1928 newspaper.**

Sea Cloth

We always wondered why it was necessary to have five hundred bucks worth of spaghetti and three pet apes to enjoy the big pull of a spinnaker. Well, it turns out that it isn't necessary at all. The single-luff cruising Spinnaker, from:

David Bierig, Sailmaker
955 W. 4th St.
Erie, Penn. 16507

You might be interested to know how this sail developed. About a year ago, Jan Gougeon (Bay City, Michigan, boatbuilder) asked if I could make a sail—for his 30' trimaran—that was the "front half of a spinnaker sewn to the back half of a genoa." We made the sail and it looked promising, so I continued to develop it and made one for my own boat. This sail measures 37' x 22' and is a real powerhouse. Even so, since most normal spinnaker gear and complication is eliminated, my wife and I can easily handle this sail. It is a great sail to use because it gives power and yet is easy to handle. It jibes just like a genoa, runs wing and wing without a pole—believe it or not, it does—and can be taken down quickly and safely without leaving the cockpit. To do this, the halyard must be led aft, and the tack shackle with trip line led aft must be used. This procedure worked well in good weather and even worked in a 40-knot snow squall on 15 November when we finished our testing for last season.

—David Bierig

The best way to keep warm when wearing a cotton shirt is to take the shirt off.

—Carl Lane

One of the frustrations of synthetic cloth sails is their almost cruel brightness. David Prior of SouWest Sails has an alternative in a treated cotton cloth called Vivatex.

SouWest Sails
West Dublin
Lunenburg County, N.S.
Canada

We carry a good stock of treated cotton sailcloth called Vivatex. This is a closely woven cotton that is highly water- and mildew-resistant. The two weights of cloth come in off-white, light green, and khaki. The 10.38-ounce, 36-inch wide costs $3.50 a yard plus tax, and the 12-ounce, 36-inch wide costs $4 per yard plus tax. These prices may increase slightly by the fall of 1978.

—David Prior
SouWest Sails

David Bierig's single-luff spinnaker in action.

Once you have used elastic sail stops, especially on gaff mainsails, you'll keep the old ones in the back of a locker for storm ties only. American Cord has all the stuff for making your own.

American Cord and Webbing Co.
505 Eighth Ave.
New York, N.Y. 10018

Our synthetic cords are mildew-resistant and water-repellent and can be furnished in bulk form, cut to any length required, and we can make the complete assembly to your particular specification. Our items are manufactured with non-rusting, lightweight, durable nylon hardware.
—**American Cord and Webbing**

Right: American Cord and Webbing's Easy Hook, just the thing to go with their elastic cord.

Fiber Technology

Dear Editors:

On page 68 of the *Mariner's Catalog, Volume 4,* you ask for information on the processing of fibers prior to the Industrial Revolution. There are five volumes of *A History of Technology* which cover the periods from the most ancient up to and including the Industrial Revolution. The work is edited by Singer, Holmyard, Hall, and Williams, and was published by Oxford University Press, London and New York, in 1956.

These volumes not only contain very interesting information on shipbuilding but also contain data on all the forms of technology which are used in spinning and weaving, tools, food and drink, etc. Volume 2 covers the period of the Mediterranean civilization to the Middle Ages. Volume 3 covers the period from the Renaissance to the Industrial Revolution. There is information covering fibers and their preparation, but there is practically nothing that covers the manufacture of sailcloth, even in the sections on shipbuilding.

—H. Talboys
Emerson, N.J.

Sailmaking: A Complete Guide to Construction, Repair, and Maintenance
by Bill Schmit
Drake Publishers, New York
135 pages, illus., index, 1974, $9.95

We have seen more detailed explanations of sailmaking for the amateur (*Make Your Own Sails,* reviewed in MC-4, p. 68; and the Sailrite Kits books, reviewed in MC-1, p. 157), but this one is all right. Its strength lies in its many good diagrams; its weakness is the very thin text. But if you are going to take the trouble and time to make your sails, you should at least look at this book.

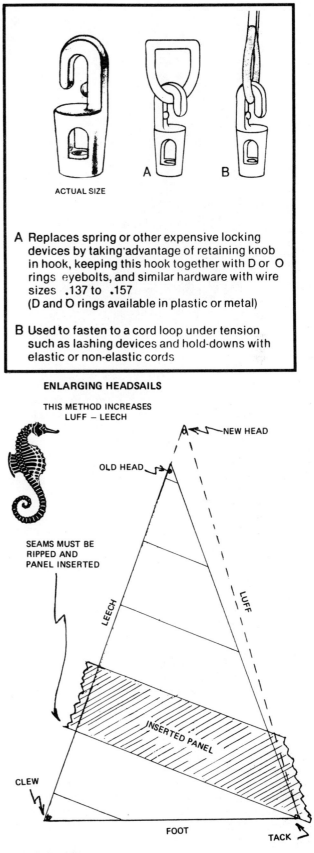

ACTUAL SIZE

A Replaces spring or other expensive locking devices by taking advantage of retaining knob in hook, keeping this hook together with D or O rings eyebolts, and similar hardware with wire sizes .137 to .157 (D and O rings available in plastic or metal)

B Used to fasten to a cord loop under tension such as lashing devices and hold-downs with elastic or non-elastic cords

ENLARGING HEADSAILS

THIS METHOD INCREASES LUFF – LEECH

NEW HEAD

OLD HEAD

SEAMS MUST BE RIPPED AND PANEL INSERTED

LEECH

LUFF

INSERTED PANEL

CLEW

FOOT

TACK

From Sailmaking.

Plate 1.

Sailing Hats

Où est mon chapeau?
—**Frédérique de la Brooks**

by John Leather

To many sailing people, any form of hat is an affectation, but to most in the hot sun, it becomes essential. To many in cold or strong winds, or relentless rain, it can be a comfort, particularly if one is thin on top.

The traditional English yachting cap is still worn or carried by some of the larger yachting centers, usually as a symbol of their association with the sport, rather as is done in the more formal sailing circles of Scandinavia or Germany where, with a navy blue jacket with club buttons, the hat forms part of the rig of the day and the traditions of organized sport.

Until the mid-19th century, many English yacht owners wore glazed top hats when afloat, practical when one considers that these helped to ease a blow from a thrashing sheet or block in the manner of the crash helmet now beginning to be worn by sponsored circumnavigators in a hurry. More practically, their crews of hardy professionals from Essex or The Solent usually wore wool stocking hats, though some south-coast crews preferred black straw hats, like those worn by contemporary naval seamen. These were called "Nab Light hats," because the crews of light vessels plaited them in spare time.

By the 1860s, the professional yacht skippers were wearing the mid-Victorian "cheesecutter" peaked cap; close fitting to the head so it stayed on in strong winds and made of navy blue material with a finely worked black band around it. Plate 1 shows the crew of Sir Alfred Paget's 107-ton yawl *Waterlily* in 1864, wearing the current headgear of cheesecutter and stocking hats.

Sou'westers were, of course, the traditional foul-weather

(Continued on next page)

Plate 2.

(Continued from previous page)

hat and some of the old-time mariners, including my great-grandfather Tom Barnard, wore them every day, gale or calm. Plate 2 shows him seated in the 1880s on the quay of our native Essex village of Rowhedge, in his sou'wester, with his bold fishing smack in the background. In contrast, grandfather preferred a round sealskin cap for his winter work fishing for sprats or trawling.

Sou'westers are still made but one seldom sees them now. Lowestoft is the place to buy one in England, and it will be genuine—stiff as a board and reaching well down the back of the neck to keep water out of the coat collar.

Plate 3 is of the crew of the famous 60-ton racing cutter *Neva* of 1874, with her skipper, Lemon Cranfield of Rowhedge, seated second from right. He was the most successful of all the many professional racing skippers in any age. He, the mate, and the steward are wearing typical cheesecutters, but the hands of this Scottish-owned racer have bonnet-style sailors caps with a pom-pom on top. Don't be deceived by their demure appearance for the photographer; this was one of the smartest racing crews in history; one season they won £1,335 in prize money when "A sovereign was a sovereign." A fantastic sum in contemporary values.

Wooly hats continued to be in vogue during the 1890s and were also worn by many "corinthian" or amateur yachtsmen sailing small craft, cruising or racing. By the early 1900s white-covered "cheesecutters" with a larger crown were popular for yacht owners and professional skippers and mates. The professional racing crews wore white sun hats—useful against glare in those legendary hot, calm summers when the great racing yachts of Britain, America, and Germany met in competition and followed the racing circuit around the British coast from Harwich to the Clyde, then back to The Solent and West Country regattas, with forays to the Baltic and the French coast. The white canvas racing suits, or blue gurnseys and white duck trousers, and deck shoes were the racing hands' uniform until the end of professional yachting in 1939. Plate 4 shows hands on board the J-class racing yacht *Velsheda* in 1935, wearing sun hats and racing suits, ruefully surveying the broken boom that has cost them the prize and some well-earned prize money.

The amateur yachtsmen, rapidly increasing in numbers after 1900, wore a variety of clothing and hats, particularly the cruising men, who were often uninterested in fashion and imitated the fishermen, pilots, and other workaday coastal sailors in having blue cheesecutter caps and, later, cloth caps, which probably keep on the head better than any of the nautical variety. I have seen people afloat in bowlers and straw hats, though these are regarded as eccentric.

During the 1920s and 1930s, a variant of the yacht hand's sun hat was taken up by many amateurs, male and female, and from childhood memories of forty years ago, was identified with retired army officers and their ladies, pleasantly sailing their one-designs or cranking the starting handles of modest launches until the ruddy military complexion contrasted well with the blue canvas hat. Having now almost reached the half-century, I can wear my blue sun hat with becoming aplomb, though my wife is reduced to the giggles when I do.

However, I have found that the best type of all-around

(Continued on next page)

Plate 3.

Plate 4.

Plate 5.

(Continued from previous page)

sailing hat is a knitted woolen cap that fits close to the head; really close, not in the sloppy manner of the ready-made variety that are sold in chandlers' shops. I have worn these wooly caps at sea in many craft and conditions, and they seldom blow off. Some fancy them with a little simple decoration around the upturned edge and/or a small bobble on the crown. Most fishermen prefer them plain, blue or white. Some English sources of blue or white sun hats (fit for corinthians or professionals), wooly stocking hats, or cheesecutters, are:

Morgan and Son
High Street
Cowes, Isle of Wight

William Wyatt Ltd.
Waterside
West Mersea, Essex

Captain O.M. Watts Ltd.
45 Albemarle Street
Piccadilly, London

Just about all nautical supply houses offer hats of the usual array—officer's, Greek, watch, swabby, bill, and so on. Here are a few better places with unusuals in their line:

A "luff" cap, from:

Commodore Nautical Supplies
396 Broadway
New York, N.Y. 10013

A real old-fashioned deep-brimmed Sou'wester, from:

Land's End
Box 66244
Chicago, Ill. 60666

The admiral's scrambled-egger, from:

Ship Shop, Inc.
294 New York Ave.
Huntington, N.Y. 11743

For those yacht deliveries in early spring and late fall (how else is a poor man to sail?), surplus flying fortress caps are miraculously still available, from:

Talbot House Textiles
Malton, Yorkshire
England

A Digression on Flags

Dear Editors:

Among the books on flags mentioned on page 131 of Volume 4 of the *Catalog*, I note *Flags, Through the Ages and Across the World* by Dr. Whitney Smith. Having purchased this mighty tome and perused it with high hopes, I would hesitate to recommend it to the usual clientele of the *Mariner's Catalog*: seafarers—professional or amateur—ship modellers, naval history buffs, or the like. Its information on nautical flags and their usage is scanty and, I suggest, occasionally misleading if not erroneous. Its lack of organization and vast mass of trivia makes it a Herculean task to ferret out such information as it does contain.

The usual captions denoting "Naval Ensign," "Merchant Ensign," "National Flag," and the like, are replaced by small code symbols requiring reference to a key in another part of the book. From a seaman's or shipmodel maker's standpoint, a great deficiency is the nearly complete lack of special maritime flags. Naval flags, such as commissioning pennants, jacks, and command flags, are generally missing. The distinguishing flags or special ensigns of lighthouse, lifesaving, and other marine services are totally lacking. However, for the nautically inclined there is a page containing a random selection of yacht club pennants and owner's private signals, and there is a page of assorted steamship funnel markings.

As the blurb on the dust jacket says, the book "... is a glorious spectacle with its astounding 2,800 full color ... ,"

(Continued on next page)

(Continued from previous page)

etcetera. A glorious and astounding spectacle it certainly is, and a worthy ornament for any coffee table. However, the needs of the sailor, model maker, and nautical history enthusiast are better met in any number of handier, cheaper publications.

W.R. Hopkins
Gibson Island, Maryland

We are always ready to stand corrected, though in this case, and others, we would appreciate hearing specifics on "any number of handier, cheaper publications." Anyone out there know enough about flags and pennants to provide a short, annotated bibliography?

—Eds.

The subject of flags brings up a nice graphic we have seen recently:

Flags of All Nations
Brown, Son & Ferguson
52 Darnley St.
Glasgow, Scotland
£2.55

A full-color wall chart that folds like a road map into its self-contained cardboard cover, this is just the thing for the person who takes his ship-watching seriously. It was compiled by the Flag Research Center (3 Edgehill Road, Winchester, Mass. 01890), an organization that publishes books on flags and a bi-monthly *Flag Bulletin.*

Heraldic Badges

Hearing from acquaintances with pretensions to the aristocracy that people who wear patches on their clothing have no taste, we quickly manifested our destiny (east coast lingo for *karma*) and found a place with a thousand of them in stock and which will do custom work for you and your fish-house gang.

Southern Emblem Co.
Box 8
Toast, N.C. 27049

Keeping Warm

Next time you think of Howard Blackburn intentionally freezing his hands to the grips of his oars, you might also give a thought to Rowing Pogies, from:

The Bonnie Hot Pogie
RFD 2, Box 85
Morrisville, Vt. 05661

Rowing pogies® are easy to use; simply slide over the end of your oar and insert hands directly onto your grip.
Rowing pogies® are constructed from GORETEX®. This new material is a 6 oz. laminate of durable oxford nylon on the outside and a soft, warm nylon tricot on the inside, sandwiching a microscopically porous film that allows small water vapor molecules to pass through, but not the larger water droplets. It is windproof, waterproof and breathable *too! One size fits all. Colors are burgundy or blue.*

—Bonnie Hot Pogie

Consider the Wetsuit

by Dave Getchell

For more than 15 years I had been surf fishing, wading out to breaking bars, leaning into pounding waves, suffering the agonies of those fishermen who push their gear to the limit in order to reach those extra few feet needed to reach fish "just beyond the next wave."

In the process, I gritted my teeth as the liquid ice of night-time combers lapped over the tops of my waders despite waterproof top and tight belt and trickled down my skinny front. Getting wet while surf fishing was a cross I bore, grudgingly if not stoically.

Then one dark night as I stood on the beach pondering the dank surf ahead, an even darker figure suddenly materialized beside me. Surprised, I saw it was a New Jersey fisherman I had met in the afternoon who had promised to join me for the night's fishing. I was clad in my usual bulky waders, raintop, and layers of wool underneath. He was slim and trim in a skin diver's wetsuit.

The tide was dropping and I knew that in a half hour I'd be able to work out onto the outer bar where I was sure to get into the stripers. As usual, I knew I'd try to go a few minutes too soon and would take a lop or two over the rubber gunnel, thus assuring myself of a cold and uncomfortable night.

"If you had one of these rigs, we could go now," my friend commented, proving once and for all that he was a true gentleman by not going out to the bar by himself.

"Oh, I guess it's about time," I replied casually, knowing full well what was in store. "After you," I added in my best sporting manner, hoping I could fiddle around a bit until the tide dropped.

(Continued on next page)

(Continued from previous page)

I watched in envy as the New Jersey hard man waded through a slough to his chest, worked up onto the bar in hip-deep water, completely ignoring the waves which swept over the bar and at times all but hid him in their froth. In the ten minutes it took for me to wade through the slough, half fill my waders with 55-degree water, and drag myself up onto the bar, he had landed one good striped bass and was fighting another. He seemed every bit as much at home as the fish he was hunting.

That cold August night on a Maine beach made a deep impression on me, and when I stood on Cape Cod's Nauset Beach a few weeks later, staring out across acres of white water tossed up by a coming storm, I decided enough was enough. It was back to town and a diving shop—$70 later my whole relationship with the surf had changed.

That was some three or four years ago. Since then, I've spent hundreds of hours in a wetsuit, as much as 17 hours at a stretch when the fishing has been good and the surf running high. I have found the suit warm, comfortable, and, unexpectedly, a real safety factor. Sure, the suits were made originally for divers, but in truth a wetsuit is naturally buoyant and goes under water easily only when a weight-belt and air tanks help carry one down. With the suit alone, you simply won't sink.

Consider the advantages: A wetsuit is warm. I'm the scrawny type, and cold water gets to me in minutes, leaving me shaking and useless. In water where I suffered in waders, I've had to dip under occasionally in my wetsuit to cool off. By contrast, when a half gale is whipping from the east and my upper half begins to get chilly in the wind, I don my raintop, which forms a dead-air barrier between the storm and my suit, and I'm quickly warm again.

And a wetsuit is comfortable—at least to me. By nature, they are snug, but a well-made suit gives with most every move. Hours of casting may chafe a bit at the elbows and miles of walking rub a bit of rawness behind the knees, but these are minor discomforts. When I'm sleepy, I lie down on the beach, impervious to bugs and pricklies; when hot, just unzip the jacket or sleeves.

The wetsuit is safe. When I step into a hole, I simply drift across or swim a stroke or two. If a big wave bears down, I just duck and let it sweep over me—chances are, it will hardly budge me. When caught on a bar in a rising tide, one paddles ashore, one-hand swimming usually being all that is required.

And consider—if the wetsuit is so great for surf fishing, and surfing, and diving, and frost-biting—what can it do for you? Are you a whitewater canoeist? Kayaker? A swimmer who likes to explore cold northern waters? A boatman with a rope in your propeller? A person whose sloop is being driven ashore in a storm? A cold-hater who is about to go on watch in a spray-strewn cockpit? My guess is that if you spend much time around water, you can use a wetsuit—more often than you might think.

(Continued on next page)

Left: First day luck. The wetsuit isn't yet dry from its first wetting and the author shows the silly grin of a contented fisherman. A stiff northeast wind and rain flattens the raintop against the wetsuit, the top being worn only to reduce the effects of the wind. The sneakers were eventually replaced with regular wetsuit boots.

(Continued from previous page)

I can't advise on types and brands since my first wetsuit, a Parkhurst, is virtually as good as the day I bought it and looks to have many more years in it. I would suggest you tell your needs to the salesman. Suits are different. You may want one that's easy to get in and out of (it can be a hassle). You may want a thick one for warmth (but these may be stiffer when moving around). Price may be a factor (but don't go too cheap; a good suit is worth the difference).

If I sound enthusiastic, it's because I am. To a waterman, the wetsuit is next thing to being a fish. And versatile? I love the story of a co-worker who was driving his foreign convertible across the country and found a desert night uncomfortably chilly. He stopped the car, dug his wetsuit out of his duffle, and then settled down to drive in comfort. And when he stopped for gas and got out to stretch, the attendant just about flipped.

Above: Off to the wars. The author, right, and his son check their gear before heading for Nauset Beach's outer bar. The side bag holds fishing lures; the coil of rope is a fish stringer; and the handles hanging from the belts and attached by telephone cords are gaffs. Notice how the tight-fitting suits offer a small target to the waves.

We have found another manufacturer of exposure suits. All the professional fishermen we know either have one or want one soon. This new source, which also offers cold-weather deck suits, is:

Bayley Suit
900 So. Fortuna Blvd.
Fortuna, Cal. 95540

Right: The Bayley Exposure Suit.

POWER

Oh Lord—I went cruising in a power boat and LIKED it!''

*My auxiliary engine and I got along just fine—
when it started, I smiled and murmured sweet noth-
ings into its air intake; when it didn't, I beat it merci-
lessly with a 5-pound crowbar.*

—Edgar Wallingford

Sweetness and Light

Very light, the lightest there must be, AquaBug is 1.2 hp
at 13 pounds and SuperBug is 3 hp at 21 pounds, $175 and
$235 respectively, from:

**AquaBug International, Inc.
100 Merrick Road
Rockville Centre, N.Y. 11570**

*This 13-pound ultralight outboard weighs less than 2
gallons of gas! And 2 gallons of gas will run it for 10 hours
at top speed, and 50 hours at trolling speed.*

*It's 11 pounds lighter and much less expensive than the
2 hp motors of the major manufacturers . . . yet it develops
35 pounds of thrust. At trolling speed, it's as slow and quiet
as an electric (to a fish), without the need for 50-pound,
$50.00 batteries.*

—AquaBug International

We had not heard of the Ocean Outboards, either. Four and seven horsepower, short and long shaft, £146 to £398, ex-factory, from:

Ocean Outboards Ltd.
132-138 Virginia Street
Southport PR8 6SP
England

The Ocean outboards, from left to right, the Ocean 4, the Ocean Super 4, the Ocean 7, the Ocean Super 7.

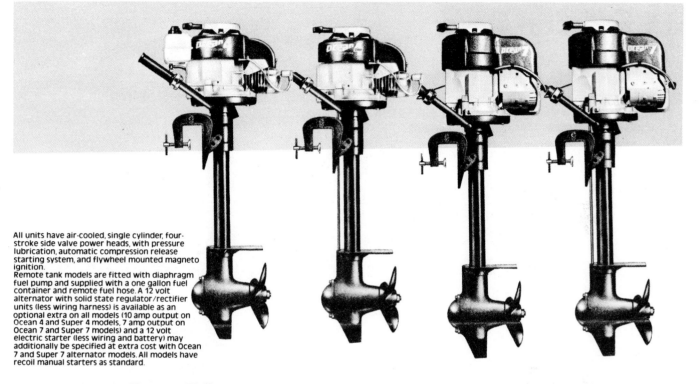

All units have air-cooled, single cylinder, four-stroke side valve power heads, with pressure lubrication, automatic compression release starting system, and flywheel mounted magneto ignition.
Remote tank models are fitted with diaphragm fuel pump and supplied with a one gallon fuel container and remote fuel hose. A 12 volt alternator with solid state regulator/rectifier units (less wiring harness) is available as an optional extra on all models (10 amp output on Ocean 4 and Super 4 models, 7 amp output on Ocean 7 and Super 7 models) and a 12 volt electric starter (less wiring and battery) may additionally be specified at extra cost with Ocean 7 and Super 7 alternator models. All models have recoil manual starters as standard.

Torque Talk

Dear Editors:

Re your dialog on Seagull "horsepower" with David Register in MC-5, page 89—ever read the article "Let's Talk Torque" by the late Gerry White? It appears in the Society of Small Craft Designers' book *Problems in Small Boat Design* (Sheridan House, New York, 1959, $7.95). Mainly, White gives the formula for the all-important torque as

$$\frac{5252 \times BHP}{RPM}$$

This is particularly meaningful to readers, especially the significant dividing by the RPMs. Some simple examples show why some old engines had "power" while newer ones (with small and high-revving props) do not.

I love the older, simpler marine engines, and believe you all noted somewhere the importance of the Seagull $1.50 accessory "Storm Cowl" over the carburetor. We were motorsailing an 18-foot Monk design in high winds around a critical headland with the weather coming over the port side. Seagull ran reluctantly, and finally quit altogether; we figured it swamped or worse. However, at home in the garage it ran beautifully. We're virtually certain its open Amal carburetor got so much wind in it that the petroil mixture leaned out too much.

Norman S. Benedict
Lomita, Cal.

Dear Editors:

I too was beguiled by your squib on Seagull outboards in Volume 1, page 146, of the *Mariner's Catalog*. Under its influence I purchased a 5½ hp Silver Century as auxiliary power for my 21-foot cruising sailboat (disp. 3,000 pounds). We lived with this motor for two seasons during which time it had the very beneficial effect of teaching us the joys of motorless cruising.

Although mechanics and other Seagull owners assured me that it was running perfectly, it would never push the hull at more than two knots. Never would it move the boat against wind or tide with any certainty. When the going got tough, it simply could not do the job. Frequently it would seem to grow tired and quit altogether. When, after two years, the Seagull developed cooling problems, I seized upon this excuse to replace it with an Evinrude 6. I have now had the Evinrude for two seasons and my experience has been that it is a better motor in every way.

The Evinrude drives the same hull at least twice as fast and it bucks headwinds and contrary currents with ease. The Evinrude has never quit in tough going. Needless to say, it is also smoother, quieter, and cleaner.

William Cheney
Rupert, Vermont

This Year's Small Diesels

Universal is one of the old names in auxiliary power. Their gasoline mills can be called standbys. Now, swept along with the rest of us into an age of power that's dear, they're offering two diesels in 16 and 24 hp. Their well-established dealerships are reason enough to consider them.

Medalist/Universal Motors
Box 2508
Oshkosh, Wisconsin 54901

Right: The 16-hp Universal diesel.

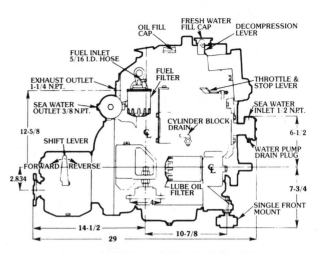

Italian manufacture and English distribution provide the Arona line of diesels. Beginning with an air-cooled 4-stroke, 6.5 hp number, the line switches to watercooling, 10 to 60 hp. Mechanical reverse/reduction gears are standard. The little air-cooled is £616.95. The watercooled run £995.50 to £2380. If VAT (the ridiculous "value added tax" they're imposing in England) and import duty don't zap you too badly, these are good values, from:

Anglo-Italian Engine Ltd.
Fordwater Trading Estate
Chertsey, Surrey
England

Above: The 6.5-hp Arona air-cooled diesel.
Below: The 60-hp Arona water-cooled diesel.

A Straight-Ahead Hydraulic Unit

There is something absurd about where auxiliary engines have to end up in a sailboat. You have to be a microscopic elf to get at them. The cramped position one must assume for servicing sends a rain of tools and parts into the nethers of the bilge. Circulation under the cockpit is always terrible, right where it needs to be good. And, of all places a hatch should not be, the cockpit, it has to be.

Hydraulics allows one to place an engine anywhere, even on deck if you want it there. Various units are available. A practical, ready-to-go system especially for auxiliaries is offered by:

Farymann Diesel
1592 Hart Street
Rahway, N.J. 07065

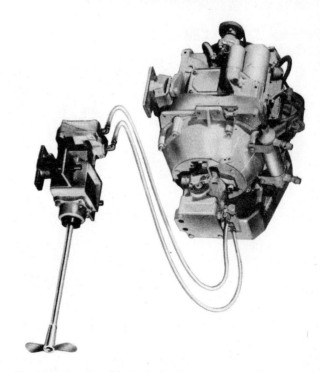

The Farymann Diesel hydrostatic drive.

Shaft, Bearing, and Wheel Tools

As do-it-yourself becomes a way of life instead of a hobby for so many people, the guys down the road with good shops really *are* cracking down on their willingness to lend tools. A friend of ours has a sign over the entrance to his shop, "The Fellow Who Loans Tools Is Out."

It is the seldom-used tool that takes the most beating and is always the one for which no substitutes exist and the loss of which is forfeiture of a right hand. There are several of these indispensable tools around boat works, including these:

A strut bearing puller, a propeller shaft puller, and a propeller puller from:

Minderman Marine Division
Port Clinton Manufacturing Co.
129 Buckeye Blvd.
Box 269
Port Clinton, Ohio 43452

Minderman also offers a complete line of shafting in tobin bronze and stainless.

Another wheel puller with a different configuration is offered by:

The Walter Machine Co.
84-98 Cambridge Ave.
Jersey City, N.J. 07307

Walter Machine carries extensive lines of drive units, reduction gears, keel cooling systems, and sundry shaft flanges.

Top: The Walter propeller puller.
Above: The Algonac propeller puller from Minderman.
Below: The Algonac strut-bearing puller from Minderman.

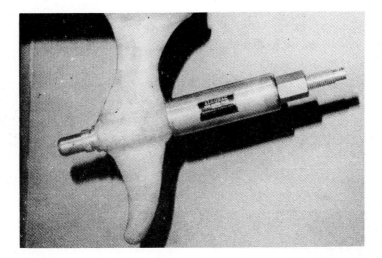

The ALGONAC STRUT BEARING PULLER eliminates the removal of the strut from the boat or the hard pounding or sawing of the old bearing. Just select the proper bushing and screw the old bearing out. Reverse the procedure and pull the new bearing into place. The puller is designed to remove and install strut bearings from 1¼" O.D. to 2" O.D.

Jet Notes

Two unusual jet configurations have appeared to feed the contemplations of the thin- or tight-water boys.

Saifjet is a small-craft unit in two sizes, and it could not be more simple. Certainly it is one to consider when converting an older wooden boat oneself. Low budgets with a Briggs and Stratton, Honda, or other small-power unit should take special notice. The Saifjet is built for them!

**Shipelle Limited
Industrial Site
King's Road
Haslemere, Surrey
England**

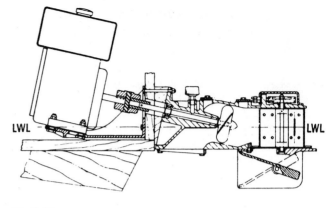

The Saifjet.

To avoid misunderstanding we would explain that the BE 150 SAIFJET is suitable for open, displacement type boats of up to 12' and the BE 250 for cabin cruisers, etc., up to 25/26' if used on canals only, or 20' for estuary or river use; these figures are only a rough guide and if you wish to exceed them please consult us. The boat must have a transom (or false transom) the bottom of which at the centre is between 2½" and 4½" under water when in service trim for model BE 150, and between 3¼" and 6" for model BE 250; if less than these figures the intake will be too close to the surface to ensure proper suction, and if more, when in reverse the flow of water from the unit will hit the transom instead of passing forwards under the boat, thus nullifying the astern thrust, though the latter can be overcome by suitable modification to the hull.

—Shipelle Ltd.

The other unit is the Dolphin Jet. Built for the bigger mills, the Dolphins are unusual in that they do not require special plumbing through the hull's bottom. The whole works is aft of the transom, giving some of the advantages of outdrive with those of the jet—especially maneuverability and practical conversion possibilities. From:

**Turbo Engineering Corp.
2444 Palm Drive
Signal Hill, Cal. 90806**

Below: From the Dolphin Jet catalog.

WHY THE DOLPHIN JET IS MORE EFFICIENT THAN CONVENTIONAL JETS

Any jet requires a vast amount of water flowing through its chamber in order to achieve maximum propulsion. This quantity of water is enough to fill a swimming pool in 3 minutes. Conventional jets draw this water from below the boat . . . their fluid foundation, actually creating a waterless hole, especially when accelerating at high power settings. Obviously, this loss of support adversely affects performance, consumes more fuel, demands higher RPM and shortens engine life.

The intake of the Dolphin Jet is located behind the boat so that the water performs its fluid support function before it enters the propulsion system.

Even the intake shape of the Dolphin Jet is superior to conventional jets. Since most of the power loss that occurs when fluid is turned comes at the beginning of the turn, the single, longer smooth turn of the Dolphin Jet suffers less loss than two shorter reversed turns which occur in conven-

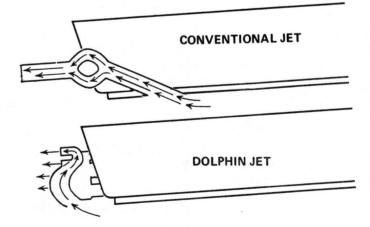

tional jets. Tests indicate that the intake loss is 8-10 horsepower more for the conventional jet than for the Dolphin Jet. Thus, smaller engines with a Dolphin can give the same performance as larger engines with conventional jets.

Sterndrives

Speaking of out- or stern-drives, Marine Drive Systems has published a comprehensive catalog on the subject, this one:

Stern Power Propulsion Equipment
Marine Drive Systems
519 Raritan Center
Edison, N.J. 08817
$2

Persons and Organizations with industrial or other heavy-duty stern-drive requirements will want to contact Schottel for their propulsion units for barges, transports, and other husky craft.

Schottel of America, Inc.
21 N.W. South River Drive
Miami, Fla. 33128

From the Schottel catalog.

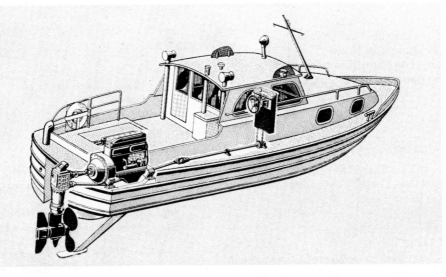

Sterngear

S.C. Ward (Engineers) Ltd. specializes in the supply and manufacture of sterngear up to 3½-inch shaft diameter. They supply from stock or to customers' requirements and offer propellers, shafting, glands and sterntubes, rudders and stocks. Shafting is in high-tensile manganese bronze, aluminum bronze, stainless steel, or Monel. Propellers are cast in manganese bronze, aluminum bronze, or aluminum alloy.

The firm also offers precision engineering, foundry work in brass, bronze, and aluminum from a stock of 800 marine and general patterns; stainless steel and chromium plating; and tank and pressure vessel manufacture.

S.C. Ward (Engineers) Limited
24 Meteor Close
Norwich Airport Industrial Estate
Norwich, Norfolk
England

—John Leather

Right: From Theory and Practice of Propellers for Auxiliary Sailboats.

Theory and Practice of Propellers
for Auxiliary Sailboats
by John R. Stanton
Cornell Maritime Press, Cambridge, Maryland
71 pages, illus., index, paperbound, 1975, $4

Recommended for yacht designers or laymen designing their own boats, but not as light, fireside reading. What you would expect is here: blade element theory, engine matching and propulsion losses, the effects of inclined shafts, vibration, cavitation, loads and materials, etc.

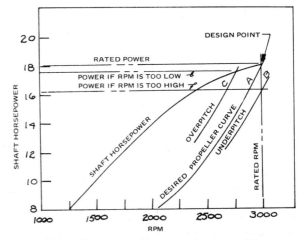

Fig. 23. Matching of engine and propeller characteristics.

New Propellers

Power Propellers specializes in the manufacture of small-craft propellers, sterntubes, propeller brackets, rudders, rudder stocks, tillers, cleats, fairleads, and associated equipment. They have thirty years' experience in the design and manufacture of propellers for fast boats and produce propellers up to 48 inches diameter in either manganese bronze or aluminum bronze and handle all types of repairs in propellers up to 10 feet diameter. Power Propellers offers technical advice and help to designers, builders and owners and will supply production runs of propellers and sterngear on contract.

**Power Propeller Company
72 Quayside Road
Bitterne, Southampton
England**

—John Leather

Old Propellers Made New

Small-craft propellers suffer from many ills—cavitation, damage by flotsam and striking the ground, and electrolysis. Besides loss of power and engine vibration, damaged or out-of-balance propellers can cause costly damage to shafts, bearings and engines.

Fleetworks of Poole, England, offers a reconditioning service to restore the damaged propeller and does a considerable volume of work at competitive prices. Reconditioning can cost half the cost of a new propeller, and Fleetworks can handle bronze propellers up to 6 feet diameter, sand cast alloy, stainless, Teflon-coated, and Monel.

Customers can have their propellers altered to a different pitch or diameter, and a variation of 1-inch pitch up or down usually can be achieved. In extreme cases Fleetworks can cut off the blades at the root and weld them on at a new pitch, usually done for racing boat engine changes or experimental designs.

Fleetworks also repairs broken castings, such as cavitation plates and skegs, which are costly to replace. They guarantee their work.

**Fleetworks Limited
Fleets Bridge
Poole, Dorset
England**

—John Leather

Cool and Silent

We have not seen neater or more get-at-able freshwater cooling systems than those offered by:

**Sen-Dure Products, Inc.
25 Moffitt Boulevard
Bay Shore, L.I.
New York 11706**

Those stern-mounted silencers you see more and more around the waterfront work! Here offered by:

**Submarine Research Laboratories
Hingham Shipyard
Hingham, Mass. 02043**

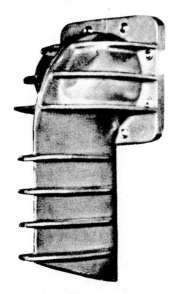

Right, top: A Yanmar diesel with a Sen-dure freshwater system.
Right: Submarine Research's rubber exhaust silencer.

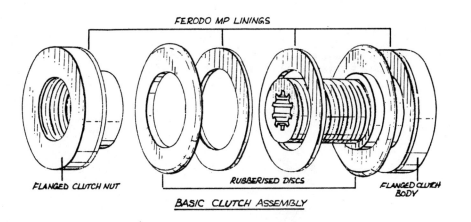

FERODO MP LININGS

FLANGED CLUTCH NUT

RUBBERISED DISCS

FLANGED CLUTCH BODY

BASIC CLUTCH ASSEMBLY

The Tuxton Torque Propeller

Propellers and driving mechanisms are subjected to forces imposed by sudden acceleration, fast speeds, and, conversely, by an engine suddenly brought up by a fouled propeller. A usual precaution is to introduce a tubular splined clutch body in the drive, which is bonded to a molded rubber bush in the cavity of the propeller hub. This bush is oversized and is compressed between the internal surface of the propeller hub and the external surface of the clutch body. During operation of the propeller, the drive is transmitted to it through the rubber bushing, which constitutes a clutch, so that if a sudden shock is transmitted to or from the engine, relative motion results between the propeller hub and the clutch body. If these forces are withdrawn, the propeller is again able to rotate normally. The principal disadvantage of this system is that, during the relative motion caused by shock loading, excessive friction can be sustained by the surface of the rubber clutch member close to the axis of rotation, resulting in rapid wear and loss of efficiency. This system can usually be readily dismantled but cannot be adjusted to allow clutch slip at a predetermined load.

Tuxton Bronze Ltd. has introduced a new approach to this problem. This incorporates a system where the clutch forces are applied to a radial surface at a relatively remote distance from the drive's axis of rotation. The clutch comprises two radial components, each consisting of two flat annular linings of Ferodo M.P. separated by a compressed, heat-resistant, rubberized disc. This is mounted on a tubular clutch body, the whole being contained within the propeller hub. The clutch body is in two threaded sections, one forming the clutch spindle on which clutch components are mounted, with a circular flange at one end. The other is the securing nut and flange for the opposite end. The drive is by a splined shaft passing through the tubular clutch body. A clutch action is obtained by drawing the two sections inward by screwing tight the flanged clutch nut until they engage against the shoulder abutment in the propeller hub.

Advantages of this method are that the pressure at which clutch slip will occur can be predetermined and varied to suit the type of craft, engine, or use. Also, it is comparatively simple to dismantle and to replace the clutch members.

Tuxton Bronze Ltd
Slape Industrial Estate
Station Road, Ilminister
Somerset
England

—John Leather

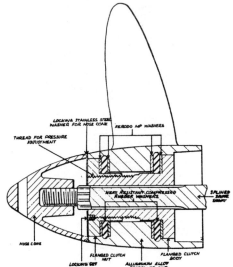

LOCKING STAINLESS STEEL WASHER FOR NOSE CONE
THREAD FOR PRESSURE ADJUSTMENT
FERODO MP WASHERS
HEAT RESISTANT COMPRESSED RUBBER WASHERS
SPLINED DRIVE SHAFT
NOSE CONE
FLANGED CLUTCH NUT
LOCKING SET SCREW
ALUMINIUM ALLOY PROPELLER HUB
FLANGED CLUTCH BODY

Top and left: The essentials of the Tuxton torque propeller.

Outboard and I/O Service Manuals

Outdoor Books carries a complete range of repair manuals for both outboards and inboard/outboards. They also have a number of factory manuals for various models. Send for their latest list.

Outdoor Books
5697 Montezuma Road
Box 15814
San Diego, California 92115

Pirates and Piracy

Many of the women begged of Captain Morgan upon their knees, with infinite sighs and tears, would he permit them to return to Panama, there to live in company with their dear husbands and children. . . . But his answer was: he came not hither to hear lamentations and cries, but rather to seek money.
—John Esquemeling

There is a pirate in all of us. There must be, else how could such a bunch of foul, rotten, murdering, thieving bastards with no humane virtues whatever have gained such a romantic attraction in the psyches of our artists and children? (*Pete asked me to write this introduction because he didn't know how to say that.*) I think that the willingness to accept piracy has to do with what economists have talked about for a long time—that anything, any thing or symbol with a value, is by definition scarce, and that all commodities are scarce, in part at least because other people *make them scarce.* Marxists, capitalists, breadwinners, and housewives know this. The larceny, then, the piracy in us, comes from our ability to say *to hell with those other people!*

If you are a person with youth, health, intelligence, vigor, and a will, *and* you can't own land, call your home

your own, enjoy the products of your own labor, pass on your estate intact, or otherwise shepherd your lot because other people prevent it, then the pirate in you is bound to emerge.

That is part of it. The other part has something to do with our feelings about how we relate to nature. Not only is the sea a natural place on which to be about as antisocial as reality allows, it is also the perfect forum for arch-exploitation. A fathom or two and everything is out of sight—it belongs to Davy. Anything I can wrestle from the sea is hard won and belongs to me because I Got It! Pretty soon everything looks like a fish, even ashore. Find, snatch, gut, dispatch. Some of us sense and suspect the script. Others read it. Some can't stand it any longer and live it.
—GP

Now, with that off our chests, we would like to talk about pirate books; actually we would like to introduce a piece by Charles Lee Lewis on pirate books. It has been excerpted from Mr. Lewis's excellent survey, *Books of the Sea: An Introduction to Nautical Literature* (United States Naval Institute, Annapolis, Maryland, 1943) and is reprinted here courtesy of the Naval Institute.

Pirates, Mutineers, and Slavers

by Charles Lee Lewis

In addition to the many works of fiction which have featured the exploits of pirates there are numerous accounts of the actual deeds of these often bloodthirsty but picturesque men, which make very thrilling stories, the pirates of reality usually surpassing in interest those of romance.

Of the standard works on the pirates who operated in American waters, that by John Esquemeling stands first not only in time but also in graphic and interesting narration. A manuscript said to have been written in 1617 by Sir Henry Mainwaring, entitled *Of the Beginnings, Practices, and Suppression of Pirates*, was published only in 1920 by the Navy Records Society. Accordingly, Esquemeling's book has the priority. He appears to have been a Dutchman who went out to the West Indies in the employ of the French West Indies Company in 1666. After the affairs of the company came to an end, he, "being like unto Adam," he writes, "when he was first created by the hands of his Maker,—that is, naked and destitute of all human necessaries, nor knowing how to get my living," became a buccaneer, or sea-rover as he called himself. In this new profession he was apparently very successful for after four or five years he returned to Amsterdam and there in 1678 he published his account of his experiences, under the title, *De Americaensche Zee-Rovers*.

This book was translated into Spanish, English, and French, the first English version appearing in 1684 under the following long descriptive title: *The Bucaniers of America: or a true account of the most remarkable assaults committed of late years upon the coasts of the West Indies, by the bucaniers of Jamaica and Tortuga, both English and French: Wherein are contained more especially the unparalleled exploits of Sir Henry Morgan, our English Jamaican Hero who sacked Puerto Velo (Belo), burnt Panama, etc. Written originally in Dutch by John Esquemeling, one of the Bucaniers, who was present at these tragedies; and thence translated into Spanish by Alonso de Bonne-maison, Doctor of Physick and Practitioner at Amsterdam. Now faithfully rendered into English, 1684.* So popular was the work that a second edition was published only three months after the first, which bore at the bottom of the title page the phrase, "The second edition, corrected and enlarged with two additional relations, viz., the one of Captain Cook, and the other of Captain Sharp." This additional material appears in the last two or three chapters of the book. It will be noted that this early form of buccaneering against the Spaniards in American waters was to a certain extent of the nature of privateering.

The same year 1684, there was published *The Voyages and Adventures of Capt(ain) Bart(holomew) Sharp and Others in the South Sea: being a journal of the same, also Captain Van Horn with his bucaniers surprizing of la Vera Cruz: To which is added the true relation of Sir Henry Morgan, his expedition against the Spaniards in the West Indies, and his taking Panama. Together with the President of Panama's account of the same expedition. Translated out of Spanish,* edited by Philip Ayres. This little book was not only a supplement to that by Esquemeling but also a rival. Accordingly, a second volume by Esquemeling appeared in 1685 with the title, *Bucaniers of America. The Second volume. Containing the dangerous voyage and bold attempts of Captain Bartholomew Sharp and others: performed upon the coasts of the South Sea, for the space of two years, etc. From the original journal of the said voyage written by Mr. Basil Ringrose, Gent. who was all along present at those transactions.*

Still another edition of Esquemeling was published in 1698, which added the "Journal of Sieur Raveneau de Lussan" and "A Relation of a Voyage of the Sieur de Montauban, Captain of the Freebooters in Guinea." A few years after Esquemeling's experiences in the West Indies, a young Frenchman of good family, named Raveneau de Lussan, went on a voyage to Santo Domingo to satisfy his passion for adventure. There after three years he found himself so heavily in debt that he turned buccaneer, as he writes, "to borrow, for the payment of my debts, as much money as I could from the Spaniards." His story may be read also in *Raveneau de Lussan: Buccaneer of the Spanish Main and Early French Filibuster of the Pacific. A translation into English of his journal of a voyage into the South Seas, 1684 and the following years...,* edited by W.E.

(Continued on next page)

(Continued from previous page)

Wilbur (1930). The other French freebooter's exploits may be followed also in a separate publication, entitled *A Relation of a Voyage Made by the Sieur de Montauban, Captain of the French Privateers on the Coasts of Guinea in the Year 1695* (1698).

In 1699 there was published *A Collection of Original Voyages*, edited by William Hacke, which included Captain C. Cowley's voyage around the world, Sharp's voyage to the South Seas, Captain John Woods's passage through the Straits of Magellan, and the adventures of John Robert with corsairs in the Levant. This collection of voyages is also to be found in the fourth volume of what is generally called Dampier's *Voyages*. William Dampier was for awhile a buccaneer himself, and it was his second venture with the "Brotherhood" that led to his famous voyage round the world. Basil Ringrose he referred to as "my worthy consort." In the same year 1699 appeared *A New Voyage and Description of the Isthmus of America, Giving an Account of the Author's Abode There* by Lionel Wafer.

The next important work on pirates, second only to that of Esquemeling, is *A General History of the Robberies and Murders of the Most Notorious Pirates from Their First Rise and Settlement in the Island of Providence to the Present Year* by Captain Charles Johnson, a somewhat vague and mysterious personage, probably masquerading for the real author who did not think it wise to make his identity known. [Recent literary historians have suggested almost conclusively that Capt. Johnson was no other than Daniel Defoe.—Eds.] This book was first published in 1724, but a reprint appeared as late as 1926, edited by A. L. Hayward, and another in two volumes in 1927 which was edited by Philip Gosse. The very next year 1725 a portion of the book was pirated by an anonymous editor and published under the title, *The History and Lives of All the Most Notorious Pirates and Their Crews, from Captain*

Avery who first settled at Madagascar to Captain John Gow and James Williams his lieutenant, etc. who were hanged . . . June 11, 1725. . . . The larger part of the 1735 fifth edition of this pirated work was published in 1915 and again in 1921 as *Pirates: with a foreword and sundry decorations* by Lovat Fraser.

Other interesting pirate books of the eighteenth century are *A Voyage to the South Sea and round the World, performed in the years 1708-1711. . . . Wherein an account is given of Mr. Alexander Selkirk, his manner of living and taming some wild beasts during the four years and four months he lived upon the uninhabited Island of Juan Fernandes* by Captain Edward Cook (1712), the Selkirk episode being the basis of Defoe's *Robinson Crusoe;* Daniel Defoe's *Account of the Conduct and Proceedings of the Pirate Gow*, who was the original of Scott's Captain Cleveland in his *Pirate*, there being only one original copy of Defoe's book and that in the British Museum; *Ashton's Memorial: An History of the Strange Adventures and Signal Deliverances of Mr. Philip Ashton, who, after he had made his escape from the Pirates, liv'd alone on a Desolate Island for about sixteen months, etc. with a short account of Mr. Nicholas Merritt who was taken at the same time . . .* by John Barnard (1725), an extremely interesting item of Americana; *The Four Years Voyages of Captain George Roberts: being a series of uncommon events, which befell him in a voyage to the islands of the Canaries, Cape de Verde, and Barbados from whence he was bound to the coast of Guiney . . .* (1726), sometimes incorrectly ascribed to Defoe and in 1930 edited by A. W. Lawrence for The Travellers' Library under the title of *A Series of Uncommon Events Which Befell Captain George Roberts;* and *The History of the Bucaniers of America* by W. H. Dilworth, the 1759 fourth edition being a small book of 140 pages, "published for the improvement and entertainment

of the British youth of both sexes" and "adorned with copper plates" of horrifying pictures.

During the nineteenth century, many books about pirates continued to appear. Of these are Johann Wilhelm von Archenholz's *History of the Pirates, Freebooters or Buccaneers of America,* translated from the German into English in 1807; S. Wilkinson's *Voyage and Adventures of Edward Teach, Commonly Called Black Beard, the Notorious Pirate* (1808); Captain James Burney's *History of the Buccaneers of America* (1816), which is confined to the exploits of the true "Brethren of the Coast," as they were called, who warred solely against the Spaniards and disappeared after the Peace of Ryswick in 1697; *The Pirates' Own Book: or Authentic Narratives of the Lives, Exploits, and Executions of the Most Celebrated Sea Robbers* by Charles Ellms, first published anonymously in 1837 and reprinted in 1924 by the Marine Research Society; Henry K. Brooke's *Book of Pirates, containing narratives of the most remarkable piracies and murders committed on the high seas . . .* (1841) and *Highwaymen and Pirates' Own Book . . .* (1845); T. Douglas's *Lives and Exploits of the Most Celebrated Pirates and Sea Robbers* (1845); H. M. Huet's *Davis the Pirate: or The True History of the Freebooters of the Pacific* and *Morgan the Buccaneer* (1853); and G. W. Thornbury's *The Monarchs of the Main* (1853). The last work, an extensive one which was published in three volumes, is by a very entertaining writer who carries the story of piracy somewhat further than did Captain Burney. His work is next in importance in this century to that of Burney, whose book John Masefield places among the great sea epics of English literature.

After Thornbury, there was apparently for a time a decline of interest in pirate books, or he covered the field so thoroughly that others were discouraged from writing books on the subject. J. S. C. Abbott's *Captain William Kidd, and others of the pirates or buccaneers who ravaged the seas, the islands, and the continents of America two hundred years ago* was published in 1874, but its lack of scholarly research is suggested by the author's noting in his preface Esquemeling and Oexemelin as different authors, whereas the latter is merely the French version of the former.

Probably Howard Pyle did more than any other person to develop the later very great interest in pirate stories. In 1891 appeared his beautifully illustrated and charmingly written *Buccaneers and Marooners of America,* which was based on that part of Esquemeling dealing with the career of Henry Morgan and on Captain Johnson's history of pirates. This work was followed by various articles by Pyle in *Harper's Magazine,* which appeared afterwards in *Boys' Book of Pirates* by Howard Pyle and Others (also published under the title of *Adventures of Pirates and Sea Rovers* by Howard Pyle, Rear Admiral J. H. Upshur, and Others) and in *Howard Pyle's Book of Pirates: Fiction, Fact and Fancy concerning the Buccaneers and Marooners of the Spanish Main* (1921), collected and edited by Merle Johnson after Pyle's death in 1911. Pyle was the author also of *The Rose of Paradise: being a detailed account of certain adventures that happened to Captain John Mackra in connection with the famous pirate Edward England in the year 1720 off the Island of Juanna in the Mozambique Channel: written by himself and now for the first time published by Howard Pyle* (1888); *Stolen Treasure* (1907), containing the four short narratives: "With the Buccaneers," "Tom Chist and the Treasure-Box," "The Ghost of Captain Brand," and "The Devil at New Hope"; and a romance of the sea, called *Within the Capes* (1885).

Under Pyle's inspiration, there was an immediate increase in the demand for pirate books. This was met by

(Continued on next page)

(Continued from previous page)

such volumes as D. Kelsey's *Wild Heroes of the Seas* (1892), which deals with pirates, buccaneers, marooners, corsairs, etc. on all seas; Thomas A. Janvier's *Sea Robbers of New York,* an episode in the career of Captain Kidd; John D. Chaplin's *The True Captain Kidd,* which appeared in *Harper's Magazine* for November, 1894 and December, 1902 respectively and was fully illustrated by Pyle; *The Real Captain Kidd: A Vindication* by C. N. Dalton (1911); *The Trial of Captain Kidd,* edited by Graham Brooks (1930); *Captain Kidd and His Skeleton Island* by Harold T. Wilkins, who claimed to have discovered Kidd's own maps, called the "Original Authentic Charts of Skeleton Island" (c. 1937); Frank R. Stockton's whimsical *Buccaneers and Pirates of Our Coast* (1897); John Masefield's exceedingly interesting *On the Spanish Main, or Some English Forays on the Isthmus of Darien, with a Description of the Buccaneers and a Short Account of Old-time Ships and Sailors* (1906); and others which will be found in the reading list at the end of this discussion. There also will be found a large number of those of a recent date. The real flood of pirate stories, based on actual fact, came after the first World War. Though this was probably only a coincidence, it is still a very remarkable one.

For interesting accounts of the deeds of the pirate Lafitte and the filibuster William Walker, one might turn to E. A. Powell's *Gentlemen Rovers* (1913). For a more detailed account of Walker's career read W. O. Scrogg's *Filibusters and Financiers: the Story of William Walker and His Associates* (1916). For a biography of the pirate, see Lyle Saxon's excellent *Lafitte the Pirate* (1930).

For information regarding the practice of piracy in the Mediterranean one may go to such books as Henry A. Ormerod's scholarly *Piracy in the Ancient World . . .* (1924), E. Hamilton Currey's *Sea Wolves of the Mediterranean,* and Stanley Lane-Poole's *The Story of the Barbary Corsairs.* For further information on pirates of the Pacific and the Far East, the following works might be consulted: Colonel John Biddulph's *The Pirates of Malabar and an Englishman in India Two Hundred Years Ago; The Pirate*

Wind: Tales of the Sea Robbers of Malaya by Owen Rutter, F.R.G.S.; *The Expedition to Borneo of H.M.S. Dido for the Suppression of Piracy* by Captain Henry Keppel, R.N. (1846); Captain Lindsay Anderson's *Among Typhoons and Pirate Craft;* and Aleko E. Lilius's *I Sailed with Chinese Pirates.* Captain H. E. Raabe's *Cannibal Nights: The Reminiscences of a Free-lance Trader* (1927), which is dedicated to "my old friend Jack London," who was once a member of one of Raabe's crews, contains interesting references to Bully Hayes, sometimes called "Pirate De Luxe," under whom Raabe served for a time. For additional information read *Bully Hayes, South Sea Pirate* by Basil Lubbock. Another book with a literary association is William Diapea's *Cannibal Jack: the true autobiography of a white man in the South Seas,* which has a foreword by H. de Vere Stacpoole, who thinks the book deserves a place on the shelf beside Melville's *Typee.*

Buried treasure, which is a fascinating subject usually suggestive of pirates, has received interesting general treatment in Ralph D. Paine's *The Book of Buried Treasure: Being a true history of the gold, jewels, and plate of pirates, galleons, etc. which are sought for to this day* (1911). Several anthologies on pirates are included in the reading list. Those by Joseph Lewis French are very useful, though he has taken his material indiscriminately from works of fiction as well as from stories of actuality. For a general bibliography on books about pirates and piracy the best work is Philip Gosse's *My Pirate Library* (1926).

Another terror of the sea is mutiny. The most famous example is that of the *Bounty,* which is described in the following books: *Bligh and the Bounty: His Narrative,* with preface by Lawrence Irving (1936); *The Mutineers of the Bounty* by Lady Belcher (1870); *True Story of the Mutiny of the Bounty* by Owen Rutter (1936); *Saga of the Bounty,* edited by Irvin Anthony (1935); and, of course, the fictional trilogy by Nordhoff and Hall. The most dangerous and appalling mutiny in English naval history took place in the fleets off Spithead and the Nore in 1797. Among the books dealing with it are the following: *The*

The Jolly Roger flown by Calico Jack Rockham. From Pirates: An Illustrated History *(The Dial Press, N.Y., 1976, $12.95).*

Naval Mutinies of 1797 by C. Gill (1913) and *The Floating Republic: an account of the mutinies at Spithead and the Nore in 1797* by G. E. Manwaring and Bonamy Dobree (c. 1935). The "Royal Oak Mutiny" is narrated in *The Navy from Within* by R. G. B. Dewar (1938). The most widely known American mutiny was that on the U.S. Brig *Somers*, which occurred in 1842. All the details are set forth in *Proceedings of the Naval Court-Martial in the Case of A. S. Mackenzie . . .*, edited by James Fenimore Cooper (1844). A chapter on this mutiny is in Hanson W. Baldwin's *Admiral Death* (1939), which contains twelve episodes of shipwreck and other perils of the sea. General works on mutinies are *Sailors' Rebellion: a Century of Naval Mutinies* by J. G. Bullocke (1938); *Mutiny at Sea* by R. L. Hadfield (1937); *Mutiny: being a survey of mutinies from Spartacus to Invergordon* by T. H. Wintringham (1936); and *Revolt at Sea* by Irvin Anthony (1934).

The slave trade eventually came to be looked upon as being as nefarious as piracy. One may learn what the early voyages of slave ships were like in *Voyages of the Slavers St. John and Arms of Amsterdam, 1659-1663 . . .*, translated by E. B. O'Callaghan (1867). That the system had not improved in the next century is shown in James Field Stanfield's *Observations on a Guinea Voyage . . .* (1788) and in Alexander Falconbridge's *Account of the Slave Trade on the Coast of Africa* (1788). In the nineteenth century, books on the slave trade multiplied. The following give experiences of slavers: *Captain Canot, or Twenty Years of an African Slaver* by Brantz Mayer (1854), which was reprinted in 1928 with an introduction by Malcolm Cowley under the title, *Adventures of an African Slaver . . .* ; *Six months on a Slaver* by Edward Manning (1879); and *A Rhode Island Slaver* by Vernon W. Crane (1922). Books which relate to the suppression of the slave trade are *Journal of an African Cruiser . . .* by "An officer of the U.S. Navy" (Lieutenant Horatio Bridge), edited by Nathaniel Hawthorne (1845), which gave experiences on an American man-of-war on the lookout for slavers; *A Three years' Cruise in the Mozambique Channel for the Suppression of the Slave Trade* by E. K. Barnard (1848); *Africa and the American Flag* by Andrew H. Foote, an officer in the U. S. Navy (1854); *A Cruise in the Gorgon . . .* by William C. Devereux (1869); and *The American Slave Trade: An Account of Its Origin, Growth, and Suppression* by J. R. Spears (1900). Another general excellent work on the subject is George Francis Dow's *Slave Ships and Slaving* (1927). Two other very good books which relate stories not only of the slave trade but also of pirates and privateersmen

are G. R. Low's *Tales of Old Ocean* and David Hannay's *The Sea Trader: His Friends and Enemies* (1912).

There are also a number of books on slave trading in the Far East and in the South Seas, where the practice was called "blackbirding" and continued until comparatively recent times. There are several books too about smuggling; such as, *Pearls, Arms, and Hashish* by Henri de Monfried, as told to Ida Treat (1930), an account of pearling, gun running, slaving and smuggling in the southern end of the Red Sea, Somaliland, and Egypt, which was very highly praised by William McFee. Other books on "blackbirding" and smuggling will be found in the reading list.

A Reading List*

Allen, G. W. *Our Navy and the West Indian Pirates.*
Anderson, Captain Lindsay. *Among Typhoons and Pirate Craft.*
Anthony, Irvin. *Saga of the Bounty* and *Revolt at Sea.*
Baldwin, Hanson W. *Admiral Death.*
Barnard, John. *Ashton's Memorial . . . .*
Belcher, Lady. *The Mutineers of the Bounty.*
Biddulph, Colonel John. *The Pirates of Malabar . . . .*
Bradlee, Francis B. C. *Piracy in the West Indies and Its Suppression.*
Brooke, Henry K. *Book of Pirates . . . .*
Bullocke, J. G. *Sailors' Rebellion . . . .*
Burney, Captain James. *History of the Buccaneers of America.*
Chatterton, E. Keble. *King's Cutters and Smugglers . . .* and *The Romance of the Sea Rovers . . . .*
Churchyard, W. B. *"Blackbirding" in the South Pacific . . . .*
Colomb, Captain. *Slave Catching in the Indian Ocean . . . .*
Cooper, James Fenimore, ed. *Proceedings of the Naval Court-Martial in the Case of A. S. Mackenzie.*
Currey, E. Hamilton. *Sea Wolves of the Mediterranean.*
Dalton, C. N. *The Real Captain Kidd: A Vindication.*
Davidson, Norman J. *The Romance of the Spanish Main . . . .*
Defoe, Daniel. *Account of the Conduct and Proceedings of the Pirate Gow.*
Diapea, William. *Cannibal Jack . . . .*

* Titles in print at this time are followed by bibliographic data in parentheses. All other titles, to our knowledge, are out of print and should be searched for in libraries and used book stores.—Eds.

(Continued from previous page)

Dilworth, W. H. *The History of the Bucaniers of America.*

Douglas, T. *Lives and Exploits of the Most Celebrated Pirates and Sea Robbers.*

Dow, George Francis. *Slave Ships and Slaving.*

Ellms, Charles. *The Pirates' Own Book . . . .* (Augustus Kelley, Fairfield, N.J., $20)

Esquemeling, John. *The Bucaniers of America . . . .* (Dover Publications, New York, $4)

Fea, Allan. *The Real Captain Cleveland.*

Finger, C. J. *Great Pirates.*

Foote, Andrew H. *Africa and the American Flag.*

French, Joseph Lewis, ed. *Great Pirate Stories* (two series).

Gollomb, Joseph. *Pirates, Old and New.*

Gosse, Philip. *My Pirate Library.* (Burt Franklin, N.Y., $18.75)

Hadfield, R. L. *Mutiny at Sea.*

Haring, C. H. *The Buccaneers in the West Indies in the XVII Century.* (Shoe String Press, Hamden, Conn., $9.50)

Harris, A. M. *Pirate Tales from the Law.*

Hawthorne, Nathaniel, ed. *Journal of an African Cruiser . . .* by "An officer of the U.S. Navy" (Captain Horatio Bridge).

Hurd, Archibald. *The Reign of the Pirates.*

Janvier, Thomas A. *Sea Robbers of New York.*

Johnson, Captain Charles. *A General History of the Robberies and Murders of the Most Notorious Pirates. . . .*

Kelsey, D. *Wild Heroes of the Seas.*

Keppel, Captain Henry. *The Expedition to Borneo of H.M.S. Dido for the Suppression of Piracy.*

Lane-Poole, Stanley. *The Story of the Barbary Corsairs.* (Norwood Editions, Norwood, Pa., $17.50)

Lawrence, A. W., ed. *A Series of Uncommon Events Which Befell Captain George Roberts.*

Lilius, Aleko E. *I Sailed with Chinese Pirates.*

Lubbock, Basil. *Bully Hayes, South Sea Pirate.*

Manwaring, G. E. and Bonamy Dobree. *The Floating Republic. . . .*

Masefield, John. *On the Spanish Main. . . .*

Mayer, Brantz. *Captain Canot. . . .*

Moray, Alastir. *The Diary of a Rum-runner.*

Morris, Mowbray. *Tales of the Spanish Main.*

Ormerod, Henry A. *Piracy in the Ancient World.* (Gordon Press, New York, $50)

Paine, Ralph D. *The Book of Buried Treasure. . . .*

Partridge, Eric. *Pirates, Highwaymen, and Adventurers* (anthology).

Powell, E. A. *Gentlemen Rovers.*

Pyle, Howard. *Book of Pirates, The Rose of Paradise . . . ,* and *Stolen Treasure.*

Raabe, Captain H. E. *Cannibal Nights. . . .*

Randell, Captain Jack. *I'm Alone.*

Rutter, Owen. *True Story of the Mutiny of the Bounty.*

Spears, J. R. *The American Slave Trade. . . .*

Stockton, Frank R. *Buccaneers and Pirates of Our Coast.*

Swan, Oliver G. *Deep Water Days* (anthology).

Thornbury, G. W. *The Monarchs of the Main.*

Treat, Ida, ed. *Pearls, Arms, and Hashish.*

Verrill, A. H. *Love Stories of Some Famous Pirates, The Real Story of the Pirate,* and *In the Wake of the Buccaneers.*

Wilkins, H. T. *Pirate Treasure* and *Captain Kidd and His Skeleton Island.*

Wilkinson, S. *Voyage and Adventures of Edward Teach, Commonly Called Black Beard.*

Some Additional Titles

The Bellerophon Book of Pirates (children's coloring book, $2.95, Bellerophon Books, San Francisco)

Defoe, Daniel. *A General History of the Pyrates* (J.M. Dent, 26 Albemarle St., London, England, £3.75). This is the same book credited above to Capt. Charles Johnson but lately determined to have been written by Defoe under a pseudonym.

Gosse, Philip. *The Pirates' Who's Who* (Burt Franklin, New York, $18.50)

Grey, Charles. *Pirates of the Eastern Seas* (Kennikat Press, Port Washington, N.Y., $12.50)

Masefield, John. *On the Spanish Main* (Naval Institute Press, Annapolis, Maryland, $10)

Mitchell, David. *Pirates: An Illustrated History* (The Dial Press, New York, $12.95)

Stockton, Frank R. *Buccaneers and Pirates of Our Coasts* (young adult book, Macmillan, New York, $5.95)

Williams, Neville. *The Sea Dogs* (Macmillan, New York, $15)

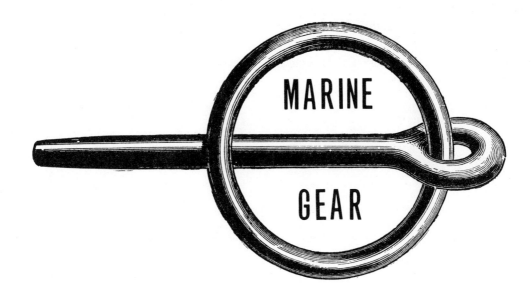

MARINE

GEAR

I approach the ideal yacht in the ideal way, here a little and there a little, gadget upon gadget . . . the gadgets roughly made and hastily shipped to be tested at sea—and, the hypercritical person will say, very obviously never finished properly, nor replaced with something more permanent. Possibly not, but what is the sense of making things permanent if you may think of something better tomorrow? It is the permanence and finish of yacht work that makes owners so unenterprising. When the time comes that I can see nothing about my ship that wants alteration, it will be a token of senility.

—Conor O'Brien

Here and there we have listed a few of the larger distributors of marine wares, but certainly not all of them. This lack of comprehensiveness has not been for reasons of policy but, rather, because there is a more natural fellowship with the smaller, more personal, less easily discovered. The big places cannot be faulted for not having the stuff; a glance at any of their catalogs shows that. Nor are they necessarily impersonal. They do have their distinctive personalities and style. And it probably is no longer fair to feel that outfits with a catalog *that* big don't need us; they do, and in many cases we need them. So here are a few more addresses of big places.

John Burns and Co., Ltd.
Ship Chandlery-Export Sales
Corner Stanley Street
Parnell, Auckland 1
New Zealand

A 246-page catalog of everything new and traditional in the Antipodes. How about copper sheathing tacks?!

As the covers of all printed matter show, printing costs are rising very rapidly and so are retail prices. Catalog prices now exist where once the catalogs were complimentary; catalogs that were always sold are seeing increases in price. They nevertheless remain interesting reading for the money. Send a card first asking the cost of a current catalog, for any prices we publish here are bound to be out of date by press time.

—Eds.

E&B Marine Supply/Mail Order
257 Bertrand Avenue
Perth Amboy, N.J. 08861

An eastern marine equipment discount house with a 184-page catalog; fair selections, good prices.

Land's End
Yachtsman's Equipment Guide
2317 N. Elston Ave.
Chicago, Ill. 60614

Over 300 pages of stylish racy-cruisey gear, this is a *guide* in addition to a catalog in that reasons are given for the choices offered. Good stuff, though a little trendy, a little expensive.

Manhattan Marine
116 Chambers St.
New York, N.Y. 10007

A good old-fashioned straight-ahead American chandlery with a loaded reference catalog. We know lots of yards that use Manhattan as a matter of course.

Goldberg's Marine
202 Market St.
Philadelphia, Penn. 19106
and
3 West 46th St.
New York, N.Y. 10036

A 22-page *Discount Accessory Catalog* showing good values on better than average choices.

National Marine and Electronics Corp.
Box 010870, Main P.O.
Miami, Fla. 33101

Another discount mailorder house. Like the others, fair choices and good prices.

M&E Marine Supply Co.
U.S. Route 130
Collingswood, N.J.

Don't know for sure, but we believe that M&E is the largest distributor in the business. They have a mailorder catalog, a fat one, but they are primarily a wholesaler. Go to your local outlet, and you'll probably find that about half of their looseleaf reference sheets are from M&E.

Sailing Equipment Warehouse
Box 2575
Olympia, Wash. 98507

Listed in previous *Catalogs,* this organization now has had its own catalog for a couple of years; they have good prices and a policy to favor folks who are building their own cruising boats.

So Onward

Over the years we've been depressed going through the catalogs of American firms offering brass and bronze fittings. Recent catalogs tend to be very old ones that are reissued with "discontinued" or "not in stock" or "now special order" written all over them. So Buck-Algonquin's catalog comes as a real joy. This is obviously a vital company, offering not only what fans of the venerable expect, but also showing evidence of experimentation and expansion of their efforts. Here are hundreds of nonferrous and malleable iron fittings from stem to stern, keel to truck.

Buck-Algonquin
Marine Hardware Division
Second Street and Columbia Ave.
Philadelphia, Penn. 19122

Below and right: From the Buck-Algonquin catalog.

TILLER STRAP & RUDDER CAP
Clevis Type Cap

Manganese Bronze				Chrome Plated
Part Number	Tiller Stock Socket	Fork I.D. Dimensions	Cap Angle	Wgt., Ea., lbs.
TSA-238	2⅜"	2" x 6"	45°	6.0

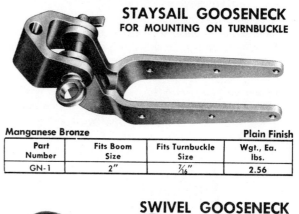

STAYSAIL GOOSENECK
FOR MOUNTING ON TURNBUCKLE

Manganese Bronze			Plain Finish
Part Number	Fits Boom Size	Fits Turnbuckle Size	Wgt., Ea. lbs.
GN-1	2"	⁷⁄₁₆"	2.56

SWIVEL GOOSENECK

Manganese Bronze				Plain Finish
Part Number	Mast Ring I.D.	Boom Clamp Ring O.D.	Overall Length	Wgt., Ea., lbs.
SG-250	2½"	1⁵⁄₁₆"	6⅜"	0.75

CROSS-OVER TILLER ARM

Manganese Bronze					Plain Finish
Part Number	Overall Length	Center to Center Dim.	Hole Sizes		Weight, Ea., lbs.
			Center	Ends	
TAC-1	16½"	7⅝"	½"	½"	2.90

On Gronicles

I think you would be well advised to drop the subject of gronicles. I have it on good authority that the Catholics have banned the use of gronicles. This goes for not only the orthodox gronicles, but also the reformed ones. Since you are an international publication with an undoubtedly large circulation in all the Latin countries, I believe you can understand how detrimental this could be to your commercial welfare.

—Darrell McClure
Talmage, California

On a tip we wrote Capt. Jack's Marine Supply inquiring about his line of gear, and he answered:

Dear Editors:

Too numerous to list. The store of a million and one items! (new and used). As they say, "If Capt. Jack's doesn't have it—forget it."

Capt. Jack

We're not sure what that means. It's your move, reader.

**Capt. Jack's Marine Supply
2521 N. Dixie Highway
Pompano, Fla.**

Below: How about a self-propelled cradle for your boat? From Airborne Sales.

Hearing that a place called Airborne offered a good crash axe, we wrote and got in return the most interesting document for this *Catalog*. Airborne is a surplus outfit in the old tradition—fantastic bargains of unheard-of stuff, just as there were after WW II. They specialize in electronic and mechanical equipment, and it would be crazy to even attempt a general inventory.

**Airborne Sales Co.
8501 Steller Drive
Box 2727
Culver City, Cal. 90230
Catalog is 50 cents**

ELECTRIC DRIVE UNIT

Used as a drive unit for an Airforce portable power unit. Will drive a unit weighing between 700-1000 lbs. Drive motor is rated at 1½ H.P. at 24 volts D.C. at 7500 R.P.M. Gear reduction through dual drive differential type gear box is 55:1. Wheels turn 290 R.P.M. no load on 24 V.D.C. and 150 R.P.M. no load on 12 V.D.C. Motor is reversible. Either wheel will drive unit Motor is continuous duty. Comes with a 38" long tow bar and eye. Wheel can be dissengaged from the drive motor by turning the wheel hub lock handle. Tires are 600-9 with tubes. Unit is 21" W. x 21" H. Removed from operating units. Tested prior to shipment. Excellent for use in electric cars or carts. Net wt. 145 lbs. Ship. Wt. 150 lbs.

No. 3644   NEW LOW PRICE **$74.50**

My husband has added so much paraphernalia, I wonder what keeps her afloat

Four Below

General Ecology (the new phrase that's reverently whispered as you share a secret handshake) now offers a water purification system for small yachts.

**General Ecology
81 Lancaster Ave.
Malvern, Penn. 19355**

General Ecology's Seagull IV is the world's finest purifier of its type, and to our knowledge, the only such unit to be tested by the U.S. Government and accepted as a "Water Purification" device according to current standards. Dozens of units are EPA-registered as bacteriostats but these, of course, are not purifiers against bacteria, cysts, asbestos, etc.

—**General Ecology**

The Ship Shop Catalog contains an entry for shatterproof acrylic safety mirror stock sold by the square inch ($.07 per). Good idea.

**Ship Shop, Inc.
294 New York Ave.
Huntington, N.Y. 11743**

*Right, above: The General Ecology Seagull IV.
Right: From the Ship Shop catalog.*

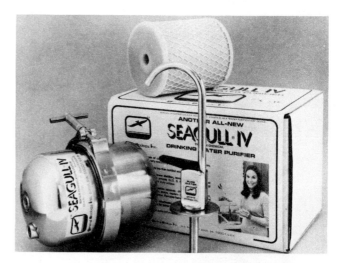

CA-245
SAFETY MIRRORS

Shatterproof, acrylic plastic mirrors fabricated to size up to 2' x 4'. Indistinguishable from plate glass mirrors. Optical quality, break and weather resistance and light

weight make them ideal for marine use, recreational areas, play rooms, etc. Their light weight permits mounting with contact cement or double backed tape, if preferred to conventional mounts or frames. The safety factor alone makes them almost mandatory for boats or areas where there is risk of breakage. Specify width and height in inches. (Minimum charge for each piece is $3.00) **$.07 per sq. in.**

West Marine, a fairly sizable discount house, carries a sane convenience, a hot-drink dispenser, for the harried watch.

West Marine Products
850 San Antonio Rd.
Palo Alto, Cal. 94304

Ken Steinmetz of Ken's Boat Shop wrote us recently about his new oarlocks, sure to be appreciated by traditional oarsmen:

Hardware for fitting out traditional boats being at a premium, I thought you would like to know that I am now having cast, and am making available to needing boat owners, manganese bronze oarlocks, size #1½ with an inside diameter of 2½". They have a burnished finish and a ½" shaft to fit standard oarlock sockets. This size oarlock is ideal for 2" to 2¼" leathered oars.

The price of the horns only is $12.50 per pair postpaid in the continental United States. Top mounted bronze sockets can be supplied *with* oarlock horns if needed, $4.93 per pair, also postpaid. Professional boatbuilders may inquire on company letterhead about quantity prices for oarlock horns.

I shall try to hold to these prices for as long as possible, but we all know what is happening to prices these days.

Ken's Boat Shop
3710 Ocean Avenue
Seaford, N.Y. 11783

Below: Oarlocks from Ken's Boat Shop.
Right: Verity's ship's bell.
Right, above: From the West Marine Products catalog.

"DISPENS-A-DRINK"

A stainless-steel one-quart vacuum bottle with bulkhead-mounted bracket and dispenser valve for keeping hot and cold drink dispensing under control in any weather. Bottle is all stainless ... inside ... outside ... cap. All metal parts in bracket and dispenser stainless. Model 270/123.
~~List $49.20.~~ **Only $41.95.**
Model 370/123 (2 Qts)
~~List $56.90.~~ **Only $48.95.**
Model 270
(1 qt bottle only)
~~List $34.25.~~ **Only $29.95.**
Model 370
(2 qt bottle only)
~~List $41.95.~~ **Only $34.95.**
Dispenser only. Fits most vacuum bottles with #4 stopper. Model U-123. ~~List $14.95.~~ **Only $12.95.**

Super Bell

Here it is, folks, the most gorgeous bell we have ever seen. We are also proud to report that Dr. Tom Clapp, when he came huffing and puffing into our offices with one of these 8-inch beauties, said that our comments about bells in Volume 3 of the *Mariner's Catalog* were instrumental in causing Verity's Chuck Bagwell to design and make this elegant piece.

Tom tells us that Chuck is a curmudgeon, at least on the outside, whose only real problem is perfection. The bell is cast of an alloy containing a high percentage of tin, which gives it a clean, sweet note. It is machined and then polished by hand inside and out to a blinding luster.

It really is, as Tom says, "22½ pounds of elegant jewelry."

Verity Incorporated
Box 274
Topsham, Maine 04086

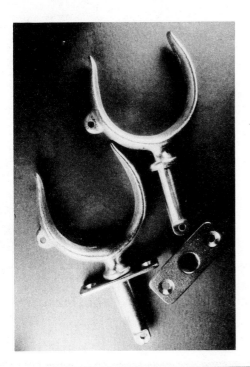

Performance Department

Resting only a moment from unrelenting simplicity, we'll look at some of the up-to-date. Since the days of McNamara at Defense, systems analysis and design has entered every phase of American life. Somewhere there is a shingle proclaiming the "Ice Cream Systems Group."

There is both bad and good news in this, bad because the getting-it-out often corrupts the what-it-is, and good because so much of what is worth keeping in the now world would not have come into being without systems design—or would not have become available to us woodchucks in any case.

Super Spar is a yacht spar systems manufacturer. They have a vast store of prepared blanks for all spars on the modern yacht and can quickly turn them out with whatever options or systems you wish to incorporate.

Super Spar
15678 Graham St.
Huntington Beach, Cal. 92649

Barient, a well-known factor of winches, has developed a self-tailing winch in sizes down to 3 inches. The self-tailer is an exclusive patent of theirs, and no doubt expensive. Singlehanders may want to consider one or two for those times when one hand, and barely that, is all that can be spared.

Barient
936 Bransten Road
San Carlos, Cal. 94070
and
557 Post Road
Darien, Conn. 06820

Right: The Barient self-tailer.
Below: Some go-fast custom spar hardware from Super Spar.

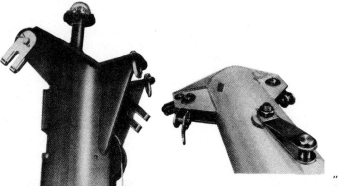

Masthead for 33' racer with externally mounted spinnaker cranes and "u" bolts for halyard blocks. Sheaves for 2 Genoa halyards.

Typical cruising masthead complete with sheaves, pins and toggles.

"Triple Header" mast head assembly. Designed to provide three interchangeable headsail halyards with internal leads. Stainless steel fairings minimize chafe. Recommended for ¼ tonners thru one ton size racing yachts.

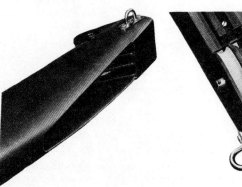

2 Ton Boom End

Jiffy Reef Arrangement

Custom fixed gooseneck mount for Maxi ocean racer.

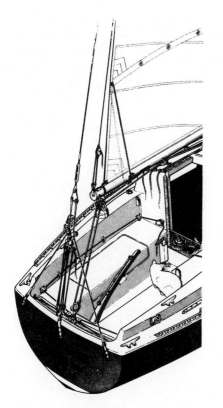

From the Oyster Bay Boat Shop catalog.

Forespar has developed some *attractive* spar systems with emphasis on downwind-foredeck sticks. Outer dimensions are large, something to get a grip on, and surfaces are spun—no glitter. Some of their poles telescope and camlock to optional lengths, and their terminals are elegant. In other words, there are some aesthetics with the engineering. They also carry the new graphite stuff.

Fore Manufacturing Corp.
3140 Pullman Street
Costa Mesa, Cal. 92626

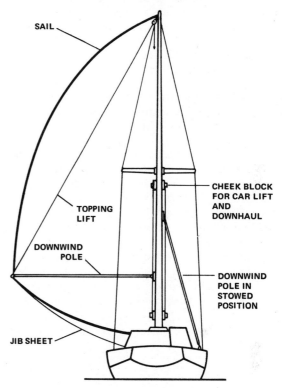

Above and below: From the Fore Manufacturing catalog.

The Oyster Bay Boat Shop has gone into class and small ocean racing rigging systems with impressive care. Many choices are offered for each fitting, drawings are provided to show possible arrangements, and prices are right on the page. If we were class racers, we'd use their catalog often.

The Oyster Bay Boat Shops, Inc.
Box 717
2 South Street
Oyster Bay, N.Y. 11771

DOWNWIND POLES

Cruising sailors have long enjoyed the pleasure of downwind passages utilizing twin headsails. FORESPAR's Downwind Pole System is a simple, convenient and safe method of rigging and controlling these sails. With FORESPAR's System more yachts can now take advantage of this effortless way of cruising.

The system is designed for either single or double poles. Most popular is the double pole system. The pole is attached to a high strength, hard anodized aluminum mast car. The mast car will accommodate either 1¼" "T" track of 1¼" x 3/16" flat track. The outboard end of the pole (our "XP" type spinnaker end) is operated by a release lanyard extending the full length of the pole.

To operate, simply remove the pole from the chock, attach the jaw end to the jib sheet, raise the topping lift and lower the mast car to the desired position. Make any minor adjustment for final sail trim.

To furl the sail, the car is raised up the mast and the topping lift eased off. The pole will swing inboard where it can be easily stowed in its chock located either on the mast, deck or next to the shrouds. When used in conjunction with a roller furling jib system, this arrangement offers the optimum in sail and pole handling. One person can easily operate the whole system.

The FORESPAR Downwind pole features 3" dia. anodized aluminum tubing and is suitable for boats larger than 30 feet. Poles are supplied in any length up to maximum of 21 feet in either "kit" form or customized to length. Each pole includes the mast car, full length release lanyard, and a rigging guide which explains what equipment is needed to complete the installation on your boat.

Your sailboat is a bow; the mast is an arrow aimed at the sea's bottom. Improper tuning, particularly on traditional craft rerigged with modern gear, can tear your boat apart. Whether the concern is for too little or too much rigging tension, the Sta-Tork can help put mind and craft at ease, from:

N-C Industries
2701 Fairway Drive
Greensboro, N.C. 27408

Remote steering problems are generally solved using hydraulics or, if mechanics are used, sacrifices in space, for the running cables must be allowed for. Orion has come up with a system that allows the quadrant to be set in any convenient position, and the cables to go around as many bends as necessary, from:

Orion Marine Products Co.
2400 Crofton Boulevard
Crofton, Md. 21114

The Orion method is a full tension, "pull-pull" system, using 3/16 dia. 7 x 19 stainless steel steering cables with a breaking strength of over 3700 lbs. But instead of running the exposed cables over individual sheaves, we send them through strong, efficient flexible conduits, which can be routed around any number of bends without outside support. The cables lead to a terminal unit on the rudder post which contains the quadrant, bearings, cable anchors, and rudder stops. This remarkably simple combination drastically reduces the number of moving parts in the system and results in safe, dependable, and highly sensitive steering.

—Orion Marine Products

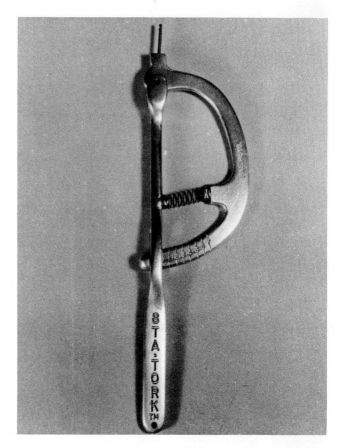

Above: The Sta-Tork from N-C Industries.
Below: The Orion Model 741 rudder quadrant.

Most commonly used on boats where cables can be routed in a straight line from the pedestal to the rudder post, keeping all cables beneath the cockpit sole. One piece terminal unit contains quadrant, bearings, sheaves and rudder stops. Highly recommended on spade rudder boats with forward raking rudders, where mounting of individual sheaves creates a problem.

Light Reading

If Hong Kong doesn't make it, Hong Kong probably sells it, and the time of the millennium doesn't seem to matter. At Tung Woo, for example, they are still making *copper* navigation lights in all the traditional patterns.

Tung Woo Navigation Light Manufactory
16 Hillier St.
Hong Kong

We knew that there had to be something between the ordinary kerosene wick lamp and the Coleman pressure gas mantle lamp that did not possess the somewhat-touchy characteristics of the Aladdins. We've found our lamp in the Tilleys. Pressurized *kerosene* mantle lamps! Better light. Better fuel.

Tilley Lamp Co., Ltd.
Dunmarry, Belfast BT17 9JA
Northern Ireland

MASTHEAD
Dioptric Lens

PORT
Dioptric Lens

STERN
Plain Lens

NOT UNDER COMMAND
Dioptric Lens

STARBOARD
Dioptric Lens

ANCHOR
Dioptric Lens

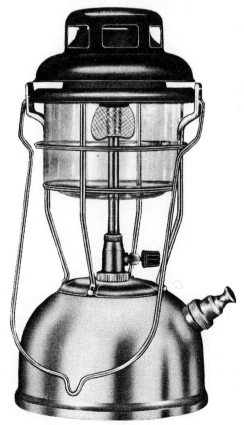

All lights on this page from Tung Woo, except the light at right, which is the Tilley Stormlight from the Tilley Lamp Co.

Owners and builders of larger working vessels will want the C and F lighting catalog in their files. Big, tough stuff mostly, lights that won't break (so easily) for every navigational purpose.

**The Carlisle and Finch Co.
4562 W. Mitchell Ave.
Cincinnati, Ohio 45232**

We've liked the look of the Bass Navigator's Light for some time.

**Bass Products, Inc.
Box 901
Marblehead, Mass. 01945**

Lifetime Flashlight

In the *Mariner's Catalog*, Volume 5, page 108, you recommended a line of flashlights. I've got another line for you. Marketed under the name Sea-Probe, these are truly an excellent value for the individual requiring a no-nonsense, dependable flashlight. They are constructed of heavy, anodized aluminum in 2- through 7-cell models. Each is waterproof down to 300 feet, is explosion proof, shock proof, and has a special "penetrator optics system," which places a light shield directly over the bulb to prevent scattered light, thus creating a very narrow, intense beam. The diamond knurling on the case provides an unbelievably sure grip, even in wet or oily conditions. Each comes with a spare bulb in the end cap and a lifetime warranty. I will testify that this light will withstand being run over by a car with absolutely no damage. None! I sincerely recommend it. The address:

**Police Equipment Division
L. A. Screw Products, Inc.
8401 Loch Lomond Drive
Pico Rivera, Cal. 90660**

—Mark C. Thomas

*Left: The Bass navigator's light.
Below: Boxed material from the Carlisle and Finch catalog.*

SINGLE OPTICAL NAVIGATION LIGHTS
Anchor, Breakdown, Whistle, Mast and Blinker

These single optical lights are also manufactured per I.E.E.E. No. 45 and are U.S. Coast Guard Listed. All the above description applies except that these lights have a single lens and lampholder.

These fixtures are available with hoisting eyes for mounting or with a tapped hole and set screw for mounting on a 1 1/4 NPT threaded pipe or stud.

Anchor light is supplied with a clear lens, breakdown light with red lens, whistle light with amber lens, and mast or blinker lights as specified.

Phenolic medium screw lamp socket for standard single filament lamps is provided unless otherwise specified. Mogul screw three contact lamp socket for use with two filament lamps can be supplied if specified at slight additional charge.

32 Point 360°

Cat. No. NL1529XA Clear
Cat. No. NL1529XB Red
Cat. No. NL1529XC Amber

32 Point 360°

Cat. No. NL2527XA Clear
Cat. No. NL2527XB Red
Cat. No. NL2527XC Amber

Light shield for reduced light angles can be supplied at extra cost. Give degrees opening required.

Tackling the Ground

These rather unusual new anchor designs have become available recently: the Mela-Stockanker from Torott-Handel in Germany, the Wishbone Nonfouling from the U.S., and the Bruce Anchor from Scotland, offered to North Americans out of the Bahamas.

Below: The Wishbone nonfouling anchor.

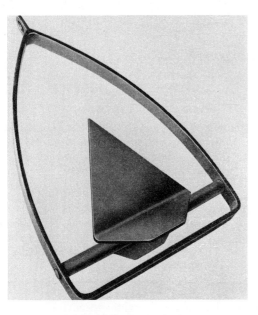

Torott-Handel
D 4270 Dorsten 2
Borkener Strasse 54
West Germany

Wishbone Marine Products
780 S.W. 9th Terrace
Pompano Beach, Fla. 33060

Bruce International Ltd.
Box N-7788
Nassau, N.P.
Bahamas

Above: Now if this won't hold ground, what will?—the Mela-Stockanker.

A little something to permit better sleep—the Bruce Anchor. It is also available in smaller sizes.

The Romantic's Boneyard

Most "marine junk" places are funky and one-man and wonderful. They specialize in on-site sales, not mailorder. We wrote off to a mess of them and heard positively from three:

Jacobson Metal Co.
Money Point
Chesapeake, Va.

Marvin Junk
Bridge Rd.
Haddam, Conn. 06438

Marine Speculator
58 River St.
Beverly, Mass. 01915

We dismantle Navy ships and carry marine hardware of all kinds, such as ship's steering wheels from 24" to 48", brass bells, life rings, hatch boards, brass propellers, cleats, electric motors, and reduction gears.
—Jacobson Metal Co.

Our new and used merchandise stock changes very often. We try to carry almost anything marine for pleasure or workboats, small boats to 80-footers, both power and sail.
—Marine Speculator

Buy It Wholesale

by Lowell P. Thomas

A couple of years ago a friend of mine who wanted to build a boat told me about some problems he was having with his wife.

"She said if I build another boat she'd leave me."

"Well, what are you going to do?" I asked, expecting to hear the latest in the psychology of soothing angry wives.

His reply was deadly serious, "Today I talked to three real nice ladies, but there ain't a single Tancook Whaler for 500 miles."

Aside from trouble with wives, amateur boatbuilders can also have a lot of trouble paying for all the stuff it takes to put a boat together. One afternoon in a marine hardware store and the would-be builder goes home and cries. What the neophyte may not know is the first rule of survival—namely, buy it wholesale. Yeah, I know, you've been told (1) it's illegal, (2) they won't sell to you, (3) you have to be in the business, and (4) besides . . . . Well, hell, here are some answers to those arguments: (1) So what, so is about 50 percent of everything else we do. (2) They will. (3) Tain't so. (4) etc., etc. Now just shut up and listen for a minute.

I don't know the laws, but as long as you pay the taxes on what you buy and don't use the name of a firm without permission and pay cash, you won't find any trouble with the law. The wholesalers I've had experience with don't seem to care too much whether you're in the business or not, as long as you buy in reasonably large amounts, which means *boxes* of screws, *coils* of line, *drums* of resin, *rolls* of fiberglass, or single large items that cost a bit, like a $65 anchor, or a $35 cabin lamp. If you can't use a whole box of screws, find another builder who needs some and split the lot with him. Is it worth the trouble? Only if you want to save 30 to 40 percent on an awful lot of items. Think about it, good buddy; it may make the difference between dreaming and actually starting that full-sized replica of the Coast Guard's *Eagle*.

So you're convinced, and you walk into Smith Marine Supplies, "Wholesale Only," and what happens? Well, generally there's a tough-looking guy, very busy, trying to wait on three customers at once. When your turn comes he'll expect you to know exactly what you want, and, unless you want to blow the whole thing, you'd better be able to quote the screw sizes, type of head, material (silicon bronze, galvanized, etc.), and thread size. If you can't remember all that at once, write it down and just give him a list. Be ready to make substitutions: "I ain't got these in flat head, can you use round head?" or "These washers come in one-pound boxes, not boxes of a hundred." Have

(Continued on next page)

(Continued from previous page)

some answers; nothing makes you look more out of place in this store than asking what the difference between truss-head and round head is, or how many washers to the pound. Also, many wholesalers have a minimum charge; don't get caught with an order less than the minimum and nothing to substitute to bring it up to the minimum. Remember that nails are going to be sold by the pound, screws by the hundred (boxed), nuts by the hundred (boxed), and washers by the pound. In the larger sizes, nuts, washers, and screws (bolts) will be sold individually or in lots of some minimum number, like a dozen or so. If you're buying paint, know the brands your wholesaler carries and give him can size and number code for color, again being ready for a substitution if he's out of a particular item.

Try to go to the horse's mouth by avoiding the middle-man when possible. If there's a resin and fiberglass distributor nearby, he'll probably sell you resin by the drum and glass mat, cloth, and woven roving by the roll (actually by the pound, as the rolls vary a bit). Cordage is best bought from a cordage company, but be prepared to buy 600-foot rolls. Just remember that your over-supply can be sold off to friends.

So finally your order is written up and the man is about to go in the back for all the goodies. Now comes a moment of truth. With a slightly suspicious tone your man says, "Who is this billed to?" If you've laid your groundwork exceptionally well, you might reply, "Jones Boat Yard, I'm picking this stuff up for Eddie, C.O.D." Which is only partly a lie, because Eddie told you to go ahead and use his firm's name, providing you pay the sales tax and pay cash. In fact, he might have called ahead for you and said, "Hey, this is Eddie. We've got a rush order and I'm sending Joe down to pick up some stuff. He'll be paying cash." Of course, maybe you don't know any Eddie; try a made-up name and hurriedly add that you're paying cash and tax, but *never* use a real firm's name without permission from somebody with authority, and *never charge anything or fail to pay the sales tax.* Actually a phone call ahead can get your order filled and waiting for you, thereby saving a bit of waiting and giving the wholesaler a chance to write it up to your "firm's" name as a C.O.D., which you can pick up without embarrassment.

Once you get to know the salesman on a first-name

basis, you've broken the Wholesale Only barrier. If you can't get permission from a boatyard friend to use the name of his yard, or if you're too disgustingly honest to try making up a name, try talking to the manager of the store, telling him that you're a boatbuilder building on specula-tion, that you buy cash and pay tax, and that you're going to be buying about $5,000 a year worth of hardware. Maybe he'll go along with the idea.

Supposing the salesman buys your story, gives you a wink, which lets you know he's on to what you're doing (and which embarrasses the hell out of you), and writes up the ticket. That yellow and pink bill he hands you is liable to curdle your blood. You're in the big time now, baby; you're buying wholesale lots, and those lovely bronze screws that cost so much each in the yacht supply store are going to run from $30 to $75 a box *even with a big wholesale discount!* You said you were going to pay cash; now you'd better have the green stuff in your pocket, and often a bit more than you thought. Carry plenty!

Now a little word on why it's sometimes so hard to buy stuff from a wholesale dealer. Aside from whatever laws may govern who they can or can't sell to, including the sales tax problems, these guys depend on high-volume, low-mark-up sales. They deal with retail stores that *you* are supposed to be buying from. If you waste their time with nickel and dime orders, or if some of their retail store customers find out they're selling to you, they're in trouble. Keep your orders reasonably large and don't send all your buddies there to try the same trick or you're apt to kill the goose that's laying those golden eggs.

Finally, if you get turned down flat, don't give up. Suppose a big wholesale lumberyard absolutely refuses to sell to you, and even their big bad-ass attack-dog snarls wickedly as you leave. Start scrounging. Find a local boat-builder who has an account with the yard and try to work a deal. Chances are he'll be happy to place an order, pro-viding you pay him a small percentage for his trouble. As a last resort you can get an occupation license, usually for a few bucks, and establish credit with the wholesalers of your choice. Actually this can really pay off if the boat you're building is big, or if you're building several. In fact, if you can borrow enough money to rent that big shed, and maybe hire a couple of helpers . . . .

Footnotes on Safety Gear

Peace of mind is important. If you don't have peace of mind, afloat or ashore, something is not right.

—Pete Culler

If the cost of fine and proper distress signal guns has you cowed, you may want to consider the less expensive but perfectly adequate Olin launchers with stainless actions but ABS molded plastic frames and barrels. Offered in two gauges, plus a combo gauge, from:

**Olin Signal Products
East Alton, Ill. 62024**

*Above: The Olin Model 25 kit.
Below: Pipe clamp from M.B. Skinner Products.*

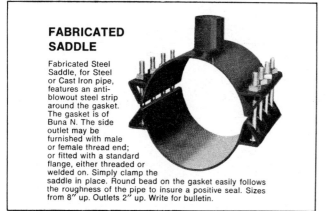

FABRICATED SADDLE

Fabricated Steel Saddle, for Steel or Cast Iron pipe, features an anti-blowout steel strip around the gasket. The gasket is of Buna N. The side outlet may be furnished with male or female thread end; or fitted with a standard flange, either threaded or welded on. Simply clamp the saddle in place. Round bead on the gasket easily follows the roughness of the pipe to insure a positive seal. Sizes from 8″ up. Outlets 2″ up. Write for bulletin.

In the business of serving industry, Skinner Products has a large line of emergency pipe repair fittings that could save your boat. In many respects the intake and outlet hoses and pipes to your engine, galley, head, bilge pumps, and cockpit drains are the weakest and most vulnerable systems on the craft. If they break, you sink. We illustrate here only one of many types of repair clamps offered. Dealers might consider carrying these.

**M.B. Skinner Products
3502 West Sample St.
South Bend, Indiana 46627**

The Automatic Halon from Convenience Marine Products.

Marine fire-suppression systems need not be complicated. Your extinguisher is required, but you need to know about the fire before the extinguisher can do its thing. Here we've found a single-component fire extinguisher that works automatically and that you can install yourself on the overhead of those places where fires can hide during their first insidious moments. The Automatic Halon at $160, from:

**Convenience Marine Products
100 Commerce Ave., S.W.
Grand Rapids, Mich. 49503**

Keeping the Fires Burning

As for several of the subjects we like to discuss, this stove section represents simply an addendum to previous coverage. If our coverage to date is not actually comprehensive, it is very nearly so.

—Eds.

Look at this beautiful, beautiful little yacht stove! It's the Queen Stove, made in England. In their letter the distributors said they had not yet sold one in North America, but were enthusiastic at the prospect. £65, from:

**Teddesley Boating Centre
Parkgate Lock
Teddesley Road, Near Penkridge
Staffordshire
England**

Some cold-climate mariners object to both liquid fuels *and* coal. For them Ratelco now offers cabin stoves in two sizes designed to burn charcoal briquets and trimmed in either stainless or brass.

Ratelco, Inc.
610 Pontius Ave. N.
Seattle, Wash. 98109

Owners of diesel-powered boats have another heating unit to consider in the Espar line, 5,800 to 48,000 BTUs. These heaters run completely independently of the engine. From:

Espar Products, Inc.
6480 Viscount Road
Mississauga, Ontario L4V 1H3
Canada

Above: The Espar diesel heater, 14,000-BTU model.
Left: The Ratelco Cole stove.

The Sure-Fire, One-Match Method

Dear Editors:

It may be criminal, or at least very poor judgment, to top your publisher, but Roger Taylor tells how to light a pressure stove with two matches in MC-5, page 130, whereas I never use more than one. We have a couple of one-burner Primus-type kerosene stoves aboard *Urchin* with which my wife turns out unbelievably great meals. Our first few weeks with the little monsters were hectic and more than once they almost got the deep six. I first tried preheating with alcohol, but some powerboat always seemed to be shoving a wake at us and slopping the stuff out of the cups. The next

move was to butter sterno in for preheat, and this stopped the slop, but when I'd try to light the burner, half the time it wasn't quite hot enough. That condition resulted in smoky flames to the detriment of the white paint on the overhead. By the middle of that summer I was desperate enough to think about the situation constructively and went to Western Auto and bought a cheap, small propane torch. So, one match to light the torch, use the nice, clean flame like a paint brush over the preheat tubes and when hot enough, pump a couple of strokes of pressure in and light the stove with the torch. That's it. If the burner isn't hot enough, use the torch some more. No trying to pour more alcohol into a hot cup.

One more refinement. We had been using regular kerosene in our stoves because I object to paying $5.00 a gallon for stove fuel. For the stoves it was fine, for the bulkhead lamp it stinks. It would drive us out of the tiny cabin. This summer we were anchored at Round Island in company with Gordon and Doris Swift aboard their lovely *Madrigal of Exeter*. From Gordon I learned that Thinex, the paint thinner, is a highly refined petroleum product which burns clean and odor-free in kerosene stoves and lamps. Maybe some chemist will tell me some day that the stuff's explosive in a lamp, but Gordon had been using it for a long time and we used it too with great success for the few weekends that were left of the summer. Thinex doesn't have a picture of a boat on the can, but maybe that's why it doesn't cost $5.00 a gallon.

—Jay Hanna
Rockport, Maine

AT SEA

Dear Editors:

Introducing Jose Francisco, the locally famous crosstree sailor. He's 82 years old, born in 1895 in Vila Nova de Milefontes, Portugal, ran away to sea when he was fourteen, spent some 22 years in the States, mostly around New York, sailed all over the world on many different ships, returning to Portugal in 1927. On board ship he used to make cork model boats and set them adrift with his name and address on them.

In 1972, he thought he'd like to expand on his model boats and had a 7-meter, 1,500-kilo cutter built, called *O Vento*. He wanted to make a singlehanded sailing trip across the Atlantic, following the course of Columbus, but his eyes started to fail him—couldn't see the stars to take a sight.

So he contents himself now with sailing his boat single-handed around the harbors of Lisbon and Cascais—from his crosstrees, up the mast. Yes sir, by God! The old guy's got all the halyards, sheets, steering lines, and even a trip line for the mooring running up the mast. He hoists himself up by hand in a bosun's chair, raises the sails, trips his mooring line, and he's off. And he sails her like a witch.

He tacked her right up next to us, dropped the sails, and glided alongside. We tied him up, he lowered himself down, and came on board *God's Bread* for a visit. "Fine boat you have here," he says. "Mind if I have a look from the mast?" And up he goes, sits up in our crosstrees for a while, checks everything out and climbs back down. "Looks good, but a little high to sail from." And this guy's 82 years old. We say, "Three cheers for Old Joe." "This whole thing is kind of silly," he says, "but it's never been done, so I do it."

His steering line is one continuous line running from the tiller, through blocks, up the mast to two blocks, and back down to the other side. He coils the halyards as he raises the sails and makes fast aloft. All sheets lead through blocks and up the mast. They are continuous lines also.

—Buck Smith & Becky Hirte
Aboard *God's Bread*
Guadalquivir River
Spain

I surely recognized the expression: it meant that we were going to put to sea come what may.
—Maurice Griffiths

Jose Francisco sailing from the crosstrees.

Organizations

Knowing that the United States has manufactured outboard motors for more than eighty years is enough to make AOMC a certainty. The Antique Outboard Motor Club, of course, with a journal *The Antique Outboarder*, a newsletter, and an annual manual (say that fast three times . . .) of parts sources. Meets, parts trading, the whole bit.

The Antique Outboard Motor Club, Inc.
c/o T.E. Bieber, Membership Chairman
1431 Kingstree Lane
Houston, Texas 77058

The Great Lakes Historical Society has a good museum and a quarterly journal, *Inland Seas*. Boatmen started this organization over 35 years ago, and if these are your waters and there's a joiner in thee, it's:

The Great Lakes Historical Society
480 Main Street
Vermilion, Ohio 44089

Collectors, historians, model builders, anyone interested in the Ohio and Mississippi Rivers and the craft that ply them, past and present, will want to know about the *Catalog of the Inland Rivers Library*. This *book* is an alphabetical reproduction of all the catalog cards in the Inland Rivers Collection, part of the public library of Cincinnati and Hamilton County, the seeds of which were planted 25 years ago by the Sons and Daughters of Pioneer Rivermen, listed in MC-4.

Inland Rivers Library
Public Library of Cincinnati and Hamilton County
Eighth and Vine Streets
Cincinnati, Ohio 45202

Left: From the Catalog of the Inland Rivers Library.

Giving Is More Blessed . . .

Having constructed more or less a thousand pages of the *Mariner's Catalog* with the underlying assumption that you want to get, receive, build, or have a boat, we feel that surely a paragraph on giving away boats is appropriate.

Many institutions are anxious to acquire boats—for scientific research, sail and seamanship training, sports programs, and even for sale on the open market to support scholarship programs and general endowment funds. The fair market value of a gift boat is 100 percent deductible from income (all at once or over five years), so if you are in that remarkable situation of having one boat too many, check with your *alma mater* or some other institution you like as to their recipient propensities. Some organizations, such as the University of Rhode Island, actually have boat acquisition programs and directors with counseling services. In URI's case, it's:

> **Director of Boat Acquisitions**
> **University of Rhode Island**
> **21 Davis Hall**
> **Kingston, R.I. 02881**

Boxed material from a URI brochure.

There are countless boat owners who have various reasons for wanting to dispose of their boats. We hope they will give serious consideration to making gifts of them to the University of Rhode Island Foundation in order to further its marine interests. Most boat owners are aware that there are important tax advantages to be enjoyed in making donations of yachts to an internationally prominent marine and oceanographic institution like URI.

Individual gifts of boats, like securities or real and tangible property, are deductible up to 30% of the donor's adjusted gross income in the year of the gift. Any excess can be carried over in the next 5 years. Corporate owned yachts are also welcomed.

Funds are not always available from tax revenue to support RESEARCH, EDUCATION and PUBLIC SERVICE in these areas:

- Commercial fisheries
- Beach erosion/ stabilization
- Marine business management
- Marine science/education
- Geographical oceanography
- Ocean engineering
- Biological oceanography
- Sport fisheries
- Chemical oceanography
- Physical oceanography
- Coastal recreation
- Water pollution
- Aquaculture
- Resource economics
- Weather
- Competitive sailing

Do you know about the Cruising Information Center? They'll help in the planning of cruises.

> **Cruising Information Center**
> **Peabody Museum**
> **East India Square**
> **Salem, Mass. 01970**

The Cruising Information Center was organized by some members of the Cruising Club of America for the purpose of assisting yachtsmen to plan cruises. By assembling detailed information about places to go and how to get there, the Center saves cruising men time and energy. Because we have time and experience, our search for information unearths data that is usually more extensive and not readily found. . . . The reports we supply our clients vary with the character of the request. We make up lists of charts, sailing directions and include information to assist in entering little-known anchorages or foreign ports. We have the basic weather information and can direct cruising men to many places having supplies and facilities. Inevitably valuable details come to light as a result of the specialized research we have the time and resources to carry on. In addition to supplying commonly needed data, we welcome specific requests for details. Sometimes these require considerable search and complete success cannot be guaranteed, but the results of such endeavors are of mutual interest.

Charges are based on the time taken to research or gather the required information. The basic charge is $50.00 for a brief description of limited information. Costs of plans for a lengthy cruise can run well over $250.00.

—Cruising Information Center

The Amateur Yacht Research Society in England lives on in grand fashion, but the former American chapter has reorganized, renamed itself, and offers a new quarterly journal:

The Experimental Yacht Society Journal
591 Island Ave.
Tarpon Springs, Fla. 33589
Membership is $12/year
Single copy price is $4

Above: Art by Buck Smith.
Below: Boxed material from The Experimental Yacht Society Journal.

Definition of a Boating Magazine: Two hundred and seventy pages of ads and thirty pages of editorial, the latter composed of (1) An interview with Gosh Hithere, winner of last year's South Shetlands to Iceland gas-guzzling Kidney Stomp, (2) A pictorial essay on the *Eagle*, (3) Useful gewgaws you can build yourself with matches and hankies, (4) New Designs, this month featuring the *Yawn*, which showed real promise in the Six-Pac, (5) How to retire on your own boat for just $200,000, (6) A list of sail-training programs to which to send your ungrateful brat, and (7) Some floozy wearing nothing, holding a stern bearing.

EYS STUDY GROUPS
We are currently organizing a series of study groups -- by correspondence -- to concentrate on specific problems, and your participation is encouraged. At the very least, we expect one good solid paper for the EYS JOURNAL to result from each group every year, and more would be welcome. Please keep the Editor informed by carbon copies of correspondence and periodic status reports. Write EYS Headquarters for more information if you wish to participate.
1. Advanced Watercraft Design and Performance - Peer Lovfald, Edmund Mahinske, Harry Morss, John Shortall, Harry Stover.
2. Boatbuilding and Materials - Bruce Roberts-Goodson, Meade Gougeon, Peer Lovfald, Edmund Mahinske, John Shortall.
3. Computer Hull Design - Edmund Gallizzi, J. A. Llewellyn, Edmund Mahinske, David Register, John Shortall.
4. Kite Sails - Gordon Gillett (Chairman), Harry Stover
5. Multihull Cross Beam Design - Wallace Venable
6. Multihull Safety
7. Sailing Hull Design - Peer Lovfald, Harry Morss, John Shortall, Harry Stover (Chairman)
8. Sailing Yacht and Boat Performance Measurement and Instrumentation - Edwin Doran, J. A. Llewellyn, Harry Morss, John Shortall.
9. Small Craft Design and Standards: Bruce Roberts-Goodson, Meade Gougeon, Peer Lovfald, William Osterholt, John Shortall.
10. Structural Design
Write EYS Headquarters for more information if you wish to join

Sailboat Survey is a new publication, self-explained in its first editorial, reprinted here. What it does not say is that its style is varied, refreshing, and friendly. It doesn't pander and soft-soap as do the so-called "evaluation" reports of most commercial magazines (those in photography and boating are the worst), nor does it take a cynical bull-in-the-china-shop approach. It reports, instructs, and entertains. We're impressed.

Sailboat Survey
1428 Oneida Street
Utica, N.Y. 13501
$10/year—6 issues

Boxed editorial from Sailboat Survey.

EDITORIAL

HOW DOES IT WORK OUT THERE ON THE WATER? THAT'S WHAT PEOPLE WANT TO KNOW ABOUT BOATS AND THE EQUIPMENT ON THEM.

SAILORS ARE MORE THAN WILLING TO SHARE THEIR EXPERTISE AND STATE THEIR PREFERENCES.

The two statements above form the foundation of this magazine.

SAILBOAT SURVEY will collect, organize and present that vital information which, first of all, allows us to determine more easily what is and what is not a quality product and secondly permits us to choose as wisely as possible the boats and accessories to outfit our dreams.

SAILBOAT SURVEY will be a positive publication. It is a sounding board — not a wailing wall. We do not subscribe to any devil theory that the marine industry is intent upon giving us the least quality for the most dollars.

We recognize, also, that the industry's leaders are as anxious as we are to see inferior and dangerous goods driven from the marketplace.

We want you to know that what we recommend is done with the full understanding that your life may depend on it. This is the kind of service we want to provide.

Can a particular yacht take a pounding without the bulkheads breaking away from the hull? What is happening to that hull-deck join meanwhile? Can the cook function in the galley when heeled at 15-20 degrees? Are the swages cracking after a month? These are the kinds of things we think need to be known by newcomers to sailing as well as by veterans.

We are convinced we can produce a publication written in a way we can all understand which will be read and re-read, pawed over, dog-eared, cussed and sworn by, used as a reference and workbook but above all respected as accurate and fair.

We know we have our work cut out for us but aside from actually sailing we can't think of anything we'd rather do.

Geoffrey Clifford
Editor and Publisher

Early multi-cylinder engines required a coil for each cylinder. They were usually kept in an oak box.

Above: From a recent issue of Antique Boating.

Antique Boating is a nicely made journal, not about elephant breeding, recommended for anyone with a love for elder craft, restoration, history of the sport, etc. Good mixture of the information, practical, and interesting.

Antique Boating
Box 199
Cleverdale, New York 12820
$10/year—5 issues

We found this useful list of antique boat organizations in a recent issue of *Antique Boating*:

ANTIQUE OUTBOARD MOTOR CLUB
Mr. T. E. Bieber, Membership Chairman
1431 Kingstree Lane
Houston, Texas 77058.
THE ANTIQUE & CLASSIC BOAT SOCIETY, INC.
Box 831
Lake George, NY 12845.
CLASSIC YACHT ASSOCIATION
Roy Newton, Commodore
13967 Marquesas Way
Marina del Ray, CA 90291.
CHRIS CRAFT ANTIQUE BOAT CLUB
Chris Craft Antique Boat Club
P. O. Box 10245
Bradenton, FL 33507.
CLASSIC YACHT CLUB OF AMERICA, INC.
Commodore Edwin Brown
19180 Peachtree Road
Dickerson, MD 20753.
PORT ELCO CLUB
Mr. Richard Cook
12 W. Main Street
Mystic, CT 06355.
MANOTICK CLASSIC BOAT CLUB
Mr. James C. Potter
P. O. Box 56
Manotick, Ontario, Canada KOA 2NO.
RICHARDSON BOAT OWNER'S ASSOCIATION
Mr. William Lindquist, President or
Mrs. William (Didi) Lindquist, Secretary
375 Parsons Acres
Ontario, NY 14519

You don't expect boats to be used just for rowing, do you? A doorway in England. Photo courtesy of Denny Desoutter, Practical Boatowner *magazine, Stamford St., London, England.*

Folks in the Seattle area can enjoy regular fellowship over small craft in the Traditional Wood Boat Society. Meeting the 3rd Friday of every month, this friendly group is developing a museum, a schedule of small craft regattas, workshops, and so on. They've a newsletter, too, $5.00/year. Meeting at:

The Old Boathouse
2770 Westlake N.
Seattle, Wash. 98109

TWBS Newsletter
c/o Land Washburn
3815 - 46th N.E.
Seattle, Wash.
$5.00

These informal groups are springing up here and there, and we would like to hear about them.—Eds.

MARCO POLO'S GALLEY GOING INTO ACTION AT CURZOLA.

The Ash Breeze is the newsletter of the Traditional Small Craft Association. Its first issue carried a succinct statement of goals by John Gardner:

1. Protection of the boating environment. Guaranteed access to the water for small boats. Provision of public landings and camp sites. Protection against excessive real estate development of the shores. Protection against pollution, contamination, noise and excessive speeds.

2. Protection of the rights of the builders, owners and users of small boats. Defense against excessive, unreasonable and unnecessary regulation by federal, state and local authorities.

3. Education for boating safety. Education of the public in the selection of worthy boats as distinguished from commercial junk, and their proper use and care.

4. Encouragement, initiation and organization of shared recreational boating activities, meets, regattas, conferences, boating festivals and cruises.

The newsletter itself needs time to develop, and we wish it well—meaning that we hope it finds its own place in the literature as a good political organ against the asinine regulations against small wooden boatbuilders. Write:

Richard and Laura Kolin
The Ash Breeze
575-B 7th Ave.
Santa Cruz, Cal. 95062

Dear Editors:

Time takes its toll. Morgan and I gave up on the Fox Islands Carry Boat. Don't know why, really. We just stopped looking one day and a few weeks later, when the supply of boiled potatoes gave out, got on the ferry boat and headed back to civilization.

I'm back at the Exchange and Morgan has his hands full with some CETA job he dredged up down at the town hall. He's cataloging topographic maps and goes out on a survey now and again. I can't figure it out—here's a guy with a PhD in romance languages, and the feds, in the name of welfare and "Comprehensive Education and Training," are paying him substantial money to play bureaucrat.

All of which got Morgan and me to thinking one day. If you can fool the government into thinking you're an untrained indigent, who else can you fool? Why, boating magazine editors, of course. We started writing bogus letters to the editor on a variety of fabricated subjects and—would you believe it?—they were published. It got us so excited that we started to think we had invented a new type of career or something, until we were brought up short by the realization that you don't get *paid* for letters to the editor. We still send in a letter or two, just for practice, you understand, but the whole thing has done something to our minds. Whenever we pick up a magazine now, we wonder how many people are doing the same thing.

Ever stop to think about some of the stuff you publish?
Fred Brooks
Prop., Wood Neck Marine Antiques Exchange
Sippewisset, Mass.

The craze for old catalogs—Sears, Roebuck being the most prominent—has been refined down to particulars recently. Tiny, even obscure company catalogs have been examined and reprinted for the pleasure of the nostalgic, collectors, historians, and restorers. The Book Sales Company has some 25 reprinted catalogs and repair manuals available, all of them having to do with early gasoline and late steam engines. Sattley, Monitor, Hercules, Schmidt, Fairbanks-Morse, and others are represented. One we enjoy particularly is the *Steam Launch Catalog* of the Chas. P. Willard and Co., 1890. Get the book list flyer from:

Book Sales Co.
Post Office Box 6147
Torrance, Cal. 90504

THE SPIDER YACHT ENGINE.

Above and below: From the Chas. P. Willard catalog, reprinted by Book Sales Co.

Nautical Quarterly
605 Third Ave., 34th floor
New York, N.Y. 10016
Published 4 times a year, $30/year

It takes an act of faith to establish a new marine publication at a time when there are plenty to go around. To make it a quarterly and charge $30 per year takes strength of character. Here's what the editor of the *Nautical Quarterly* had to say:

Dear Editors:
   ...We expect to give issues as much variety as there is in the madness itself of owning and using boats of all kinds, and to try to express what that's all about with more elegance and intelligence than has previously been the standard. We are, for one thing, not an advertising medium; we are also physically larger and graphically and editorially deeper than the normal run of magazines of any kind; and we are not up against the monthly deadline pressures of a monthly. Actually, we are not a magazine; we're a four-times-a-year book. We expect to get into subjects at greater length and depth than other boating magazines, and we expect to be able to exploit that enormous fund of yachting and small-boat history that existing magazines, with their economic interest in the here and now, either will not or cannot. We are trying to be a better magazine, relating the past, present and future one to another, and generally glorying in boats and boating experience with the best writing, photography and art we can manage. The $30 subscription tariff is pretty high, but it's the only way a magazine like this one can work. We hope it works. We hope that there are enough people around to make it pay.

                       Joseph Gribbins

We have seen the first few editions and find them to be excellent in every way; the design, the layout, and especially the color work give the publication class.

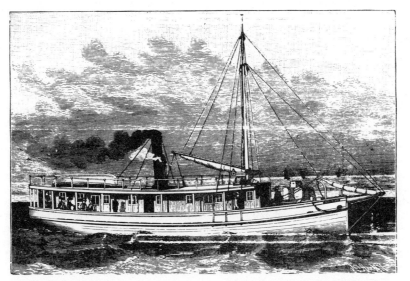

LIGHT DRAFT TWIN-SCREW COASTING STEAMER 70 FT. LONG 16 FT. BEAM, BUILT FOR RIVER AND COASTING TRADE IN SOUTH AMERICA.

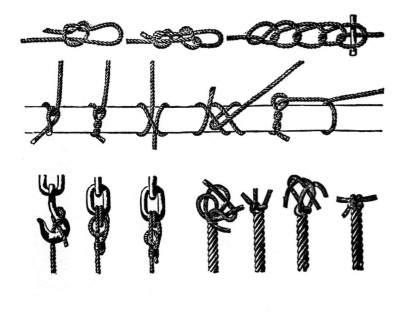

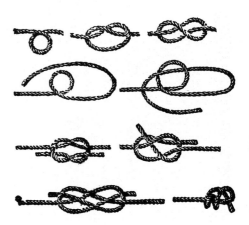

Knot Books

Dear Editors:

This letter concerns the review in MC-2, page 136, by Burt Coffey and Karen Eggert of Day's, Ashley's, and Graumont and Hensel's respective books on knotting and splicing.

As a student of all three volumes and as one who makes a living with knots, I can agree with their assessment of Day's *Art of Knotting and Splicing* as "the best . . . to keep aboard for quick reference of basic to moderately specialized knotting and marlinspike skills." However, I must take serious exception to their opinion of the other two books.

The Encyclopedia of Knots and Fancy Rope Work (Graumont and Hensel) is certainly superior in sheer numbers of knots represented to the other two books, and it is this exhaustive thoroughness that makes it a very valuable book, but it does have some serious shortcomings: Like Day's book, its knots are shown with photographs, but Day's photographs are very clear half-tones that show subtle (essential) distinctions, while the *Encyclopedia's* murky black-and-white shots can be bears to decipher at times. This is compounded by the fact that most written instructions are pages away from the photographs they describe, necessitating much leafing back and forth with hands full of line. What is even worse, those descriptions are often maddeningly inadequate.

Take, for example, their description of the four-strand irregular Turk's Head, ". . . first tying an overhand knot around the hand or any suitable object, then working the crosses back and forth, over and under in the usual fashion, until it comes out correctly." Perhaps I missed something, but *I* could never tie the thing by those instructions, and have never known anyone else who could, and even this cursory style breaks down in more intricate work when the reader is (frequently) asked to simply look at the photograph since the construction is supposed to be self-evident. Well, in some cases it is self-evident, but when it is not, one suspects that the authors have simply avoided a difficult description at the expense of their students.

The Ashley Book of Knots, on the other hand, seems to meet with near-unanimous approval. It is true that, as your reviewers stated, it is, "a very valuable historical reference," and "fine winter reading," but it is much, much more, and there are good reasons for considering it as the best all-around book on the subject.

Day, for example, calls it, "the definitive encyclopedia of knots," in his preface to *The Art of Knotting and Splicing,* and goes on to say in the bibliography that it is "authoritative, systematic, complete, readable."

As for the "roughly sketched rope for teaching purposes leaves something to be desired," comment by the reviewers, I recommend a closer look. Ashley was a marine artist of considerable note, and his drawings, far from being roughly sketched, are clear, concise representations, devoid of extraneous detail and as easy to follow as such complications might conceivably be. Moreover, the written instructions are always on the same or facing page, and are as complete as the *Encyclopedia's* are abysmal.

The crowning touch is the extent of Ashley's *original* work in every aspect of knotting, and a collection of it, alone, would make an enviable work. His bend #1452 is as strong, secure, and easy to untie as they come, and was subsequently named in his honor, thus putting him in a league with Matthew Walker. He was an innovative splicer, an unparalleled button designer, a master at Turk's Heads (have you *looked* at his chapter on Turk's Heads?), and ever so much more. Enjoyable as his writing style and sense of humor are, I fail to understand how they could obscure the awesome quality of his skill.

Summing up, then, I would have to recommend Ashley's as *the* book for those interested in extensive ropework and the *Encyclopedia* as a work of great value for those who can put up with it, in which case it is an excellent companion volume.

Brion Toss
Seattle, Washington

Looky Sea

Binoculars for use at sea should probably be more powerful than those one would use on land if one wants to look *at* things. It is fair to say that 8-power, 10-power, or 12-power are usable at sea. If, however, one wants to look *for* things at sea, then a lower power, e.g., 7-power, is all right, and one might want the high light-transmitting qualities of 50mm front lens. 7x50 binoculars were used successfully as "lookout" binoculars in the Navy. If one wants to look *for,* binoculars that have "individual focus" are all right, and these are less subject to becoming fogged with moisture with long exposure to the elements than are "central focusing" binoculars. Also, because one does not usually carry binoculars around one's neck all day when on a boat, it is practical to have somewhat heavier binoculars. The heavier ones tend to be better able to take dropping and to be cheaper for equivalent quality.

Even so, I doubt that it is cost effective (in terms of the weight and inconvenience of the binoculars) to have the bulky 7x50s, unless you know why you want them to be that size. Binoculars that are 7x35 will do the job and consistently be smaller and lighter. Also, one can perfectly well use 8x30 and 9x35, which have the advantage of higher power, yet retain their light-gathering abilities.

Binoculars of 7x35 but especially of 8x30 have traditionally been those that most people use, and thus they tend to be the model most industriously designed by the companies. I think that it is safe to say that the least bulky of the full-powered binoculars are usually 8x30—that combination seems to be an especially happy one.

The higher the power the binoculars, the harder they will be to hold steady. This starts to be felt at 10-power and is usually felt with 12-power, so again unless you know why you want them, don't get 12-power binoculars.

As to make and price: the cheaper makes are not only more expensive than they were a couple of decades ago, but they are also better made. Lightweight binoculars are not as fragile as they were, but it is still safe to say that the cheaper models will not hold up as well. By that I mean that they will get out of adjustment so that the horizon in one eye is higher than it is in the other. From that one can get a headache, though some people do not notice it.

Of more constant concern is the observation that cheaper binoculars, and in fact most binoculars, will have "soft focus" around the edges of the lens. This can be an annoyance or, if you use the binoculars a lot, it can produce headaches. Many people do not notice this effect even when it is pointed out. I think it depends on how sharply people are used to seeing things in their usual experience.

One of the most unexpected findings is that the quality of the image, that is, how sharply one sees, is not necessarily correlated with expense. Some inexpensive binoculars are very sharp; some expensive and otherwise excellent binoculars are (to my eyes) soft. I would repeat that the less expensive ones are likely to get jolted out of adjustment and then to be irreparable.

The costs are pretty closely associated with quality. Swift and Bushnell are the least expensive of the lines that carry a diversity of models. In my experience Bushnell has models that are preferable to Swift, but I

(Continued on next page)

(Continued from previous page)

think it is safe to say that the Bushnell models tend to be bulkier. There are some models (I know there are in Bushnell and I don't know for Swift) that are in the "roof prism" design. In these, all the focusing is done inside the binocular, so they are relatively invulnerable to moisture. This design is primarily found among the very expensive types. I know some people who are satisfied with their Bushnell binoculars, including those that are "roof prisms."

If one is going to use binoculars a lot, it is safe to say that one should spend more than one would expect. I know many people who have saved money and regretted the action. The above makes are in the category of saving money.

I would add Bausch & Lomb binoculars roughly in a category above Bushnell and below or with Nikon, though somewhat cheaper and somewhat heavier/bigger. Anyone interested in 9x35 binoculars should compare Nikon with Bausch & Lomb. I think they are equally good.

For really good binoculars, it is necessary to spend over $150, I think. For example, Nikon makes a superb 9x35 that is as good as any of the most expensive makes and models. Then if you are willing to spend big money ($350 to $450), Zeiss and Leitz make very high-quality binoculars. I don't think that they are worth the difference in price, unless one is going to use binoculars heavily and wants sharp focus without tiring one's eyes. Leitz makes several models in "roof prisms." The 8x32 is perhaps the

smallest and most convenient of all binoculars that one can use for hard work. I think that the Leitz 10x40, although good, is soft on the edges of the field, and the binoculars tend to give things a yellowish tinge. I have used Zeiss 10x40 for many years and still hold to them as the hard-working workhorse, but they are not true "roof prisms" in that the front lens actually moves when focusing. Thus these glasses are more subject to moisture.

As you can gather from my criticisms of Leitz and Zeiss, they are not necessarily the end-all. Since the American dollar has fallen to half of its value against the German mark, these makes are priced above their real value. They were clearly the best in the early 1960s, but now personal preference when combined with relative costs make it equally clearly preferable to get other makes. Really, the ultimate choice is a very personal one: which binoculars "feel" best when you are looking for something or when you want to watch something for a while?

—William Drury

William Drury is one of the country's foremost authorities on sea and shore birds. For years he was director of research for the Massachusetts Audubon Society and is now a professor at the College of the Atlantic in Bar Harbor, Maine. Several months of each year find him in the Aleutians of Alaska using binoculars like you wouldn't believe.

—Eds.

Just for fun, thought you'd like to know that the huge Japanese factory ships use these Fujinon 25 x 150 binoculars on their bridge-cowls. If you'd like a dozen or two, it's:

Fujinon Optical Co.
Dept. 19
672 White Plains Rd.
Scarsdale, New York 10583

Finally, sensible mariner's shades. They flip up, are polarized, and float! The Aqua-mates, from:

Foster Grant
Leominster, Mass. 01453

Left: The Fujinon 25 x 150s at $4,370.
Above: The Aqua-mates from Foster Grant.

For instance, you could handle a boat around this semi-submersible drilling rig moored over the Baltimore Canyon. (Continental Oil Co. photo)

The Petromarine Wants You

In MC-2 we reviewed a book about careers at sea and made a pointed remark or two about the problems of getting a berth in the Merchant Marine. But our careers were pretty well set, anyway, so we never looked further into the subject. Now we find someone who has:

Dear Editors:

I read with interest your description of D.X. Fenton's *Sea Careers* (*Mariner's Catalog*, Volume 2) and especially a reference to "the merchant marine" being a "closed corporation." The interest I speak of here stems from my own efforts to describe in a recent publication another kind of merchant marine with very real opportunities. Fenton's work apparently assumes a well-traveled course that other authors have taken with their usual comments about the academies, the rigorous licensing exams, and the inevitable union hiring halls. Beneath the surface there exist some disconcerting facts about the decline in the number of American ships being built, the number being retired, and the predicted decline in manning requirements for these ocean-going vessels.

The "merchant marine" I seek to describe is an elusive subject because it is the product of the ever-changing offshore oil industry that began in earnest after World War II. Today, this unconventional petromarine demands men who have the gutsy disposition to maneuver specialized vessels at close quarters with an offshore platform. Small vessel handling is the single most important set of skills sought by the marine companies. In fact, one can possess a Master or Mate, Unlimited, Oceans License and still must serve an apprenticeship until he learns by actually doing or until he loses his nerve—and quits.

Without getting into the merits (or obstacles?) of union-

ism in the maritime occupations, suffice it to say the Louisiana marine industry is not unionized, and it is not a "closed corporation" by any means. Companies hire, fire, and otherwise employ who they want—occasionally hiring an individual as "master" or "mate" of their vessels without a license. Those days are just about over, though. If marine companies need an ordinary seaman, they hire first, arrange for a quick physical, and send the person off to sea after he has acquired a temporary seaman's document. Slovenly or dangerous conduct or, reportedly, even unionizing conduct brings immediate dismissal. Fortunately (or unfortunately due to several marine disasters), captains no longer risk losing their jobs when tool pushers take leave of their senses and demand that a cargo be delivered in gale force winds. Times indeed are changing. Still, this merchant marine has a rough, devil-may-care, frontier-like style that O.S.H.A. and the U.S.C.G. are trying to tame.

John R. Rochelle
Offshore Research Service

Mr. Rochelle has written a booklet on employment opportunities in the Louisiana petromarine, and in it he tells how to go about finding a job that pays reasonably well and does not have the built-in impediments found in the regular Merchant Marine. We wish the information were more detailed, but if $5 can get you started on the road toward a career, it is an expenditure worth making.

Employment Opportunities in the Louisiana Offshore Marine Industry
by John R. Rochelle
Offshore Research Service
P.O. Box 2606 NSU
Thibodaux, La. 70301
27 pages, 1976, $5

Kaboom!

Gorgeous muzzle and breech-loading cannon, from:

**RBG Cannons
2022 Avenida Chico
Newport Beach, Cal. 92660**

Below, left: RBG's solar-fired gun does its thing at noon. It fires black powder. Desk model is $395; trophy model is $525.
Below: RBG's Herreshoff saluting cannon. It is 16 inches long and fires 10-gauge blanks. Price is $625.

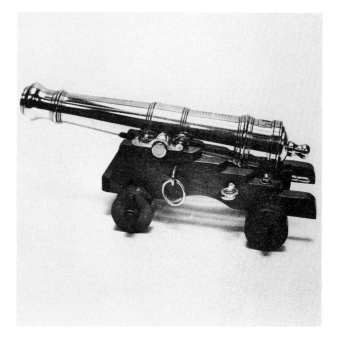

And these guys in England don't fool around either, 'cept you can't fire them. These are kits.

**H.L. Pearson
5 Ruskin Avenue
The Straits
Sedgley, Dudley
West Midlands
England**

Below: H.L. Pearson's 1/8-scale 68-pounder, circa 1800. This car-ronade measures 13 inches. As of 1977 it was £27.50 plus £13.50 postage and packing.

Crafts at Sea

There are certain hand crafts that do not mix well with cruising boats. The potters will have to wait some more, but the weavers have a good friend in Big Cypress Loom Company. For about $75, plus shipping, here's a loom *designed* for use aboard boats.

Big Cypress Loom Co.
3043 Grand Ave.
Coconut Grove, Fla. 33133

Above: The Big Cypress loom doing what it's supposed to do, where it's supposed to do it.

Nylon for Towing

Dear Editors:

I noticed a brief discussion on the pros and cons of towing with nylon lines in MC-5, page 144. I fail to see how someone can condemn nylon for towing. It is an ideal material due to its stretch characteristics. What should be condemned is the fools who build boats with cleats and fittings of insufficient strength, and those who buy them. Any vessel designed for towing has a bitt able to take full power with a safety margin for surge and shocks. I laugh at the well-known advertisement of the boat lifted clear of the water by her cleats. This load is far from the forces the cleats are subjected to when towing, or even when the boat is moored in rough water. The combination of the boat's momentum and the shock loading on the cleats causes much greater strains. When you buy a boat with racy-looking cleats, the ones with the vinyl, color-coordinated inserts, and fastened to the deck with sheet-metal screws, for God's sake throw them away and install quality cleats, of proper size and properly backed up. Or, better yet, don't buy such a boat in the first place.

But back to the argument: nylon for towing. The basic problem in towing is to eliminate the shocks, the sudden strains, and to provide a fairly constant tension on the towing line. Commercial tugs are often equipped with auto-matic towing winches, which pay out and take up line to maintain a constant pull. Others use a very long line, allowing the sag or catenary to eliminate any sudden surges. It may surprise you to learn that nylon lines are being used more and more in large tows. The elasticity allows a shorter line to be used, which significantly reduces resistance and allows the tow to make better time. Something very vital when towing over long distances.

Nylon should present no problem when towing small craft if the proper size line is used and each vessel is soundly constructed. Dacron can actually cause a bitt or cleat to fail because shocks are not absorbed as well as with nylon. I do not condemn either system, but rather wish to point out that both can be safe if their limitations are realized.

Mark C. Thomas
Bay Village, Ohio

A Quiet Time.

Tanks Alot

We've given very little space to the subject of tankage. (Hmm, wonder when we'll ever give a lot a space to it?) A company that specializes in marine tankage is Tempo. They have a very impressive inventory of made-up tanks ready to install—write them for details. It's their outboard fuel tank that caught our eye; very handy, well-shaped, and it has a *reserve* built in.

Tempo Products Co.
6200 Cochran Rd.
Cleveland, Ohio 44139

Meanwhile, one of the cleverest gadgets for the small boat ever devised *has* to be this portable sink that is also its own tank. The guy in *The Graduate* was right—Plastics! From:

Reliance Products Ltd.
1830 Dublin Ave.
Winnipeg R3H OH3
Canada

Left: Tempo Products' portable fuel tank.

Be Kind to Your Red Gas Cans

It's seldom that the terne-plate steel outboard fuel tank gets much maintenance. As a consequence, after several years of hard use, a serious corrosion problem often develops. It's especially severe around salt water. Personally, I've never encountered rust as stubborn as this stuff—so much so, in fact, that removing it from the deeper pitting can involve chemical treatment. Wire brushing just glazes the rust, which remains as firmly entrenched as ever.

Actually, the best approach is to sandblast the tank, so if such equipment is available to you (auto-body shops), forget about the rest of this piece. On the other hand, you may find yourself on your own for one reason or another, in which case you can do a reasonably effective clean-up job as follows:

Chuck a rough sanding disk in your hole-shooter and knock off as much scale as possible. Make sure the tank cap is on tight, as you don't want to get any crud inside, and you certainly don't want a stray spark to land in there. You'll probably have to switch to a stone to get inside the rim around the bottom. When you've done as much as you can, you'll have a lot of clean metal, but you'll also notice much rust-filled pitting that will raise hell with premature repainting. That rust has to come out.

The next step is to soak a number of small rags (cotton, preferably) in full-strength muriatic acid and drape them over about half the can. Muriatic is 20 percent hydrochloric and is available in most hardware and paint stores. It's not what you would call "vicious" stuff, but it's hot enough to respect. Use rubber gloves, old clothes, and eye protection—and do the job outdoors where the fumes won't get to you. Soak time is about half an hour. Wet down the rags, if necessary, to keep them dripping.

While we're waiting here, and for what it's worth, I haven't had any luck at all with the proprietary rust removers such as Jelly de Rust or Naval Jelly. Their active ingredient is phosphoric acid, which just isn't equal to the job—at least, not in the quantity used in these preparations. Muriatic acid works and works quickly. Also, it's cheap.

When you pull off the rags, you'll find that most of the pitting is now clean and bright. Now fill a pad of fine steel wool with the acid and go over the wetted area. This will remove loosened rust and pull more from the deeper pits. Repeat the process until you've treated the whole can, and then flush liberally with water. Now dry the can thoroughly so it won't begin to oxidize again, prime and repaint. I've found that Rust-Oleum zinc chromate primer and finish paint do an excellent job—better, as a matter of fact, than the factory finish—but there are doubtless others that work just as well.

The whole business is a bit messy and tedious, but with the prices charged for these cans nowadays, it's worth the effort. I've never seen one rusted clear through, but then I never thought I'd see a Cadillac rusted through, either.

—David Register

Left: Reliance Products' Port-A-Sink.

THE MARINER'S CATALOG / 113

Well-Kept Secrets

Boat theft is SUCH A DRAG! Just about everything necessary to stop theft is almost as bad. (Definition of a cruise—a boat, a course, mom and pop, the kids, and two Coast Guard boardings.) So an outfit in California has developed a system of secret markings for boats. They'll stand up in court.

A-1 International Marine Recovery
P.O. Box 42
Redondo Beach, Cal. 90277

Of course, if you'd built your own boat out of wood, you wouldn't need any secret markings at all—you'd know every mistake in it!

Below: From Shaping Up to Ship Out.

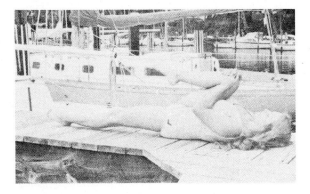

Shaping Up to Ship Out
by James Holechek
with exercises by Hy Levasseur
Cornell Maritime Press, Cambridge, Maryland
143 pages, illus., ring-bound, biblio., index, $7

We were initially at a loss as to how to take this book—perhaps it was the salacious thoughts aroused by the models used to illustrate the various exercises; sort of jolted us back to our boyhood when magazines such as *Cavalier* assaulted our imaginations rather than our sensibilities. At any rate, we soon discovered that the point of the book is that we should be in shape if we intend to fight runaway spinnakers or wrestle winches. The author assumes that we are not and provides simple exercises to ensure that we will. By gum, there's even a halyard-hauling exercise, to be done alone or with a partner.

Supine Leg Hugger
Start: Lie on back, legs straight and together with arms down at your sides.
  a. Raise right leg and bend knee up toward your chest.
  b. Grasp knee with both hands and pull in as closely to the chest as possible.
  c. Repeat with left leg for one repetition.

The Cat
Start: On your hands and knees.
  a. Lower your buttocks back toward your legs as far as you can, keeping your arms extended to the front and the chest and face facing the deck.
  b. Now, lean forward until your legs are fully extended and your arms support the body from the waist up.
  c. Head up, chin up.
  d. Repeat the desired number of times.

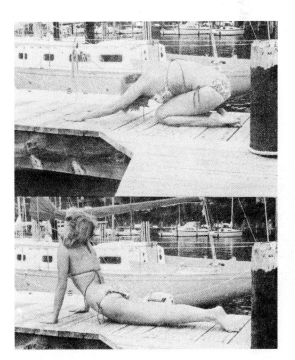

Waterfront Guide

The Maritime Association of the Port of New York publishes an annual handbook on the port and its facilities. If you are a wharf rat and waterfront crawler, you might find this publication worthwhile as a guidebook. If you are curious about what makes a big port work, you'll find it educational reading.

New York Port Handbook
Maritime Assoc. of the Port of New York
80 Broad Street
New York, N.Y. 10004
184 pages (1977 ed.), illus., maps, paperbound, $5

We suspect that other major ports of the world have similar publications. If you know of any, we would appreciate knowing about them.

Interport Pilots Associates, Inc.

The Interport Pilots Associates provide pilot service to American-enrolled coastwise vessels entering all harbors, including the New York-New Jersey Port, from Cape Henry, Virginia, to Searsport, Maine. The organization operates two 40-foot pilot boats from berths at Atlantic Highlands, New Jersey. Interport pilots are federally licensed and also licensed by the State of New York to move vessels in Long Island Sound. They also operate in ports along the Atlantic Seaboard and in the Cape Cod Canal.

Inquiries relating to pilotage rates may be obtained by writing to any of the organizations listed under that title in the "Directory" section of this book.

Above and right: Boxed text and map from the New York Port Handbook.

The Hand of God: Whaling in the Azores
by Trevor Housby
Abelard-Schuman, New York

Re: Kenneth R. Martin's "Introduction to Books on Whaling" in MC-5, an interesting additional variation on that theme is *The Hand of God* by Trevor Housby. This is a first-hand account of contemporary open-boat whaling in the Azores, and by that token probably the description of a disappearing way of life (and not so very rarely, death). Azorean whalers, with whom the British-born author lived and worked for half a year in 1969, are perhaps the last group of people for whom sailing and rowing their canoes is still an integral part of their chase—which may sometimes turn into a deadly duel between the game and the hunters, which has inspired many of the often sad Azorean folk songs. The book contains some 80 very interesting photographs.

—**Karl Freudenstein**

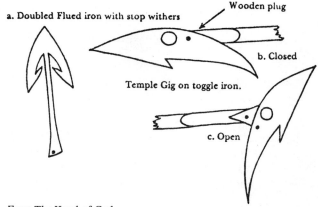

From The Hand of God.

War at Sea

We haven't gone into the war story at sea—yet—but a friend of ours has been walking around in a daze after reading what he considers to be the best of the genre. So let's hear about it.

—Eds.

The Boat, by Lothar-Günther Buchheim
Alfred A. Knopf, New York
1975, $10

Torpedo, periscope, depth charge, pinging ASDIC, moldy sausage, swinging crazy, stinking fear, stinking bodies, cracking, groaning hull plates, popping rivets, manometer needle at 600 feet and falling! The Captain like a rock; old at 30. A crew of children 17, 18, and combat hardened.

Dead, burned bodies floating, gesturing in the oily wake, a burning freighter, men dropping like scorched moths into fuel-covered water.

A terrific storm in the midwinter Atlantic; creeping into the Med through the gauntlet of Gibraltar.

There are already rave reviews about *The Boat*. This is another. A classic war-at-sea story in Cinemascope and Technicolor. If you don't read anything else, read this book.

—Robin Adair

Cruising Around

Adventures, by Gum

Times have changed. It used to be that people *had* adventures. Now they pay for them. Not too long ago, if you wanted to row a boat a long distance, you merely grabbed your water bottle, lunch pail, and oars, and did it. If you wanted to be awakened at 5 A.M. with a cold shower, flogged around an obstacle course, harassed by wiseguy experts, you joined the Service and Uncle Sam paid you for it. If you wanted to shoot some rapids, you found a friend with a canoe and begged him to take you along. Today, that's outmoded. Instead you write a check to Outward Bound, Klondike Safaris, Orange Torpedo Trips, or the Infinite Odyssey, and they guarantee an authentic, certified, genuine, unsurpassed, fantastic *Adventure*. Never having had an adventure of such sterling quality, we won't pass judgment; rather, we'll refer you to:

International Adventure TravelGuide
ISBS, Inc.
Box 555, Forest Grove, Oregon 97116
500 pages, illus., index, annual, paperbound, $9.95

"Describing 2,000 worldwide adventure trips and expeditions—land, sea, air, and underwater—open to public participation." And, if you want to join with others who enjoy *Adventure*, and receive a magazine, a newsletter, a membership card, a shoulder patch, a scroll, and discounts on adventure equipment, get in touch with:

The American Adventurers Association
Suite 301
444 N.E. Ravenna Blvd.
Seattle, Wash. 98115 (dues are $15)

Arctic Alaska River Trip: Two weeks of river running on the Kobuk River on the southwest side of the Brooks Range. Departures July and Aug., 1 each month. Over 150 miles of the Kobuk are traveled, from Walker Lake to the Eskimo village of Kobuk, all of it above the Arctic Circle. The region is quite isolated and has a variety of wildlife, including wolves, and offers fishing for grayling, lake trout, arctic char and sheefish. $1,200 includes all group equipment, guides, 16-foot inflatable rubber boats, food, fly-in transportation. Contact: Alaska Wilderness River Trips, P.O. Box 1143, Eagle River, AK 99577, USA; phone (907)694-2194.

Diving in the Virgin Islands: Daily, year-round scuba diving trips with the Dive Shop in Cruz Bay, St. John in the Virgin Islands. Operator offers instruction for novices, night dives, photography dives and wreck dives. $10 to $45 for various dives, locations and instruction. Contact: Jack Bosh, The Dive Shop, P.O. Box 161, Cruz Bay, St. John, Virgin Islands 00830, USA; phone (809)776-6256.

From the International Adventure TravelGuide.

After 50,000 Miles, by Hal Roth
W.W. Norton, New York
328 pages, illus., index, notes, 1977, $12.95

Hal Roth has sailed a lot of miles, and, as you can expect, he has a lot of advice to give after all that experience. In this book, he tells us things seldom heard, such as how to deal with paperwork when entering and leaving foreign ports, how to live with cockroaches, choosing and using ground tackle for all conditions (i.e., not textbook conditions), and making your boat visible at night.

There are plenty of ocean cruising books by people who *think* they know how to do it. Hal Roth *does* know how to do it. He has been there and back.

Below: From After 50,000 Miles.

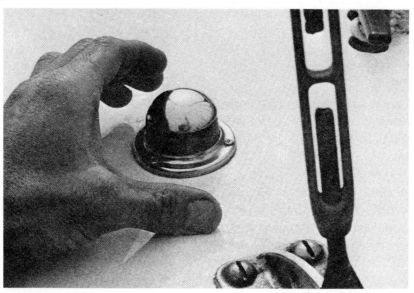

How ridiculous can you get? The maker of this tiny and widely sold fixture claims that it puts out enough red and green light to be seen at two miles. In my judgment, however, the light is not much better than a flashlight, and I would hate to trust my life to such a paltry scrap of hardware. If this light passed Coast Guard tests as stated, the inspector must have been watching the light with a telescope. Not only is the fixture inadequate for safety and common sense, but the location means that a sail on deck, a sailor's foot, the rigging, or even a piece of line can mask the light. This small yacht needs larger and better placed navigation lights. On looking around, we also see that the forestay turnbuckle lacks both locking cotter pins and a toggle to take care of side-to-side movements.

Anti-fouling: A very expensive paint, which, when applied to the bottom of a boat, apparently encourages marine growth.
Bastard: A knot which will not come undone; a tangled rope; a person who hoards alcohol to himself.
Batten: A plastic or wooden stiffener, designed to fall out of the sail. Strongly attracted to water.
Beam: To smile broadly.
Beneaped: To go aground at the top of a spring tide and thus be stuck for several weeks until the next exceptional tide. If you desire to impress other sailors, however, why not use the word 'bespringed'? It sounds much more impressive and should mean the same.
Bosun: A sailing club official, a seeker of power, who delights in removing unregistered tenders from the club yard.
Bow: Either the front of a boat or what your wife has tied the ropes in. Also what you do if the Queen visits the sailing club.

From The Art of Coarse Cruising.

Laughter on the Broads

In MC-4 (p. 181), Wallace Venable mentioned the Norfolk Broads in England as an area with "a high position on our places-to-go-back-to list." Having spent a wonderful fortnight there myself, a couple of years ago, I can only confirm that judgment. The area is, however, also known to addicted readers of English author Michael Green, who described a fictitious sailing holiday on the Broads in his book on *The Art of Coarse Sailing* (Hutchinson, 3 Fitzroy Square, London, England). One doesn't have to be familiar with the waters haunted by the book's hero, yacht *Merryweather* and her crew, to appreciate this absolutely hilarious story.

In the light of the success of this first venture into sailing literature, Michael Green must have been tempted to produce another such gem—*The Art of Coarse Cruising* (also published by Hutchinson of London), which contains a

(Continued on next page)

(Continued from previous page)

wealth of vital bits of information such as the *Coarse Signal Guide* (e.g., Barrel of Tar Alight on Deck, Conventional Meaning: —SOS—; Coarse Meaning; I have just lit a barrel of tar on deck) and a Glossary; a typical sample: Gather Way: What you do suddenly when trying to come alongside under sail.

The Norfolk Broads are also an important area for Charles Gardner, author of *Trogs Afloat**), published by Midas Books, 12 Dene Way, Speldhurst, Tunbridge Wells, Kent, England. It is particularly the waters around Yarmouth, where incidents of various types seem to be the inevitable destiny of the unsuspecting strange yachtsman (a theory borne out by expert Michael Green in *The Art of Coarse Sailing*). Which just goes to show that—as anyone who has some experience in sailing will be able to confirm—Murphy's Law, as quoted by author Gardner in most scientific terms, seems to be particularly valid in this great field of human endeavor.

Further evidence that this is indeed the case can be found by the more visually oriented, in a series of cartoon collections by Mike Peyton:

*The exact meaning and origin of the term *trog* has the professional linguist baffled, but there is some credibility in the etymological theory that it is actually an acronym for *Terrible Road Hog*, in the light of Gardner's earlier political study, *The Great Trog Conspiracy.*

Best of Peyton (Illustrated Newspapers Ltd., Holborn Hall, 100 Grays Inn Road, London WC1, England)

Come Sailing with Peyton (BlackJAC Group, 12 Frogmore Road, Apsley, Hemel Hempstead, Hertfordshire, England)

Come Sailing Again with Peyton (Nautical Publishing Co. Ltd., Lymington, Hampshire SO4 9BA, England)

Peyton is also an author who has frequently contributed to British yachting magazines. He has an uncanny capability of visualizing scenes that "as far as I know, have never happened. However, I have that niggling feeling that they will. All I can suggest is that you allow yourself a smile at them, now. You won't later." (From his introduction to *Come Sailing with Peyton.*)

Now that the *Mariner's Catalog* has commented on sailing primers (MC-5, p. 83), perhaps a brief mention is in order, concerning another erudite work on that subject: *Three Sheets in the Wind,* or *Thelwell's Manual of Sailing* (published by Eyre Methuen Ltd, 11 New Fetter Lane, London EC4P 4EE). Along with useful notes on technical terms, there is, of course, also a series of illustrations on the author's interpretation of the Beaufort Scale.

—Karl Freudenstein

Below, left: From The Art of Coarse Cruising.
Below: Boxed material from Trogs Afloat.

A Pearl from the Mudbanks

Many a good sail makes a bad honeymoon

I tell you all this just to make the point that lowering the mast takes time, and that the onlooker can soon — from the much practice offered — form an excellent judgement as to whether the operation has been started in good time in relation to the speed of the ebb and the proximity of the bridge, or not. Usually not. There then follows a cliff-hanger sequence — with the helmsman dancing up and down and various crew calling out to "slow her down" — especially those actually working on the mast who will be casting calculating glances at the rapidly narrowing gap between them and the bridge. They know that, on the foredeck, they are the exposed and expendable troops.

About now betting can break out among Yarmouth locals which will give you a good guide as to eventual outcome. The usual "favourite" is that the skipper will, at the last moment, opt for the bank, with the results already mentioned. Such a decision wins for him the whistles of derision one hears at football matches when there is a long safety pass back to the goalkeeper. Now and then — as in the "frozen on the controls" case — the incident comes to its natural thrilling climax and this can be of wide general interest if, at the moment of mast/bridge impact, the mast was already unpinned ready for lowering. The betting then concentrates on the stage at which all hands will abandon ship — voluntarily or involuntarily.

Inland Cruising Companion, by John Liley
Stanford Maritime, 12 Long Acre
London, England
159 pages, illus., 1977, paperbound, £2.50

If you were to give in to temptation and head overseas to rent a canal boat in England or Europe, you might find this book a valuable pocket companion. It is essentially a seamanship book for canals and contains all the information you would expect to see in such a book, from canal boat construction and maintenance to working a lock and dealing with engines and other on-board equipment. You'll like the chapter entitled, The Things That Happen—you know, those unexpected mishaps that could spoil your idyllic week on the Thames if you were not prepared.

The author, John Liley, is an experienced canal man. He has written another book on canal cruising in France, which will convince you as nothing else can that you will not be whole until you see France by canal.

> *France, the Quiet Way*
> by John Liley
> Beekman Pubs., 38 Hicks St.
> Brooklyn Heights, N.Y.
> 1975, $15

Right, above: Boxed material from the Inland Cruising Companion. *Below: Map of European waterways from a Floating Through Europe brochure.*

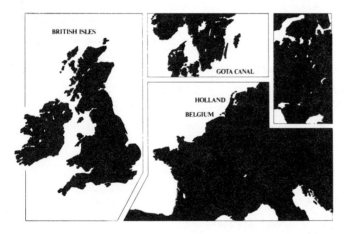

European Canal Books

We've located a new source in the United States for books and maps about European waterways:

> **Floating Through Europe, Inc.**
> **501 Madison Ave.**
> **New York, N.Y. 10022**

These folks have a number of titles on British, French, and Dutch canals, and in addition act as booking agents for canal-boat rentals, trips, and package deals. Their book and map list, plus brochures on some spectacular trips, are available on request.

Bow hauling

This is the old waterway term for manual towing, 'bow' for some extraordinary reason being pronounced as in Bow Bells. Pulling a boat from the bank requires surprisingly little effort (and therein lies its efficiency as a means of propulsion). The secret is not to pull too hard, but to lean gently on the rope and let the boat travel at her own pace.

Bow hauling can be useful after a breakdown, and it is best accomplished by forming a bridle, as in the diagram. If the line were attached to the bow, the boat would be pulled towards the bank, if at the stern it would be turned away from it. A bridle combines both, and with experimentation it is possible to pull the boat quite easily with no-one steering her at all. If she turns towards you lengthen the rope a little; if she turns away, then pull it in. Provided the wind is not strong, a boat can be steered quite accurately by this method.

Bow hauling, with one person both pulling and controlling the boat.

ON A NORTH HOLLAND CANAL

Sod's Law of the Sea
by Bill Lucas and Andrew Spedding
Stanford Maritime, 12 Long Acre, London
152 pages, illus., 1977, £1.96

We notice that few American nautical book reviewers have been able to figure out this book. Quite simply, it's a very good, very practical book about sailing on yachts and dealing particularly with situations that other books ignore—successfully mooring where you're not allowed, dealing with all manner of fools and incompetents, sex, and so on. But the book is terribly English and funny. Americans don't like their serious subjects to be funny, and the English habit of dwelling on eccentricity seems like so much irrelevance to many readers. The *Mariner's Catalog* finds a brother in this book. Useful, enjoyable reading with terrific drawings.

Shantyboat: A River Way of Life
by Harlan Hubbard
The University Press of Kentucky
Lexington, Kentucky
352 pages, illus., reprinted 1977, paperbound, $4.95

In the 4th *Mariner's Catalog* (page 121), we reviewed Harlan Hubbard's *Payne Hollow,* which we found a thoroughly satisfying book and which caused us to search high and low for his out-of-print earlier work, *Shantyboat.* You can imagine our joy when the University Press of Kentucky saw fit to reprint the book at what today can only be termed a reasonable price.

Get this book. It tells about a shantyboat voyage by the author and his wife down the Ohio and Mississippi Rivers in the late 1940s. The Hubbards were living then what we now call an "alternate lifestyle," a life that on the surface seemed aimless and purposeless but that gave them a sense of inner peace. Their story makes great reading.

The manual for the engine will say, for instance:
> 'Changing the filter is a simple operation; remove the retaining nut at the top, drop down the filter bowl, change the XYZ cartridge and replace taking care to see the retaining gasket is properly seated.'

To do this in your boat means taking up the cockpit floor, and then finding you cannot squeeze down the hole – in desperation you hire the small boy from the boat on the outboard end of the trot. Give him a Coke and lower him down the hole with simple instructions. The wing nut on the top does not give up easily, but after you have adjusted the Mole Grips several times he gets it loose and takes off the filter without difficulty.

An accessible engine

Unfortunately he drops the wing nut down the sump. You spend half an hour fishing from the front of the engine with a magnet tied to a stick trying to retrieve it, before the helpful neighbour tells you that that is the only non-ferrous part of these particular engines. You charm your slim helper with promises of funds for the fun fair to keep him down the hole trying spare nuts you have in the tool kit. After another half hour your friendly neighbour comes back to tell you that those engines are all Universal threads . . . you have a selection of Whitworth and metric. You bodge the whole thing up with boat tape for that weekend, and the boatyard charges you £27.30 to fit a new filter unit. When this sort of thing doesn't happen you are becoming in sympathy with the Character of your engine.

Above: From Sod's Law of the Sea.
Below: From Shantyboat.

Sailing Round Ireland
by Wallace Clark
B.T. Batsford, 4 Fitzhardinge St.
London, England
176 pages, illus., biblio., 1976, $8.95

The cruising story is so all-pervasive that it takes something really different to get us to read one. We regularly pass up man-alone-against-the-Atlantic stories, or woman-with-companion-along-the-trades tales, but being unrepentent fanciers of Ireland, we couldn't miss this one, and we're glad we didn't.

But just why is it that we're bored with the stock cruising story? If the truth be known, it's the aimlessness of it all. Handing the jib, making the soup, taking the sights, streaming the warps, fixing the gear, lashing down the dinghy—for what purpose? To get to the next port, or to cross the next meridian. To make the fastest passage or sail nonstop the longest distance. No thanks. We want our story to talk about sailing with a purpose, about work. In short, about real life, not an endless summer. We found it all right, in just about the finest nautical book published in 1977:

Alaska Blues, by Joe Upton
Alaska-Northwest Publishing
Anchorage, Alaska
236 pages, illus., 1977, $14.95

Joe Upton is a fisherman, a salmon fisherman. His book tells about a typical season during which he sailed from Seattle with his wife and dog for southeastern Alaska, living on his boat and using his boat to make a living. He saw as much scenery as someone who might have cruised the same waters that year, but you *know* it's not the same. His perspective was entirely different, of course, because he was a participant in a culture, not an observer.

If you ever wondered what modern commercial fishing is like—with the 19th-century romance and grizzled picturesque-fisherman-meets-the-sea-on-his-own-terms garbage stripped away—here's a book that will reveal the truth. The Alaska salmon fishery, to be sure, is quite a bit different from the Northeast ground fishery, or any other for that matter, but the fisherman's frame of mind is not. Upton puts you there, with first-rate text and photographs not to be believed. And the publishers, to their credit, wrapped it all up in a finely produced book, complete with maps of clarity and detail seldom seen in publications of this type.

If you pass up everything else in this Catalog, don't miss Upton's book. It's worth every penny of its purchase price.

Photo and boxed quote from Alaska Blues.

JULY 6—The day came chilly with a smell of rain in the hills. Overhauled the net this morning and changed a section to a lighter color. I'm very nervous about this 24-hour fishing period; there's too little room for error and not any troll fishing to fall back on yet. The afternoon was clearing and fine after a threatening morning, so we rigged a spritsail to the skiff for a lazy evening sail, ghosting through the back channel and around the cove with the dying evening breeze. All was quiet and still in the cove, just old Flea out for a walk along the shore in the last rays of the sun. Tonight at dusk, as we ate in the cabin, an old double-ender troller slipped into the cove below; his anchor chain rattled, then all was still.

"Somewhere a fur, fur piece back yonder you done a noble job of gittin' losted"

Go South Inside: Cruising the Inland Waterway
by Carl D. Lane
International Marine Publishing Company
Camden, Maine
192 pages, illus., index, 1977, $15

One of our favorite nautical writers—also known as Mr. Inland Waterway—describes the delights and techniques of cruising the East Coast's Intracoastal Waterway.

Quote from Go South Inside.

The great fear is the West Indian hurricane. October is the very height of the hurricane season, and it behooves all skippers to keep an eye peeled for possible trouble. Fortunately, hurricanes do not occur every year, and there is an excellent warning system, giving every vessel ample opportunity to seek shelter. Radio, television, marinas, marine police, and the Coast Guard all have coverage and hourly reports that should leave no boat unwarned. The prudent skipper will pay attention and play it safe . . . lay over. Select a location (advised by locals) where the storm damage could be the least, and prepare . . . and don't move until advised that the threat positively has passed. Local watermen usually try to get away from other boats, from docks and wharves, from open stretches of water, from nearby structures, from trees, overhead wires, and microwave towers. This takes them up a creek more often than not, deep in the marshes, in narrow waters: good holding ground and the right place for the ultimate defense if necessary . . . to pull the plug and let 'er sink to safety. To be sure, we don't want to do that with our sleek yachts; nor will we have to, if plenty of time is taken to plan ahead. By all means, if at all possible, depend upon many stout lines or chain run to immovable objects ashore rather than depend upon your anchor(s). High water will surely come, and anchors seldom hold against the seas then built up by increased wind fetch. Fortunately, the Waterway is generously laced with creeks and bayous that can be entered with caution and that might provide the safety needed . . . first from the hurricane, then from other boats, then from wreckage, and finally from high water.

Better Sailing, by Richard Henderson
Contemporary Books, Chicago
223 pages, illus., index, 1977, $10

Richard Henderson is one of those lucky fellows who has managed to carve a niche for himself, preempting his little corner and mining it for all it is worth. His niche, of course, is seamanship, and he has written a number of books and articles on the subject that can only be termed solid and respectable. There probably isn't a seamanship writer alive today who considers all angles of a problem with the vigor and diligence of Henderson.

Here we have a book subtitled "Error analysis in sailing and seamanship"—learn from your mistakes and those of others. We've always believed in correcting mistakes before they happen, and here's our opportunity. You won't find flavorful writing, but you will find some worthwhile advice.

The hardcover edition is out of print and not widely available, but a paperbound version is in the works.

We understand Henderson's newest book is as opportune as ever:

East to the Azores, by Richard Henderson
International Marine Publishing Company
Camden, Maine
192 pages, illus., index, 1978, $10.95

Subtitled "A Guide to Offshore Passage-Making," it is just that—a learning cruise with the Henderson family from the Chesapeake Bay to the Azores.

Right: From Better Sailing.

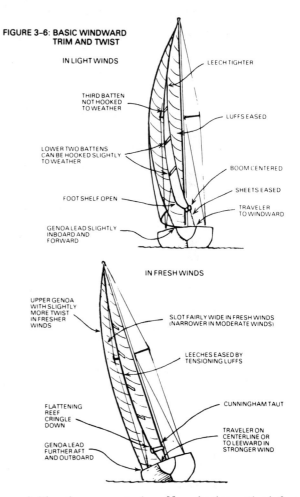

FIGURE 3–6: BASIC WINDWARD TRIM AND TWIST

IN LIGHT WINDS

LEECH TIGHTER

THIRD BATTEN NOT HOOKED TO WEATHER

LUFFS EASED

LOWER TWO BATTENS CAN BE HOOKED SLIGHTLY TO WEATHER

BOOM CENTERED

SHEETS EASED

FOOT SHELF OPEN

TRAVELER TO WINDWARD

GENOA LEAD SLIGHTLY INBOARD AND FORWARD

IN FRESH WINDS

UPPER GENOA WITH SLIGHTLY MORE TWIST IN FRESHER WINDS

SLOT FAIRLY WIDE IN FRESH WINDS (NARROWER IN MODERATE WINDS)

LEECHES EASED BY TENSIONING LUFFS

FLATTENING REEF CRINGLE DOWN

CUNNINGHAM TAUT

GENOA LEAD FURTHER AFT AND OUTBOARD

TRAVELER ON CENTERLINE OR TO LEEWARD IN STRONGER WIND

Adventures of a Red Sea Smuggler
by Henry de Monfried
Stonehill Publishing, New York
287 pages, paperbound, 1974
(first published in France, 1935), $3.45

I guess we all wanted to be pirates for a while. I always wanted to be a decent pirate. You know, capture the ship, take the gold and jewels, kiss any available succulent females, and sail away with Jolly Roger flapping at the masthead and my victims saying things like: "Who was that masked man?" or "He may be a no-good pirate, but by gad, he's a gentleman." Then I found out that pirates had to be rotten. There didn't seem to be any way out of it; if I was going to be a pirate, I was going to have to be rotten. Even the most gentlemanly of the pirates I found in my reading seemed to indulge in occasional outbursts of savagery that had more in common with my idea of butchers than with pirates.

Then I discovered smugglers! Smugglers do not rape or pillage, and if they dispose of an occasional sentry or customs agent, it's more in the nature of a skirmish than a wholesale butchery. Soon we all became smugglers. We put away our red bandanas and wore gray coats. We tied strips of cloth around our rowlocks. We looked out the corners of our eyes.

It's been several years (or more) since we stopped smuggling Nesbit's Orange across the lake in our old pram. The authorities never did catch up with us—it hardly seemed like they were trying. Now having retired from smuggling, I content myself with reading about other smugglers. Henry de Monfried has written a book to gladden the hearts of all smugglers.

Here is a man who, finding himself broke and hearing about the immense profits to be made smuggling hashish, travels to Greece and buys 600 kilograms of hashish without ever having seen it before or knowing anything about it. Unfamiliar with the normal channels for smuggling, he ships his goods on a steamer to Djibouti, at the southern end of the Red Sea. At Djibouti, he picks up his consignment (listed on the manifest as "hemp flowers") and loads the eight zinc-lined cases onto his 12-ton boutre and sails up the Red Sea to Suez.

De Monfried tells his story with a mixture of Huck Finn exuberance and Arab fatalism, spending as much time telling about the characters he meets as about the places and events he sees. The places he tells about are places of the past—sleepy colonial villages that the radio has since tied inescapably to the twentieth century—but the people he writes about are the people of forever. They may change their guise or their garments, but we can recognize in De Monfried's descriptions people we have known or met.

Perhaps the most entrancing thing about this book is this very paradox of the known and unknown, the familiar and the exotic. De Monfried is neither a cynic nor an innocent. He is both. The events and people he writes about are at once strangely familiar and completely extraordinary.

—Stephen Bird

PONDERINGS AT THE CHART TABLE (NAVIGATION, ELECTRICS, TOYS)

*"You and Your * !!—% ** !! Gunk Holes!"*

The officers who are over-sure, and "know it all like a book," are the ones, I have observed, who wreck the most ships and lose the most lives.
—Joshua Slocum

Charts

No mariner can resist a chart on the wall—you *have* to go look at it. Charts are like Brueghel or Bosch paintings; always something new to discover on/in them, even if you've looked a thousand times. The usual nautical charts are wonderful, of course, but try a *bathymetric* chart of the waters you ply. NOAA has a new and very handy "Map and Chart Catalog 5, Bathymetric Maps and Special Purpose Charts." This is a foldout catalog that lists and shows the many bathymetric, coastal zone, marine boundary, weather service, mineral leasing, tidal current, storm evacuation, and other "odd" charts offered by this agency. Whoever designed this catalog should be loaned to the IRS.

Distribution Division C44
National Ocean Survey
6501 Lafayette Ave.
Riverdale, Maryland 20840

Right: From the NOAA Chart Catalog 5.

MAP AND CHART CATALOG 5

UNITED STATES
Puerto Rico and the Virgin Islands

BATHYMETRIC MAPS and SPECIAL PURPOSE CHARTS

Section of Wilmington (NJ 18-2 OCS) Topo/Bathy Map

NATIONAL OCEANIC AND ATMOSPHERIC ADMINISTRATION
NATIONAL OCEAN SURVEY

Chart tubes, binders, and cases of clear plastic are very practical now that chart prices no longer allow laughing off the big dollop in the cockpit when thrashing to windward. A good range of them is offered by:

Halsted-Porter Co.
Box 3095
Burlington, Vermont 05401

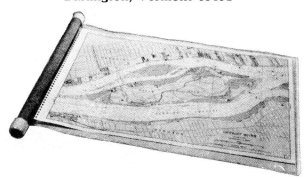

Below: Text and photos from a Halsted-Porter brochure.

WATERPROOF PROTECTIVE PLASTIC CASES

THE USE OF THE MARINE NAVIGATIONAL CHART, SINCE IT IS USUALLY LARGE AND IS OF FRAGILE PAPER WITH PRINTED NOTATIONS IN THE SMALLEST PRACTICAL TYPE, IS A REAL PROBLEM ABOARD ALL BUT THE LARGER POWER AND SAILING CRAFT. DUE TO WIND, SPRAY OR RAIN, THE LIGHT PAPER ALMOST ALWAYS GETS TORN, WET, WRINKLED OR FRAYED AND THE CHART NOTATIONS BECOME BLURRED DURING NORMAL USE. DURING EVEN LOWER WIND VELOCITIES, THE SPRAY OF A SAILBOAT COCKPIT OR THE WET BILGE OF THE SMALLER POWERBOAT MAY WET OR SOIL THE CHART SEVERELY. ALTHOUGH LACQUER APPLIED TO THE CHART YIELDS SOME PROTECTION FROM WATER OR SOILING DURING HANDLING, LITTLE PROTECTION FOR THE CHART FROM MECHANICAL DAMAGE BY WIND OR HANDLING IS PROVIDED.

A FLAT, WATER-CLEAR, TRANSPARENT, FLEXIBLE PLASTIC CASE WITH A WATER-TIGHT CLOSURE NOT ONLY PROTECTS THE VALUABLE CHART FROM DAMAGE BUT ALSO PROVIDES ADDITIONAL CHART WEIGHT AND STIFFNESS FOR USE ON WINDY DAYS. THE CASE DUE TO THE "MEMORY" OF THE PLASTIC MATERIAL HAS A TENDENCY TO LIE FLAT RATHER THAN ROLLING-UP, EVEN IF USED ONLY A FEW MINUTES AFTER REMOVAL FROM A STORAGE TUBE. SHOULD THE CHART CONTAINING CASE INADVERTANTLY FIND ITS WAY INTO A DIRTY BILGE NO LOSS OF READABILTY ORDINARILY TAKES PLACE BECAUSE THE CASE IS WATER-TIGHT. THIS WATER-PROOF, PLASTIC CASE IS AN EXCELLENT WAY TO PRESERVE AND TO USE VALUABLE NAVIGATIONAL CHARTS AS WELL AS ADDING EASE OF HANDLING.

SPECIAL PROTECTIVE CHART BINDER

WHILE PROVIDING COMPLETE PROTECTION FOR CHARTS BY THE USE OF CLEAR, PLASTIC ENVELOPES SIMILAR TO CASE #12X20 SCC AND 19X25.5C THIS BINDER PERMITS USE OF LESS EXPENSIVE ENVELOPES BY THE USE OF BINDER CLAMPING PRESSURE TO CLOSE AND TO MAKE WATER-TIGHT THE OPEN END OF THE ENVELOPE WHERE THE CHARTS ARE INSERTED. THE RESULT IS A WATER-TIGHT, LOOSE LEAF CHART BINDER. THE BINDER WILL HOLD UP TO SIX OF THE ENVELOPES BELOW. (THE BINDER CAN ALSO BE USED WITH THE APPROPIATE PLASTIC CHART CASES: BINDER B-12 WITH CASE #12X20SCC, BINDER B-19 WITH CASE #19X25.5C, BINDER B-31 WITH CASE #31X41C AND BINDER B-37 WITH CASE #37X49C.)

WHEN THE BINDER IS NOT IN USE THE CHART CONTAINING ENVELOPES ARE WRAPPED AROUND THE ROD-CLAMP TO FORM A COMPACT ROLL WHICH IS SECURED WITH A RUBBER BAND. (FOR EVEN MORE PROTECTION OF THE CHARTS IN ADDITION TO BINDER PRESERVATION THE BINDER ROLL MAY BE INSERTED INTO A 3'' CHART STORAGE TUBE: CHART TUBE T-14X3 ACCEPTS BINDER B-12, CHART TUBE T-21X3 ACCEPTS BINDER B-19, AND CHART TUBE T-36X3 ACCEPTS BINDER B-31.)

You can carry *in your pocket* every chart you'll need for a month of cruising. Oh yes you can(!), if you have a Latady Microview. It's a microfilm reader for hand use, and, at the time of writing, they had the whole east coast "in the can." From:

Latady Instruments, Inc.
Box 39
Accord, Mass. 02018

The Latady Microview provides a means of storage and viewing microfilmed maps, charts or printed material in a lightweight, water-resistant container. It also provides a means of finding your position and plotting a course. A high resolution 15X lens moves in X and Y to cover the 1-1/4 X 1-3/4 inch image. This lens contains a reticule for sighting, and a reference azimuth ring for determining a heading. A luminous compass swings out when needed. Accessories include a light for night use and a vinyl carrying case.

NOAA charts of the East Coast from Maine to Texas have been edited into chart strips of approximately ten charts per strip. These high resolution black and white films give a continuous coverage of the coast utilizing, where possible, large scale charts.

—Latady Instruments

Below and right: From the Latady catalog.

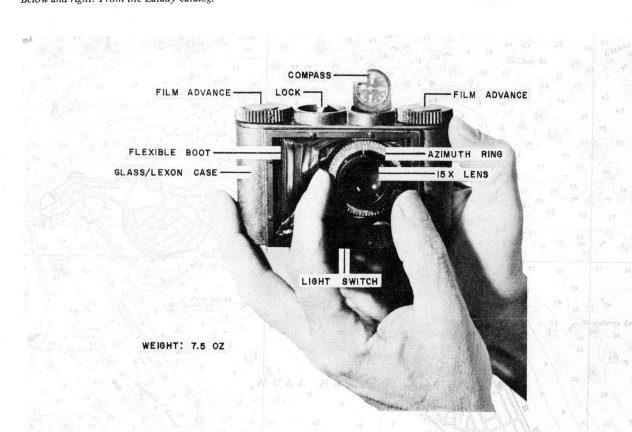

FILM ADVANCE · COMPASS · LOCK · FILM ADVANCE

FLEXIBLE BOOT · AZIMUTH RING

GLASS/LEXON CASE · 15 X LENS

LIGHT SWITCH

WEIGHT: 7.5 OZ

Compasses

For $38.50 you can own your own authentic Chinese junk compass with the most interesting descriptive literature you can imagine. Our kind of good stuff, from:

**Argosy Services
Box 1655
Sausalito, Ca. 94965**

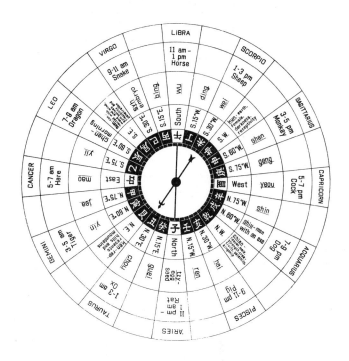

All material on this page from Argosy Services.

The Chinese compass points

Chinese navigators reduced the compass they inherited from the geomancers to its simplest form, using only 24 points, or even reducing them to 12 or 8. The concentric circles which appear around the dial above are for explanatory purposes only and do the represent the way the compass actually looked.

The innermost circle, or the dial itself, is divided into segments of 15 degrees each, represented by 24 Chinese characters. These are the compass points, which scholars say were the basis for calulations by diviners and geomancers in ancient times. These compass points were stabilized in their present system by at least the early eighth century.

The corresponding directions of these characters are noted in the second circle from center. The third circle from center gives the pronunctiation of these characters in "pu-tong-hua," the language spoken throughout China today (often called "Mandarin"), together with the early meaning, where known. Bearings are always given in the form, for example, of "sail with the needle between **geng** and **shen**" if the intended direction is W.S.W. The instruction to sail S.S.W. would be "sail between **ding** and **wei.**"

These characters used on the compass dial are not the characters commonly used in China to represent directions. Their origin or etymology is, for the most part, lost in the mists of antiquity. But scholars have traced many of them back to over 4,000 years ago when they appeared on "oracle bones" used to look into the future. These were animal bones which, according to the cracks produced by scorching them in a fire, yielded "answers" to questions put by oracles. The oracles would then scratch or inscribe these questions onto the bones.

Twelve of the characters **tzy, chou, yin, mao, chen, syh, wu, wei, shen, yeou, shiu,** and **hai** have been traditionally grouped together and referred to as the "12 branches." Eight of the characters (**jea, yii, bing, ding, geng, shin, ren, guei**) are part of the traditional grouping known as the "10 stems." The remaining four characters (**chian, kun, ken,** and **suen** derive from one of the earliest Chinese works on divination, the **I Ching** or "Book of Changes."

In very ancient times, the "12 branches" were applied to the months of the tropical year and the "10 stems" were used to name the ten day week. Diviners used the stem/branch combinations of the day, month and year of birth as the basis of their calculations and conclusions.

The "12 branches" are also associated with the following symbolic animals — the rat, ox, tiger, hare, dragon, serpent, horse, goat, monkey, cock, dog and bear — which compose a kind of Chinese zodiac. Each of these creatures is supposed to exercise an astrological influence over a particular two hour period of the day, and one year out of every twelve. (See 4th circle from center).

In later years, the "12 branches" also came to be associated with the zodiac signs familiar to the rest of the world, and this correlation is shown in the outermost circle.

Baker, Lyman and Company is a place we must add to the list of outstanding sources of navigational equipment of all sorts of craft large and small, working and pleasure. We like their range of compasses and binnacles, including one with a projecting telltale for both above and below decks use.

Baker, Lyman and Co., Inc.
308 Magazine Street
New Orleans, La.
or
Cotton Exchange Building
Houston, Texas

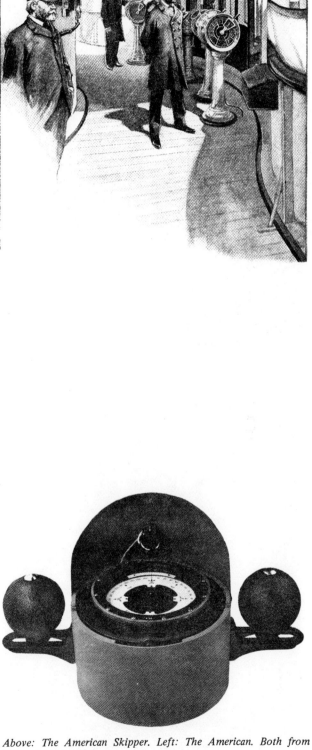

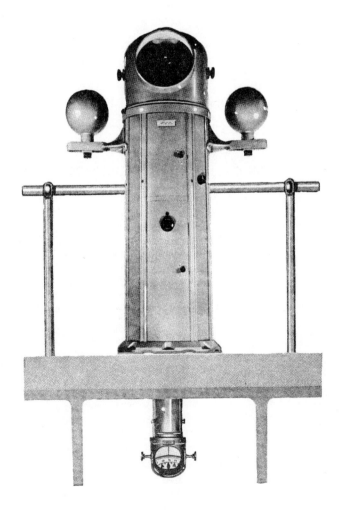

Above: The American Skipper. Left: The American. Both from Baker, Lyman and Co.

A case of time being money, as always, but not very much: The Quartz-Z Time Bowl chronometer kit at $29.95!

Time Bowl-Chattanooga
Box 8202
Chattanooga, Tenn. 37411

The original Time Bowl Quartz-Z kit was designed to take advantage of the new crystal-controlled movement developed by Precision Products Division of General Time Corporation which pulses in 1/2 second increments. It uses a mass-produced quartz crystal as used in TV sets. Amazingly, it keeps as good time, or better, than the best of chronometers which were available until only a few years ago. Using a plastic bowl, the case has enormous practical and economic advantages. Selling for $29.95, apparently this clock is fulfilling a need for a low-priced timepiece of supreme accuracy—which is both easy and fun to assemble.
—Norman Hatker, Time Bowl

Above: Time Bowl's Quartz-Z.
Below: Photo and specs of the Memochron from Ensign Electronics.

Then again, time can be *real* money: the Memochron portable digital chronometer, $295 worth of *Now*, from:

Ensign Electronics, Inc.
Box 168
Brookhaven, L.I., N.Y. 11719

SPECIFICATIONS
FOR MODEL NDC 24 MEMOCHRON

CASE : Aluminum, 5-3/4 x 4 x 2 inches, weight 20 ozs.

MODES :

    1) RUN: Time of day updated each second showing hours, minutes and seconds in 24 hour format. Daily rate is better than 0.1 sec/day at 70°F. Temperature co-efficient is less than 0.25 sec/day over range 50-90°F.

    2) HOLD: Internal memory stores time of operation of HOLD switch indefinitely. A remote HOLD switch on a 6 ft. cord is also provided.

DISPLAY : 6 each 0.3 inch Light Emitting Diode display of high efficiency orange with polarized filter.

POWER : 3 'C' size alkaline batteries provide approximately one year of operation with normal use of the display.

GUARANTEE
    Unconditional for one year.

PRICE : $295 post-paid in the U.S. New York State residents add tax.

Pocket RDF

How about a pocket-sized RDF? What with your binoculars, camera, churchkey, and the Seamark RDF, you can go to Mardi Gras as a Christmas Tree. From:

Nautech
445 Sacramento Blvd.
Chicago, Ill. 60612

Below: Nautech's pocket RDF.
Bottom: Photo from Calculator Navigation Institute.

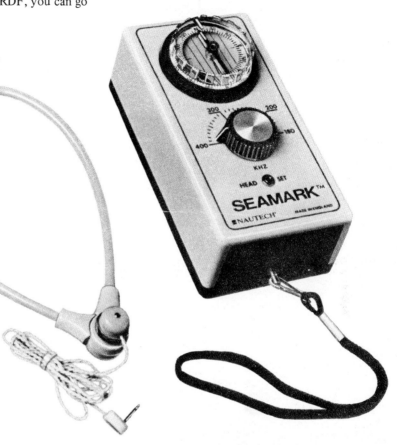

Pushbutton Navigation

By the way, with Nautech and other outfits offering calculators for navigational purposes, you may want to know about the:

Calculator Navigation Institute
Box 3299
Alexandria, Va. 22302

The Calculator Navigation Institute offers two programs for learning celestial navigation via the calculator. The first is a 9-lesson home study version (price as of this listing $147), which covers a review of piloting and dead reckoning, the complete calculator system, and a back-up system of navigation using the HO-211 Table. All materials (except the calculator) are furnished. Calculators covered include: Tamaya NC-2, Texas Instruments 58/59, TI-52, TI-56, TI-51 series, and the HP-25 and 25c. According to the company, the materials are written in plain English and avoid technical terms that confuse the navigator. The home study course can be completed in 25-30 hours.

In the Washington, D.C., area, CNI offers a combination classroom/home study course. The program starts off with a one-day classroom session where participants learn to

work complete celestial problems using calculators, practice with sextants, and plot results on a chart. At the end of the day, everyone receives the complete 9-lesson home study package so they can continue to learn and practice on their own. The combination program is, as of this listing, $169.

Piloting/Navigation with the Pocket Calculator
by Jack Bychanek and Ed Bergin
Tab Books, Blue Ridge Summit, Pa.
405 pages, illus., index, paperbound, 1976, $8.95

Navigating with a pocket calculator is hot stuff, and anyone with half a brain can see why. All you have to do is learn a few simple rules, program your machine, punch in your variables, and sit happily by while the answer pops up in bright red numerals. Simple, huh? Sounds like it is, but you better pray to God your batteries don't go dead while you're crossing the Indian Ocean in the monsoon season.

We recommend you learn how to navigate with tables before you go the calculator route, and we recommend that you take those tables with you when you set sail. Then, and only then, are you ready to play with your calculator; this book will show you how. (By the way, the machines that are used for examples in the book are the Texas Instruments SR-50, SR-51, and SR-56, and the Hewlett-Packard HP-21 and HP-25.)

Problem from Piloting/Navigation with the Pocket Calculator.

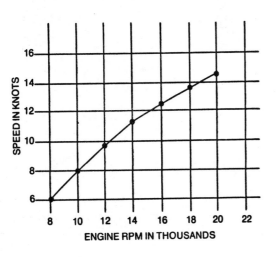

Fig. 2-2. Speed curve.

HOW TO FIND THE STRENGTH OF A CURRENT

Using the same data you just gathered for your speed curve, you can also compute the strength (but not the direction) of the current when you made your runs. The formula for finding the speed of the current in knots is

$$C = \frac{60\,D(T_U - T_D)}{2\,T_U\,T_D}$$

where
  C = current (kn)
  T_U = time upstream (min)
  T_D = time downstream (min)
  D = distance (naut. mi)

Now, for the preceding problem involving the two runs at 800 rpm, suppose that we want to know the speed of the current we encountered. Just use one of the following calculator programs. The answer is 0.26 kn.

ENGINE RPM	SPEED KNOTS
8,000	6.1
10,000	7.8
12,000	9.6
14,000	11.2
16,000	12.6
18,000	13.8
20,000	14.7

Fig. 2-3. Speed table.

SR-50 Program for Strength of Current

STEP	UNITS	VARIABLES	CALCULATOR OPERATIONS	DISPLAY
1. Clear machine			C	0
2. Enter whole seconds of time downstream	SS.	25	÷ 60 +	0.42
3. Enter whole minutes of time downstream	MM.	9	= STO	9.42
4. Enter whole seconds of time upstream	SS.	15	÷ 60 +	0.25
5. Enter whole minutes of time upstream	MM.	10	− RCL = × 60 ×	50.00
6. Enter distance (one way)	NN.n	1	× RCL 1/X × 2 1/X	0.5
7.			= STO	2.65
8. Enter whole seconds of time upstream	SS.	15	÷ 60 +	0.25
9. Enter whole minutes of time upstream	MM.	10	= 1/X × RCL =	0.26
10. Answer is speed	KK.k			0.26

SR-51 Program for Strength of Current

STEP	UNITS	VARIABLES	CALCULATOR OPERATIONS	DISPLAY
1. Clear machine			C 2nd FIX 5	0
2. Enter time upstream	MM.SS	10.15	2nd 17 STO 1 −	10.25
3. Enter time downstream	MM.SS	9.25	2nd 17 STO 2 = ×	0.83
4.			60 ×	50.00
5. Enter distance (one way)	NN.n	1	× 2 1/X ×RCL 1	10.25
6. Answer is speed	KK.k		1/X × RCL 2 1/X =	0.26

RA-ALERT SYSTEM™ (patent pending) is an anti-collision alarm and sensing system for pleasure boats, off-shore cruisers, and commercial fishing vessels not equipped with their own radar. The system detects another vessel's radar beam and helps determine that vessel's direction of travel and relative proximity.

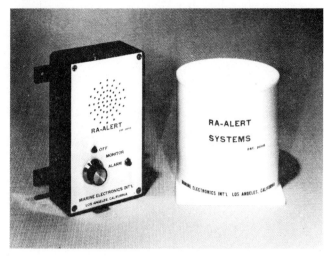

Radar Alert

Two radar alarm/alert systems have appeared on the market, the Ra-Alert for general alarm in the $200 range, and the Drom with quadrant indicator at around $475. Both systems detect the radar emissions of ships, giving warning of their proximity. One of these could be a good shipmate when shorthanded and two weeks out in a shipping lane.

Ra-Alert
Marine Electronics International
7449 West Manchester Blvd.
Los Angeles, Cal. 90045

Drom
Regent Marine and Instrumentation Inc.
1051 Clinton Street
Buffalo, New York 14206

Words of Caution
Wherein We Do Our Modern-Technology
Hard-Case Soft-Shoe Spiel

Before going on with a bunch of gadgets to plug in, a word of our litany: to go to sea pleasurably and safely, you don't need any of this stuff. There.

Now then, tell you what we're going to do. We'll go to one of those New Jersey ship-breaking yards where they kill subs and get a foot-diameter sonar transducer. Then we'll build a synthesizer into the cockpit, rev up the mill to about 10,000 watts, and go marry a whale.

Top: The Ra-Alert.
Below: The Drom.

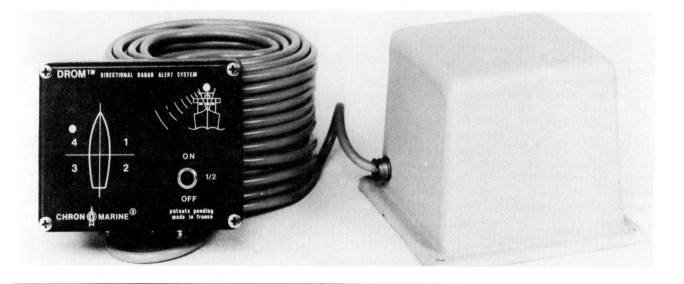

Battery Gauge

A good, big, tough, battery-checking gauge that monitors systems and units. The Battery-Check Monitor, $74.95, from:

Electronic Specialists
Box 122
Natick, Mass. 01760

Above: The Battery-Check from Electronic Specialists.
Below: The Aquair 50 from IMTRA.
Right: The Ampair 50 from IMTRA.

Charge It

Electric charging devices are springing up like crocuses in spring—and are as welcome. Here are three new systems to add to those listed in previous *Catalogs.*

The Ampair 50 for wind power and the Aquair 50 for water power from Ampair Products in England. The American agent is:

IMTRA Corp.
151 Mystic Avenue
Medford, Mass. 02155

The Ampair 50 should not be regarded by any manner of means as a trickle charger, but rather as a means of keeping the batteries charged. Given fluorescent lights below deck and a single tri-colour masthead light plus careful conservation of electricity, the Ampair 50 will provide most if not all the electricity needed on a small cruising boat. As long as the wind is abeam or forward of the beam, with any sort of decent sailing breeze offshore, one can regard the Ampair 50 as producing the same amount of electricity in a 24 hour period as the average sized diesel engine generator will put out in 45 minutes to 1 hour's running.

—Don Street, Jr.

The Eodyn Windgenerator from:

Proengin Eodyn of N.A., Inc.
Box 455
Port Isabel, Texas 78578

The HydroCharger from:

Regent Marine and Instrumentation
1051 Clinton St.
Buffalo, N.Y. 14206

The HydroCharger is a quiet, water-driven, 12-volt D.C. generator for boats. It can deliver up to 16 amps at 10 knots boat-speed. During a typical 100-mile day offshore, it will produce over 100 amp-hours, enough energy for 1,200 watts electrical consumption and sufficient to operate most onboard electronics, including refrigeration, without depleting stored battery power.

—Regent Marine

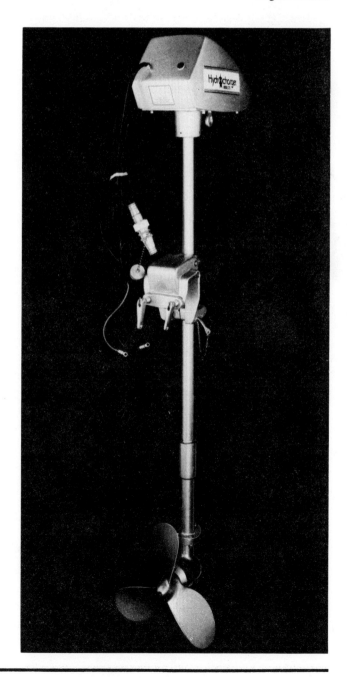

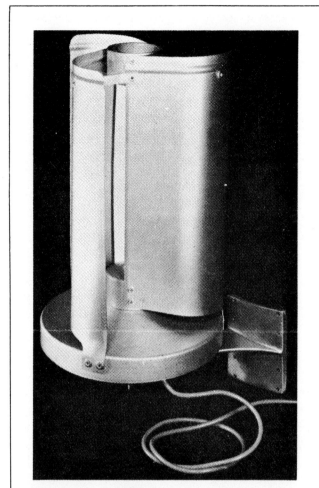

Eodyn Windgenerator

GENERAL:
The Eodyn Windgenerator is a special piece of energy saving equipment for use on land or sea for maintaining storage batteries at peak efficiency. The turbine type vanes require no orientation to the wind thus making the location a matter of convenience with no maintenance for continuous operation. There is no vibration or noise to disturb the surroundings nor are there fumes. With proper location the shape avoids the fouling of lines, halyards, sails, etc. Since the Windgenerator is made entirely of metal it will function as a radar reflector aboard sailing yachts.

CHARACTERISTICS:
Charging capability is a function of the wind velocity and is shown as a graph on the enclosed chart. A diode in the interior circuit rectifies the current from AC to 12 volts DC. The electrical operation is entirely static.
A fuse protects the diode in case of inversion of the polarity at the time of hook-up. Two models are available. Model BR consists of the windgenerator, mounting bracket, 16m of special double strand electronic cable and a rectifier. Model BB consists of the windgenerator, mounting bracket, 16m of special double strand electronic cable and a control panel containing indicators for intensity of charge, battery charge level and wind speed indicator with manipulating control knob.

CONSTRUCTION:
Anodized lightweight oxide alloy and stainless steel. Generator impregnated with watertight electronic circuits.
Daimeter---200mm (approx. 7 7/8'')
Height---310mm (approx. 1'-0¼'') w/o mounting bracket
Weight---2.7kg (approx. 6lbs.)

Successful Celestial Navigation with H.O. 229
by G.D. Dunlap
International Marine Publishing Company
Camden, Maine
160 pages, illus., index, 1977, $15

A simplified celestial navigation book that doesn't ignore theory. Includes problems, solutions, and excerpts from *H.O. 229* and the *Nautical Almanac*.

Self-Contained Celestial Navigation with H.O. 208
by John S. Letcher, Jr.
International Marine Publishing Company
Camden, Maine
240 pages, illus., 1977, $12.50

Hailed by many as the first truly different book on navigation to be written in years, this book describes the use of Dreisonstok's tables and much, much more.

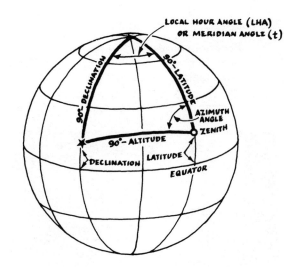

FIGURE 1-17   The celestial triangle.

From Successful Celestial Navigation with H.O. 229.

I rediscovered lunar distance under a sort of self-imposed necessity. On my first ocean passage, from Los Angeles to Hawaii singlehanded (in the *Island Girl*, June 1963), part of the experience I sought was to be totally independent, isolated, and self-contained for the duration of the voyage. Receiving radio time signals from shore would be a form of outside assistance, and besides, how could I rely on Station WWV to keep its signals coming? Thus, I chose to sail without even a receiver. For a chronometer, I had an eight-day aircraft clock that I had carefully rated and tested. But in the third week of the passage, as I approached the latitude of the islands, I began to wonder about my $22 chronometer: was there any chance it had lost time, so that I was much closer to the islands than my time sights were indicating? Of course there was a chance, so maybe I'd better start worrying about running ashore at night. On the other hand, if the chronometer had been gaining time, I would have farther to go than I thought, and heaving to at night would greatly prolong the rest of the passage. It had gradually become very, very important to my peace of mind to have a single verification of my actual longitude. The *Island Girl* was steering herself day and night under twin running sails, and I had little to do all day but puzzle over this problem. In discovering a way to solve it using only the *Nautical Almanac* and the ordinary sight reduction tables I had on board (H.O. 214), I experienced one of the great intellectual triumphs of my life. On the twenty-fifth day of the passage, with 500 miles to go, I was able to prove beyond all doubt that my clock was correct, within one minute of true GMT, so my longitude was found within 30 miles or so—ample precision for the upcoming landfall.

Boxed quote from Self-Contained Celestial Navigation with H.O. 208.

Control

Some boats have everything and with all this juice you're going to need a control and monitoring panel. This splendid affair, the Model 650, is from:

**Marinetics Corp.
Box 2676
Newport Beach, Cal. 92663**

For those craft with less than everything, but at least *something,* Marinetics also has a range of lesser switches and panels.

Anyone doing a major zapping of their cruising vessel should get in touch with National. Offering dozens of brands of every sort of electronic device at reduced rates, you're bound to find they beat the next fellow on something. Lots of the digital gear.

**National Marine Electronics
Distributors, Inc.
P.O. Drawer 1308
Lake City, S.C. 29560**

*Left: The Model 650 from Marinetics.
Below: Digital units from National Marine Electronics.*

The BRISTOL DK-15 is a flush mount digital knot meter that reads from .3 to 15 knots. It may be calibrated in knots or MPH.
   Other outstanding features include:
   • one tenth of a knot resolution.
   • impeller has a bronze thru-hull fitting.
   • 6/10″ red digits for easy reading.
   • choice of 5″ clear or black anodized aluminum bezel.
   • draws only .6 amp.
   • 5 year limited warranty.

LIST PRICE . . . $269.00   **YOUR COST . . . $199.00**

This new BRISTOL wind speed indicator has 6/10″ digits that may be read the full length of the cockpit or wheelhouse.
   Other advantages include:
   • clear readout from 3 to 99 knot range.
   • accurate to ± 5% over the entire range.
   • your choice of 5″ clear or black anodized aluminum bezel.
   • draws only .6 amp.
   • 5 year limited warranty.

LIST PRICE . . . $269.00   **YOUR COST . . . $199.00**

Peripheral Vision

Now *you* can have side-scanning sonar. Why not? The mob'll have the bomb soon. . . . Seascope, from:

Wesmar Marine Systems Div.
905 Dexter Ave. North
Seattle, Wash. 98109
good descriptive pamphlet for $1.00

Und den vee go feeshing, ya? But first we read the temperature and oxygen content, with a Ray Jefferson Sentry II Monitor.

Ray Jefferson
Main and Cotton Streets
Philadelphia, Penn. 19127

Left: From the Wesmar catalog.
Below: Boxed material from a Ray Jefferson brochure.

Without scanning sonar . . .

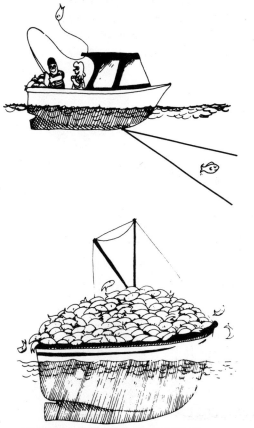

I told you to get scanning sonar, Fred.

Later, with scanning sonar . . .

I'd say this is the biggest haul yet, Harry. Wouldn't you? Harry? Harry . . .?

Two units in one. The "Sentry II" reads both dissolved oxygen content and water temperature to depths of 50 ft. It measures and shows oxygen content from 0 to 16 parts per million and also reads water temperature from 30° to 90° F. Fish thrive where dissolved oxygen measures between 5 and 13 ppm and where water temperature meets their needs. The "Sentry II" combines the measuring of these two essential elements — dissolved oxygen and water temperature — into one easy to use electronic fishing aid which shows you where fish have to be!

To use, simply turn it on, select oxygen or temperature function, and lower to combination probe into the water. The probe is attached to 50 ft. of high tensile wire marked in 5 ft. increments. The "Sentry II" shows you on a color coded meter and calibrated scale whether there's enough dissolved oxygen to sustain fish life. Green means fish, red means no fish. If oxygen is right, flip the function switch and read water temperature on a separate calibrated meter. (Or, read water temperature first, then read dissolved oxygen content).

THE "SENTRY II" INSTANTLY ELIMINATES NON-PRODUCTIVE WATER. It operates from two 9V alkaline batteries (included). A wraparound wrist safety lanyard prevents the unit from falling out of your hand and overboard.

The unit features the latest in solid state, transistorized circuitry. It's portable and is housed in lightweight, rugged, weather resistant case.

SPECIFICATIONS:

Size:	6¼" x 4" x 3" (exclusive of 4¼" handle)
Power:	2-9V alkaline batteries
Depth Capability:	50 ft.
Weight:	2 lbs. with batteries

Marine Electronics Users & Buyers Handbook
Electra Yacht
10 Wallace Street, Stamford, Conn. 06902
106 pages, illus., paperbound, $4.95

This is a tough book to categorize. Electra Yacht is a dealer in marine electronics—loran, radar, ADF, VHF, SSB, depth-sounders, automatic pilots—and this is essentially their catalog. Yet it goes beyond a catalog, since there is editorial material on how various types of gear work, performance data on the equipment sold, installation data, and details on the government's relationship with marine electronics. No matter who you buy your electronics from, Electra Yacht's handbook can be very useful for comparison-shopping and all-around information.

Shoreline and Sextant
by John P. Budlong
Van Nostrand Reinhold, New York
214 pages, illus., index, 1977, $11.95

There are three things that we like about this book: (1) Its subject matter; there are plenty of books on celestial navigation, but not much of a selection on the coastwise variety. (2) Written by a Canadian and published by an American publisher, there is considerable discussion of *both* Canadian and American sources of charts, navigational publications, and navigational systems. (3) As the title implies, the author favors the use of the sextant for coastline use; a lot of navigators who should know better think that sextants are only used for celestial observations.

From Shoreline and Sextant.

Another application of the horizontal angle comes about when you're more interested in knowing where you're *not* located than where you *are* located, as often occurs in avoiding hazards. Suppose you're cruising in a generally westward direction from the inner fairway buoy HB, and you want to keep at least half a mile away from the Brig Rocks. The chimney with the fixed red light and the Cape Entry light will make useful markers. Using them as a baseline, draw a circle of position which gives the desired clearance, as shown in Figure 10-8. From any point on the circle, draw lines to both lights, and measure the angle between the lines. In this case it is 70 degrees. Then, as you sail along, check the horizontal angle periodically. So long as it's less than 70 degrees, you are outside the circle. If it becomes more than 70 degrees, look out.

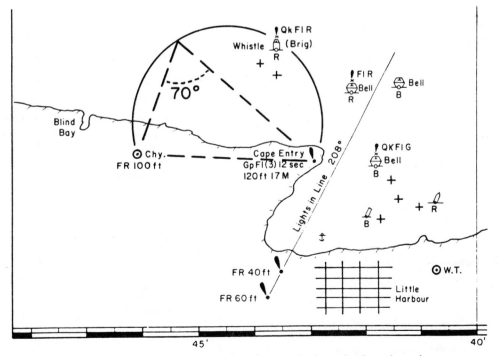

Figure 10-8 Using the horizontal angle as a check on clearing a hazard.

Zapp 'Em

Illegal in some places, unsporting in most, electronic fishing equipment for boat and backpacking is made for research scientists, state agency taggers, and their ilk. Using electrical impulses, the Electrofisher attracts fish. From:

    Smith-Root, Inc.
    14014 N.E. Salmon Creek Ave.
    Vancouver, Wash. 98665

Electronic Antifouling

We heard about using sonic transducers on the inside of boats to prevent bottom-fouling. The company making these Sonar Shield units is:

    Aquarius Agencies, Inc.
    104-1601 Granville Street
    Vancouver, B.C. V6Z 2B3
    Canada

The SONAR SHIELD system consists of a control unit and several transmitters (depending on boat size). The system is mounted completely inside the hull—there are no through-hull fittings. The unit operates on 12 volt DC battery power or 110 volt AC shorepower with an incredibly low power drain of 50 milliamps on the basic system. The SONAR SHIELD runs continuously to prevent the infestation of barnacles and mollusk and, at the same time, greatly impairs the growth of marine vegetation which plagues commercial and pleasure boat owners.

—Aquarius Agencies

Below: Text from Smith-Root.

For many years it has been known that fish will react to an electric current in the water. Depending on the type and intensity of current used, the fish will be frightened, attracted, stunned or killed. These phenomena offer the fisheries Biologist an efficient alternative to older methods of capturing fish for research purposes. Basically, an electrofishing operation consists of a system where a high voltage potential is applied between two or more electrodes that are placed in the water. The resulting field surrounding the electrodes will affect the fish in or near the electric field. The type of reaction observed in fish varies with a number of important parameters; the magnitude of the applied voltage, the type of current employed (i.e., AC, DC pulsating DC), and the species of fish involved. Alternating current will effectively stun most species especially where the water is highly conductive. If the applied voltage is too high, however, severe muscular contractions will occur in the fish resulting in gross physical damage or death. For this reason, AC is seldom used to capture fish except in hard water areas. Furthermore, the immobilized fish may be scattered over a relatively wide area around the electrodes making netting difficult. The problem is complicated by stream currents that sweep the stunned fish downstream away from the netting operation. Direct current minimizes the physical damage encountered with AC but suffers the same disadvantage of difficult collection. An effective compromise can be obtained by using pulsed direct current. Using this technique, fish exhibit a peculiar physiological response known as galvanotaxis, where they swim toward the positive electrode or anode. Since the fish tend to concentrate themselves near the anode, netting is a relatively simple operation. While the reaction is not as severe as that encountered with AC, pulsed DC can also cause physical damage in fish. Therefore, care must be taken to avoid damaging the catch.

Weather Reports

For $3,000 you can have a current radiofacsimile weather chart whenever you want one with an Alden 11 Marinefax Recorder, from:

Alden Electronic and Impulse
Recording Equipment Co., Inc.
Alden Research Center
Westborough, Mass. 01581

The ALDEN 11 Marinefax receives radiofacsimile weather charts 11" wide by any length from radio transmitters throughout the world sending at 120 scans/minute. Charts provide surface analyses which show current weather patterns, weather progs that indicate future weather patterns on a 24 to 36 hour basis, extended progs that forecast fronts and systems 2 to 5 days ahead, wave analyses, sea temperature and sea ice data. The printing process is quiet and odorless.

—Alden E&IRE

Revised and Better

Way back in MC-1 we reviewed Kotsch's *Weather for the Mariner,* then as now considered one of the best books on the subject. There's a new edition out, and aside from the outward manifestations of change—the shape, design, and binding are different (an improvement) and the author has been promoted from captain to admiral (another improvement)—it is an even better book. If you don't understand the principles of weather development at sea after reading this book, then you should consider artichoke farming in southeastern Iowa.

Weather for the Mariner
by William J. Kotsch
Naval Institute Press
Annapolis, Md.
272 pages, illus., index, 1977, $14.95

From Weather for the Mariner.

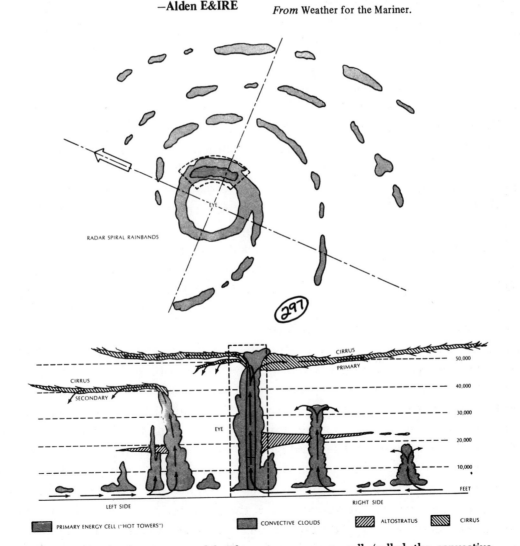

Figure 8–7. The hurricane model. The primary energy cell (called the convective chimney) is located within the area enclosed by the broken line. (From Project *Stormfury* Annual Report, Appendix D, 1965.)

The Last Word

We heard about Telesonic being the largest marine electronic distributor in the world and inquired. This letter came back with a copy of the catalog. Holy Mackerel! It's our final word on the subject.

Telesonic Marine Ltd.
243 Euston Road
London, NW1 2BT
England

Dear Editors:

Our current 570-page catalogue is out of print. We are compiling a new 600-page catalogue which we believe will be the most comprehensive directory of marine equipment available anywhere. Like you, we are attempting to publish a catalogue which contains listings, descriptions and applications of all equipment suitable for fitting onto, into or under vessels of 20 ft or over. We are recognized experts in the field of marine electronics and we supply all types of equipment for yachts, power boats, fishing vessels and small commercial vessels.

Our new catalogue will cost £3.50, the airmail postage charge to the U.S.A. will be £5.71 or £1.28 by surface mail.

A.J. Brooks
Telesonic Marine

Commonsense Celestial Navigation
by Hewitt Schlereth
Contemporary Books, Chicago, Ill.
231 pages, illus., index, 1975, $12.95

"*Commonsense Celestial Navigation* is the first navigational instruction book to strip away the mystery of navigation."–publisher's jacket blurb. Now, where have we heard that before? Don't be fooled by that claim or by this one, from the front of the jacket: "Contains everything—instruction almanacs, sight-reduction tables—you will need to locate your exact position and to sail on course anywhere in the world." On the contrary, there are only samples of those documents in the book for learning purposes; for real navigation, you have a few more purchases to make.

Extravagant claims notwithstanding, this is a solid book that gives the reader a number of different methods to fix his position at sea. The tables that get most of the treatment are *H.O. 249* and *H.O. 229,* and both the *Air Almanac* and the *Nautical Almanac.*

Boxed problem, from Commonsense Celestial Navigation, *shows how to reduce the navigational triangle directly using logarithms. An electronic calculator here will make things easier.*

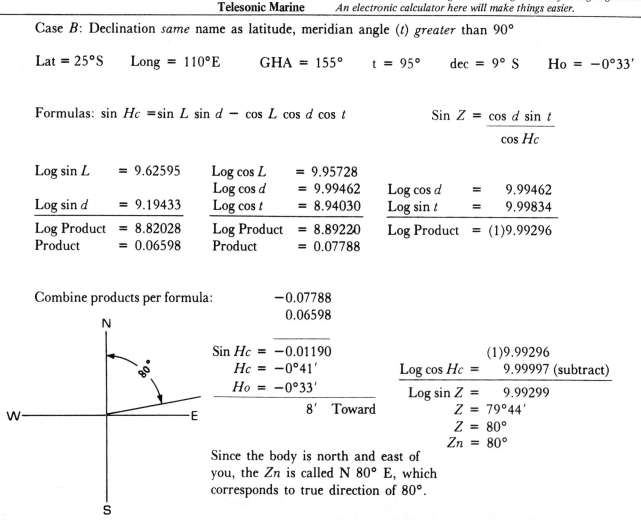

Case B: Declination *same* name as latitude, meridian angle (t) *greater* than 90°

Lat = 25°S   Long = 110°E   GHA = 155°   t = 95°   dec = 9° S   Ho = −0°33′

Formulas: sin Hc = sin L sin d − cos L cos d cos t Sin Z = $\dfrac{\cos d \sin t}{\cos Hc}$

Log sin L = 9.62595	Log cos L = 9.95728			
	Log cos d = 9.99462	Log cos d = 9.99462		
Log sin d = 9.19433	Log cos t = 8.94030	Log sin t = 9.99834		
Log Product = 8.82028	Log Product = 8.89220	Log Product = (1)9.99296		
Product = 0.06598	Product = 0.07788			

Combine products per formula: −0.07788
                                    0.06598
                                    ─────────

Sin Hc = −0.01190
Hc = −0°41′
Ho = −0°33′
─────────────
8′   Toward

(1)9.99296
Log cos Hc =   9.99997 (subtract)
───────────────────────────
Log sin Z =   9.99299
Z = 79°44′
Z = 80°
Zn = 80°

Since the body is north and east of you, the Zn is called N 80° E, which corresponds to true direction of 80°.

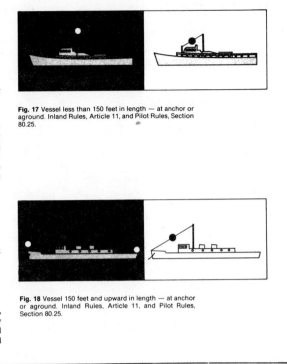

VESSELS AT ANCHOR AND AGROUND
(Court Interpretation)

Figure 17

Required lights

One 32-point white light forward

Dayshape

Black ball in forward part of vessel, required if length of vessel greater than 65 feet

Note

In special anchorage area: a vessel not more than 65 feet in length is not required to show anchor lights; where two or more barges, canal boats, scows, or other nondescript craft are tied together as a unit, the anchor light need be displayed only on the vessel that has its anchor down.

Fig. 17 Vessel less than 150 feet in length — at anchor or aground. Inland Rules, Article 11, and Pilot Rules, Section 80.25.

Figure 18

Required lights

One 32-point white light forward
One 32-point white light aft and at least 15 feet lower than forward light

Dayshape

Black ball in forward part of vessel

Note

In special anchorage area: a barge, canal boat, scow, or other nondescript craft may show only one white light, and if two or more are tied together and anchored as a unit, only the vessel with anchor down must display a light.

Fig. 18 Vessel 150 feet and upward in length — at anchor or aground. Inland Rules, Article 11, and Pilot Rules, Section 80.25.

A Mariner's Guide to the Rules of the Road
by William H. Tate
Naval Institute Press, Annapolis, Md.
138 pages, illustrated, 1976, $10.50

How many are aware that the International Rules of the Road were revised, effective July 15, 1977? How many are aware that the definition of U.S. inland/international rules boundaries has been changed so that many waters that were classed inland are now classed international? A couple of small matters, you might think, but just become a party to a collision at sea and you'll think otherwise.

We've seen a number of books on the Rules of the Road, some simplified and some highly complex, but this one seems to have the right balance. It has the latest data on the new regulations, including the complete text of the new International Rules of the Road, and is must reading for anyone who sails on a regular basis.

Canadian West Coast Books

I'd like to recommend two books, both "specialized" in that they are about and for the Canadian west coast. The first is:

A Guide to Coastal Navigation
by Capt. John A.T. Llewellyn
Division of Post-Secondary Education
Dept. of Education, Province of British Columbia
Victoria, B.C., Canada
$10

It was to be used as a textbook for a government-sponsored course called "Fisherman Upgrading," primarily

Boxed material from A Mariner's Guide to the Rules of the Road.

geared toward people raised into fishing and who know the local coast like the back of their hand, but don't know which side to pass a red buoy. Chapter Two is called addition and, I swear to God, starts out, "The sign of addition is the plus sign +." Try the following:

$$\begin{array}{ccc} 2 & 3 & 6 \\ +4 & +5 & +3 \quad \text{etc.!''} \end{array}$$

But by the end of the book you're doing compass deviation and know the collision regulations, etc. Unfortunately, the provincial government cut out the course from their budget a few years ago, but the book is still available.

The other book is:

Pacific Fishes of Canada
by J.L. Hart
Publishing Centre
Ottawa, Ontario
Canada
$14.40

It's a book about every fish known to Canadian Pacific waters. On each fish it gives the common name and Latin name, then description—fins, scales, color, size, recognition, life history, distribution, and references. Did you know that white sharks, barracudas, and electric rays have been found on the Canadian west coast? Or that 69.2 million pounds of halibut were landed in 1961? Or that the white sturgeon can grow to 20 feet long? The book is also good for winning a round of beer, too. Just bet any fisherman that a ling cod is not really a cod (it's not, it's a greenling). At any rate, the book is packed with information about fish found from California to Alaska.

—Peter Rothermel

Books & Things

. . . all of us, through reading, can live five or six lifetimes in one.

—Norman Cousins

A *Dictionary of Sea Terms*, by A. Ansted
**Brown, Son & Ferguson, 52 Darnley St.
Glasgow, Scotland
328 pages, illustrated, 1928 (2nd ed.)
reprinted 1977, £4.80**

That this dictionary hasn't been revised since 1928 might make it seem useless for the modern era, but we think not. We like it because of its traditional bent and preservation of proper sea terminology without pretension. We also appreciate the illustrations, which supplement many of the definitions and are rendered with true style. There are problems with this dictionary, however—obvious ones, such as British meanings and spellings that are contrary to American ones (*goodgeon* for gudgeon, which is fair enough, but who would think to look it up under that spelling?). Yet, for the serious-minded, the volume is nice to have on hand when reading historical works, especially British ones. And besides, who would want to miss some choice expressions seemingly lost to this age, such as: "*Cheat the devil*—Using soft expletives where strong ones would most naturally occur." Yes, this one sits nicely alongside De Kerchove's *International Maritime Dictionary*.

Marry.—To join ropes together, as it were in the bond of matrimony. Thus :—1. (In splicing rope.) To join one rope to another in such a manner that the join may be reeved through a block. 2. (In working ships.) *To marry ropes, braces, or falls.* —To hold two such ropes together, and, by pressure, to haul in on both equally.

Marryat's code.—The code of signalling for many years used at sea, but now superseded by the International Code. (*See* SIGNALS.)

Martello towers.—The name given to the small circular forts, or towers, met with along the East and South-East coasts, and placed there in view of the meditated and boasted invasion of England by Bonaparte. "The name is usually supposed to be derived from a fort in Mortella (Myrtle) Bay, Corsica, which, after a determined resistance, was at last captured by the British in 1794."

MARTELLO TOWER.

From A Dictionary of Sea Terms.

Another dictionary of more ancient origin, has recently been reprinted:

Falconer's Marine Dictionary (1780)
by William Falconer
David & Charles
North Pomfret, Vermont
412 pages, illus., $25

William Falconer was a British seaman of considerable ability, and his dictionary should be of help to modelers as well as historians. There are some fine illustrations, though not as many as one would like. The definitions in many cases include the origin of words, there are helpful cross-references, and the last section of the book includes an 80-page English translation of French sea terms and phrases. This is a facsimile reprint, so you will have to come to grips with "s" printed like "f," as in this definition of *parrel*: "A machine ufed to faften the fail-yards of a fhip to the mafts."

From Falconer's Marine Dictionary.

KNEE *of the head*, *(poulaine*, Fr.) a large flat piece of timber, fixed edgways upon the fore-part of a fhip's ftem, and fupporting the ornamental figure or image, placed under the bowfprit. See the article HEAD.

The knee of the head, which may properly be defined a continuation of the ftem, as being prolonged from the ftem forwards, is extremely broad at the upper-part, and accordingly compofed of feveral pieces united into one, YY, plate I. PIECES of the HULL. It is let into the head, and fecured to the fhip's *bows* by ftrong knees fixed horizontally upon both, and called the *cheeks of the head*, Z Z, plate IV. fig. 10. The heel of it is fcarfed to the upper end of the fore-foot, and it is faftened to the ftem above by a knee, called a *ftandard*, expreffed by &, in plate I. PIECES of the HULL.

Befides fupporting the figure of the head, this piece is otherwife ufeful, as ferving to fecure the boom, or *bumkin*, by which the fore-tack is extended to windward; and, by it's great breadth, preventing the fhip from falling to leeward, when *clofe-hauled*, fo much as fhe would otherwife do. It alfo affords a greater fecurity to the bowfprit, by increafing the angle of the bob-ftay, fo as to make it act more perpendicularly on the bowfprit.

The knee of the head is a phrafe peculiar to fhipwrights; as this piece is always called the *cut-water* by feamen, if we except a few, who affecting to be wifer than their bréthren, have adopted this expreffion probably on the prefumption that the other is a cant phrafe, or vulgarifm. It appears a material part of the province of this work to call the feveral articles contained therein by their proper names, and to reject thofe which are fpurious, however fanctified by the authority of official dulnefs, or feconded by the adoption of dignified ignorance. Accordingly we cannot help obferving, that when a term of art has been eftablifhed from time immemorial, and, befides being highly expreffive, produces the teftimony of foreign nations * to it's propriety, nothing more certainly betrays a fuperficial underftanding, than the attempt to change it, without being able to affign the fhadow of a reafon for this alteration. For although *knee of the head*, being invariably ufed by the artificers, is of courfe explained in this work as a term of naval architecture, wherein practice has indeed rendered it natural and intelligible; it is neverthelefs very rarely ufed by feamen, efpecially in common difcourfe, unlefs when it is intended to imprefs the hearer with an idea of the fpeaker's fuperior judgment.

Boxed material from Seglerlexikon.

Foreign-Language Dictionaries

Seglerlexikon, by Joachim Schult
Klasing & Co., GMBH
Bielefeld, West Germany

There is now an up-to-date German sailing dictionary containing over 4,000 sailing, navigation, boatbuilding, and other related terms, which—although definitions are given in German only—can also be used as a German-English bilingual dictionary because English equivalents are indicated for the terms themselves. An alphabetical reference index of those English equivalents is also provided, referring back to the page where the corresponding German entry will be found. The book is exceptionally well illustrated with numerous clear and easy-to-read drawings.

The author, who has also written—apart from many other publications—the six volumes of the *Blue Water Sailors* series mentioned in MC-5 (p. 96, Verlag Gerhard Stalling), is a leading authority on German nautical terminology. Less than a year after the publication of the first edition, a second (revised) edition is now in print, and if it sells as well as its predecessor, a third one may already be coming up on the visible horizon.

A similar (hardcover) French nautical dictionary has just been published:

Dictionnaire de Marine, by R. Gruss
Editions Maritimes et d'Outre-Mer
17 rue Jacob
F-75006 Paris, France

As in the case of Schult's German *Sailing Dictionary,* this book contains English equivalents for the French terms, which are defined, and an English index giving page numbers. As the name indicates, the dictionary is not restricted to sailing but is based on a more general maritime and naval approach. There are fewer illustrations than in Schult's book, but nevertheless it is a most useful aid for readers of French nautical and naval literature.

—**Karl Freudenstein**

Cruising Guides

We've been meaning to say something about cruising guides for a long, long time. The publisher dropped by the other day and threatened bodily harm unless we produced a comprehensive guide to the subject. We're sensible journalists, so we promised, but our hearts weren't in it. If there's one thing we find impossible to do, it's to become enthusiastic about someone else's cruising grounds, especially when you consider that, as we write this, it is the heart of winter here in Maine—a time when it can only be termed heartless to ask a person to review a book on the delights of sailing along the Leeward Islands. Besides, how are we to tell whether a cruising guide is any good or not if we've never sailed in the waters it purports to describe?

It's easy to see that we're not the ones for the job, but a promise is a promise. A cop-out is in order. We found two places that have a comprehensive stock of cruising guides for waters primarily in the Western World. If you plan on sailing in unknown waters, they probably have something to help you find your way.

The Dolphin Book Club
485 Lexington Ave.
New York, N.Y. 10017

BOAT/US
880 South Pickett St.
Alexandria, Va. 22304

To buy from Dolphin, you have to be a member, but they make that easy for you (see MC-3, page 108). You don't have to be a member of BOAT/US to buy books from them, but membership will provide a discount (see review on page 148).

Voyager's Cruising Bibliography
Box 32
East Aurora, N.Y. 14052
$7.50

Boating bibliographies come and go. This is a new one and consists of loose, mimeographed sheets listing magazine articles and books of interest to the modern cruiser under a variety of headings: literature of cruising, cruising psychology, income while cruising, choosing a boat, etc. We're not convinced by some of the short annotations of books (if *Knight's Modern Seamanship* is really "probably aboard more boats than any other book," there are a lot of cruisers who are making a big mistake), but there are enough references in the bibliography to keep you reading for a long time. The price is steep for a mimeographed format, but you're buying research, not a physical object. The compilers plan to update and re-edit the bibliography either semiannually or annually, and promise to change soon to a more readable medium.

Nautical Book Publishers

In past volumes of the *Mariner's Catalog*, we have discussed publishers of nautical books. We missed a few and here catch up on them. All will send you a catalog on request.

Ye Galleon Press
Fairfield, Washington 99012

Ye Galleon specializes in regional history on esoteric subjects. They have a small maritime list, which includes *Early Voyages in the North Pacific; A Voyage to the North Pacific; A Five Years' Whaling Voyage;* and *A Narrative of the Shipwreck, Captivity and Sufferings of Horace Holden and Benj. H. Nute, etc.* These are reprint editions.

Editions des 4 Seigneurs
39 rue Marceau
3800 Grenoble, France

The Four Lords publish some magnificent books, nearly all on maritime history. They're in French, of course, but if you can read the language, you'll delight in such titles as *Bateaux des Côtes de France; Les Barques du Léman; Bateaux Bretons et Vie Maritime Traditionnelle en Bretagne Atlantique;* and *Souvenirs de Marine Conservés.*

David McKay Company
750 Third Ave.
New York, N.Y.

McKay is a general publisher that in recent years has released a large number of nautical titles, most of them on boating. They have published a number of cruising yarns (*Woman Alone* by Clare Francis, and a reprint of *The Riddle of the Sands,* for instance) and quite a few practical books: *Bowditch for Yachtsmen, The Happy Ship Cookbook, Multihull Seamanship, The Book of Ropes and Knots,* etc.

Windward Publishing
Box 371005
Miami, Florida 33137

Windward publishes books about the Florida area. Subjects are primarily the natural history variety: *The Shell Book, The Shark Book, Diver's Guide to Florida, Birds of Sea, Water and Shore.* They also have a few sportfishing titles, a notable one being *How to Build Custom-made Handcrafted Fishing Rods.*

Below: From Les Barques du Léman, *Editions des 4 Seigneurs.*

Sea Fiction Guide
by Myron J. Smith and Robert C. Weller
Scarecrow Press, Metuchen, N.J.
256 pages, index, 1976, $10

This is the first sizable, published bibliography of nautical fiction we have been able to locate. With 2,525 entries, it's a formidable work, though some of the introductory essays by various authors seem a little shallow. Many of the titles and authors listed are annotated, some more than others depending on importance. Some of the annotations are inaccurate, and there are books and authors missing from the discussion, but all in all, if you are interested in nautical fiction, this can be your guide.

An Unpretentious Publisher

You can count on one hand the number of authentic nautical book publishers in the United States. We're not talking about the general publishers with a strong list of nautical books, or the tiny, specialized publishers who put out a title or two a year. We're talking about genuine publishers who know the field and consistently publish good books about the sea.

The granddaddy of nautical publishers in this country is Cornell Maritime Press. They've been in business for years and, through sheer force of will, have remained solvent while many of their competitors have not. We have reviewed many of their books in past *Mariner's Catalogs* and will probably review many more in future ones.

Cornell publishes solid-core practical books. You won't find fancy volumes puffed up like toasted marshmallows on their list. No slick tomes with titles like *The Wonderful World of the Square-Rigger*, or *Sailing Barefoot to Bora Bora*. Instead, you'll find utilitarian books, plainly designed and plainly priced, on a wide range of maritime subjects: *Blue Book of Questions and Answers for Third Mates, Boatbuilding in Your Own Backyard, Encyclopedia of Knots and Fancy Ropework, Hydraulic Dredging, Marine Cooks and Bakers Manual, Modern Marine Engineers Manual, Naval Architecture of Planing Hulls*, etc.

The major share of Cornell's publishing effort is directed toward the merchant-mariner, but there are plenty of titles for the small-boatman and fisherman. We've always admired Cornell's lack of pretension—they make no claim to the best of anything. They merely get up in the morning, work on their books, and get them out. The results speak for themselves.

Cornell Maritime Press
Cambridge, Maryland 21613

British Marine Books

Pendragon House of Connecticut has set up a welcome service for purchasers of new British books. They carry over 300 marine titles in their Fish and Ships catalog (available on request) from the following publishers and others:

Boat World
Brown, Son & Ferguson
Conway Maritime Press
Leo Cooper, Seeley Service
Fishing News (Books)
Her Majesty's Stationery Office (full service agent)
Model and Allied Publications
Nautical Publishing
Stanford Maritime Press

> **Pendragon House of Connecticut**
> **Box 255**
> **Old Mystic, Conn. 06372**

European Publishers Representatives, Inc.
11-03 46th Avenue
Long Island City, N.Y. 11101

This outfit acts as a subscription agent for a number of periodical publishers in foreign countries—specifically France, Italy, Spain, Great Britain, Germany, Poland, Portugal, Mexico, and Czechoslovakia. The procedure is simple: you send U.S. dollars to them, and they arrange the subscription for you. The advantage? If something goes wrong, you have someone to deal with in this country who speaks your language, rather than a petty bureaucrat in Warsaw, whose only other language is Croatian.

Obviously, there are a limited number of nautical magazines available through EPR. Their British selections, for instance, are *Motor Boat & Yachting, Ships Monthly, Yachting World,* and *Sea Trade*. For detailed information, send for their free brochures.

Using the Sponge Hook.

Nautical Books at Discounts

If you buy nautical books on a regular basis, it might be worth your while to investigate the Boat Owners Association of the United States. We described BOAT/US in the *Mariner's Catalog,* Volume 3 (p. 150), and came to the conclusion that theirs is a service worth exploring. Indeed it is, especially when it comes to books. They have a comprehensive list, including government publications, and for their members, offer good discounts: "Commercial books are offered at savings of at least 15%, often 20%, and some as high as 25%, depending on publishers' terms. Although less dramatic, discounts are also provided on most U.S. Government publications, usually around 10%." Find out about becoming a member by writing:

> **BOAT/US**
> **880 South Pickett St.**
> **Alexandria, Virginia 22304**

22 This photograph is included because it shows a different aspect of the reality of a late nineteenth century port—a river with heavily industrialised banks, miles of railway sidings with steam cranes, miles of bleak industrial wasteland, which were as characteristic of the age as in a different way they are of ours and which were the only background and playground of far too many children like these two little boys. This quayside camera caught also two of the most famous small British sailing ships of the period, the wooden two-masted schooner *Isabella* of Barrow and her sister ship of the same fleet, the steel three-master *Result*. The *Result* is still afloat. She belongs to the Ulster Folk Museum and it is hoped to restore her to her appearance when this photograph was taken.

Photo and caption from A Quayside Camera.

Two Worthy Picture Books

You can almost hear it. Once a year, perhaps twice, in half the publishing companies across the face of this land, into the editor-in-chief's office walks a rosy-cheeked fellow, tall and blonde, wrapped in a double-knit suit, his collar held together with a paisley tie, his shoes polished. His message is simple: "Excuse me, sir, but isn't it time for us to do this year's (or half-year's) gorgeously illustrated, all-stops-pulled-out, great age of sail book?" The editor-in-chief stops fondling his Brazilian rosewood flow-tip blue pencil for half a second, looks thoughtful for the first and only time that day, and then says, "Brilliant idea, Twitchard. Give Slatterly a call and tell him he has a week to put together the text, and tell Fenstermaker to go through last year's culls and see what we have in house for illustrations."

If 85 percent of the nautical picture books published today aren't put together that way, things are worse than we thought they were. But we're getting negative, and that won't do. . . . As we were saying, 15 percent of the nautical picture books published today are put together with intense research, scholarly flair, and editorial acumen. That's a fair percentage for the captains of industry in publishing, and we congratulate them.

Since we are making an effort not to be negative, for the moment at least, we'll forget about the 85-percent books and tell you about two of the 15-percenters:

A Quayside Camera: 1835-1917
by Basil Greenhill
Wesleyan University Press, Middletown, Conn.
original publisher David & Charles, England
112 pages, index, 1975, $8.95

The Medley of Mast and Sail: A Camera Record
Naval Institute Press, Annapolis, Md.
original publisher Teredo Books, England
330 pages, 1976, $21.95

These books are everything a nautical picture book should be. They are historical works, and as such, they are compiled, edited, and written by people who know what they are talking about. They show us scenes from the world of the past, freed of the bindings of romantic drivel and filled with lives as they were lived, not as we wish they were lived. Though both are English books, they have value for us all: Basil Greenhill even made a studious effort to include many photographs of scenes in the United States.

We commend them to you. They put the 85-percenters to absolute, unadulterated shame.

Mystic Paperbacks

With an overall title that sounds much too much like a men's magazine come-on, Mystic Seaport has begun publishing a paperback series: The Mystic Seaport True Maritime Adventure Series. Even the individual titles sound like something out of the pages of *Argosy*:

Mutiny on the Pedro Varela
The Wreck of the Steamer San Francisco
The Long Arctic Search
Disaster on Devil's Bridge

But they're legitimate—"In the earliest days of the Seaport some of these titles, gleaned from the growing manuscript collection of the new museum, were printed in limited editions and given to members as a token of gratitude for their support of what was then an undertaking almost unique in the museum field. The present series reproduces these books as they were then printed, with no apologies for typographical errors or an often appealing quaintness of style." Get them for $3.95 apiece from:

The Mystic Seaport Store
Mystic, Conn.
or
The Pequot Press
Chester, Conn.

UNDER FULL SAIL.

The Mystic Seaport Store, by the way, has a catalog of gifts, prints, books, and whatnot. We are surprised at the high number of nautical kitsch items offered for sale by what purports to be a museum, but you will find quality gifts here and there among the, shall we say, lesser stock.

Used-book Dealers

Our collection of nautical book dealers who sell through the mail increases (see additional listings in past *Catalogs*). Here are our latest finds:

Editions
Boiceville, N.Y. 12412
A sizable used-book clearinghouse. Since they specialize in a wide variety of subjects, ask for their Ships & the Sea list. Catalog has no annotation; prices are reasonable. $1 gets you on their regular mailing list (a catalog every 5 weeks).

Graham K. Scott, Bookseller
2 The Broadway
Friern Barnet
London, England
List issued once a year. Also sells new books on all subjects: "We are particularly keen to introduce ourselves as a supplier of reasonably priced British books. We understand that for the overseas book buyer the purchase of British books from us rather than from his local bookstore in his home country can show him considerable savings. We find that overseas book suppliers seem to charge very high prices for British books."

Schooner Books
5485 Inglis Street
Halifax, Nova Scotia
Canada
Their specialty is books about the maritime provinces, and as a result carry a number of nautical items. Their catalog is very well annotated and prices seem moderate.

Ted Stone
21 Sunset Trail
Croton on Hudson, N.Y. 10520
Has a small list of naval books, pamphlets, and cards. Listing updated periodically. "My specialty is photographs of U.S. naval vessels which I sell by mail. Lists are available, but I also work from want lists. Am also interested in purchasing collections of old naval photographs and negatives."

The Book Cabin
Uffa Fox Ltd.
53 High Street
Cowes, Isle of Wight, England
Carries titles on most marine subjects; heavy on yachting. Prices are moderate. Catalog is lightly annotated.

P.G. de Lotz A.B.A.
20 Downside Crescent
Hampstead, London
England
Carries used and new books on mostly naval subjects. Catalog, which is lightly annotated, also includes military, political, and aviation titles. Prices are moderate.

Atlantic Book Service
Box 218
Charlestown, Mass. 02129
Carries both used and new books. Subjects are primarily maritime and boating. Catalog is well annotated and prices are reasonable.

Mammals of the Oceans
by Richard Mark Martin
G. P. Putnam's Sons, New York
1977, 208 pages, illustrated, appendices,
selected bibliography, index, $12.95

Martin's book is a handy reference, two thirds of it being one- to three-page summaries of information about each species of marine mammal preceded by characteristics and problems of survival for each order as a whole: cetacea, pinnipedia and sirenia. Otters and polar bears are given a chapter as well.

Martin's focus is on stages and styles of adaptation to marine life emphasizing the fact—or the assumption—that these mammals are in the process of recreating ecological niches for themselves in the sea, having opted for the better opportunities there compared to competition on land. The evolutionary history and particular adaptations of each species seem to fade in importance as Martin lunges into a final chapter on "the future," barely suppressing his horror and rage that men continue to exploit sea mammals to the point of extinction. This brings us back to the forcefulness and compassion of Martin's preface, which includes a compliment to Friends of the Earth: with branches in eleven cities around the world, it is a powerful force in creating legislation to protect whales. Between the lines you read that what is owed is not protection but a treaty.

—Charlotte Putz

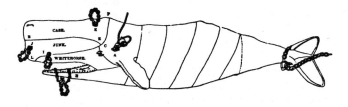

Whales, Whaling and Whale Research
A Selected Bibliography
Compiled by L.R. Magnolia
The Whaling Museum, Cold Spring Harbor
Long Island, New York 11724
92 pages, paperbound, 1977, $5.30

A bibliography of books and periodical pieces, most of which were published between 1946 and 1976 (though the earliest reference is 1820). There are approximately 1,000 references, and they range from the highly technical (*On the Historical Structure of Cetacean Lungs*) to the general (*Whales on Parade*). There is no annotation.

When the Whale Came to My Town
by Jim Young
Scholastic Book Services
Division of Scholastic Magazines, Inc.
by arrangement with Alfred A. Knopf, Inc.
1974, 31 pages

This is a gem that appeared in one of those Weekly Reader book orders. It's written by a school boy from Provincetown, Massachusetts, who stayed with a whale during the three days that it lived on the beach behind his house. He went home to sleep but remained with the whale in dreams. He was alone on the beach when he first saw "... a big grey thing ... bigger than a bus." And he was alone with the whale the first night when he looked at the whale's eye for a long time, "and his eye looked at me. Then he blinked. And I wasn't afraid anymore." He describes the turmoil in town of old men and kids and dogs and gulls, of whale doctors and Coast Guard boats, and the five times that the whale was towed off and swam straight back. Finally, he was alone with the whale on the third evening to say good-bye when the whale died.

—Charlotte Putz

Marine Education

Compiling and editing *The Mariner's Catalog* is quite simple. We get together once a year for a knock-down, drag-out marathon editorial session in which we make lists, argue about principles, threaten each other, promise that This Is The Last Year, and generally act like civilized people. With our aggressions sated, we adjourn to the local saloon and come to an Understanding, which usually takes the form of a neatly typewritten sheet, xeroxed for all who care to see it, simply entitled Things to Do. We then go back to our respective corners and ignore the damn thing.

Marine education has been a Thing to Do for years. It was ignored at first out of orneriness, then stabbed at in an idle sort of way, and then we *promised* some time ago that we would get serious and publish a piece on it that would restore order from chaos. We failed, though not because we didn't try. We just found it impossible to determine whose program was for real and whose was nothing more than a shuck for putting together a Galápagos cruise, or garnering loose grant money, or putting indigent marine science majors to work. The result is that we have listed a program here and there, but we have not done a *catalogue raisonné*.

To their credit, the University of Delaware Sea Grant College program is moving in that direction. They have produced three publications to date that make an attempt to analyze the goals of marine education and to describe the programs now offered around the country.

An Introduction to Marine Education is a free paperbound statement on the importance of marine education. The purpose of the study is to get people thinking about the future direction of marine education.

Americans and the World of Water ($2.50, paperbound) is a collection of essays on the meaning of the sea, sort of an educated argument for investing resources in marine education. We especially liked "Images for a Sea People: Arts, Letters and Science of the Sea."

But the truly valuable publication for those who want to know what is going on in marine education today is *Marine Affairs and Higher Education* by Gerard Mangone and John Pedrick, Jr. ($5, paperbound). This book is the result of a survey recently taken of college courses in marine affairs, which includes such subjects as law, ocean policies, coastal zone policies, marine resource economics, maritime history, geography, anthropology, transportation, and fishery ecology. There is a list of colleges offering courses in marine affairs and degrees in marine subjects; and a list of faculty members teaching courses. The real meat of it, though, is reprints of course outlines and bibliographies of courses taught throughout the country.

All three publications are available from:

**The College of Marine Studies
University of Delaware
Newark, Delaware 19711**

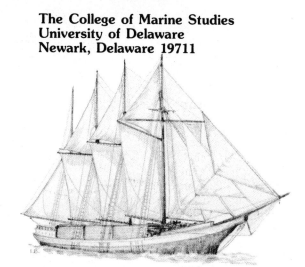

From Americans and the World of Water.

6. American Society and the Uses of the Sea

Pessimists, viewing traffic congestion, have predicted dourly that some day a monumental highway jam will take place covering hundreds of miles of superhighway, and that it will be so bad that people will just get out and abandon their cars forever. Should that happen before the petroleum crunch drives many cars from the roads, it will undoubtedly be on a Sunday as people all try to go home at once from the sea and lake shores.

One of the great phenomena of our time is the increase in aquatic recreation which has taken place so gradually that it is most noticeable by the clogged highways and waterways during weekends and vacation times. There are many causes: more leisure time, more disposable income, the fact that aquatic recreation can be as simple and inexpensive as swimming or fishing from a pier or as expensive as anyone cares to make it. Above all, there is the attraction of water.

We mention aquatic recreation because it is a highly visible and useful manifestation of the social value of the world of water. To be sure, there are economic values, too; next to offshore petroleum and gas in economic impact is the recreation business, according to some estimates, with fisheries third. The phenomenon of water recreation has created such oddities as Arizona, a state with severe water problems but also with one of the highest rates of pleasure boat ownership in the land; and beaches crowded past belief with scarcely a square yard of sand unoccupied and the salt smell of the seashore completely lost in a miasmic haze of sun-tan lotion effluvia. Of course crowded beaches in some places are not new. Some years ago John Steinbeck characterized Coney Island as a place *"where the surf is one-third water and two-thirds people."* The difference today is that once-remote beaches are now becoming equally crowded. The estimate is that more than 150 million Americans will seek aquatic recreation by century's end, and this figure may be conservative.

"What else did ye expect? Going about ye streets proclaiming boats would someday be fashioned of GLASS!"

Sea Grant, Wisconsin Style

The Sea Grant programs conducted at various American universities might sound similar in goal and substance, but as in everything else, some are better than others.* There are those that have the appearance of just going through the motions, and there are those that seem genuinely interested in getting the results of their research and analysis into the hands of those who really could use them. The University of Wisconsin, which specializes in Great Lakes studies, fits in the latter category. To see what we mean, send for their information packet "Sea Grant Portfolio," which lists their reports, books, studies, films, and projects. The subject areas are minerals, law, socioeconomics, water quality, transportation, living resources, and ocean engineering. They have something for everyone, and a handy order form to get it to you fast. It's an appealingly designed portfolio, and, though we're not the ones to be taken in by slick presentations, we found ourselves wanting to know more, not wishing that they would go away.

We tip our hats to the folks in Wisconsin.

**Communications Office
University of Wisconsin
Sea Grant College Program
1800 University Avenue
Madison, Wisconsin 53706**

*For a rundown on the purposes and objectives of Sea Grant, see the *Mariner's Catalog,* Volume 2, page 125, and Volume 3, page 151.

We notice that many of the Sea Grant Programs around the nation have compiled marine resources and information directories during the past year. If your state hasn't one yet, no doubt it will soon. Locally, we got hold of copies from Massachusetts and New Hampshire (*A Citizen's Guide to Sources for Marine and Coastal Information in Massachusetts,* and *Marine Resources Directory State of New Hampshire*), and they both are well organized and useful. They cost one dollar and are a deal for that. Contact your own state's Sea Grant College.

**Sea Grant Program
Massachusetts Institute of Technology
Cambridge, Mass. 02139**

**Sea Grant Program
Kingsbury Hall
University of New Hampshire
Durham, N.H. 03824**

**Maritime Book Society
P.O. Box 6
Newton Abbot, Devon
England**

This is the English equivalent of America's Dolphin Book Club (485 Lexington Ave., N.Y., N.Y. 10017), which was described in the *Mariner's Catalog,* Volume 3, page 108. The method of operation is about the same—when you join, you choose three books at 25 pence each, plus 60 pence postage; you agree to purchase 4 books in the next year at club prices, which are up to 25% off the publishers' prices; and you receive the club newsletter once every two months.

We have heard rumors of two other nautical book clubs in the formative stage in the United States. We'll report on them in future catalogs if they should ever break out into the open.

Dear Editors:

In MC-4, page 176, you listed Pioneer Marine School only as an ex-drug addict training program. This is not quite accurate.

When started in 1970, the school was indeed open only to former drug users who had spent a minimum of six months in a half-way house environment. The funding at that time was from Addictive Services Agency.

As the school developed and the curriculum was broadened, it was felt that a wider range of students would benefit from the program. In 1974 application for funding was made to the New York State Department of Employment, and since January 1975, this agency has been the principal source of operating funds.

Admission criteria are as follows: Applicants must be over 18, residents of New York City, drug free (including alcohol), unemployed, able to pass a series of math, mechanical comprehension and reading tests (administered by the staff) and acceptance by two staff members following an exhaustive screening interview.

The results of this have been very positive on at least two levels. The interaction between people from a more diverse range of backgrounds has made for a more stimulating teaching atmosphere for all concerned (including the instructors). Secondly, since we stress a policy of helping each graduate find his or her own job, placements have been more successful and better related to the boating industry.

Don Meisner
South Street Seaport Museum
16 Fulton St.
New York, N.Y. 10038

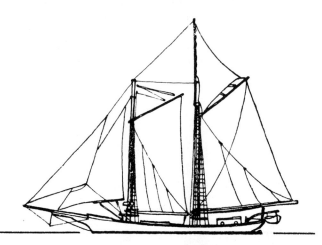

The Rand McNally Atlas of the Oceans
Rand McNally & Co., Chicago, Illinois
208 pages, illus., index, 1977, $29.95

We are generally hesitant to recommend books that rightly fit in the "gift book" category. After all, the purpose of the *Mariner's Catalog* is to help our readers find primary, or hard-core secondary, source materials that can truly help them get along in marine-related endeavors. Coffee-table books are hardly our stock in trade.

When we picked up this book, we thought we would see page after page of detailed maps of the ocean's surface and the ocean's floor. Instead, we got a mixed bag of things, all related to the sea, of course, but not what we expected. Yet, after spending time with the book, we realized that it is indeed valuable, if for no other reason than to force the reader to consider aspects of the ocean usually left to scientists and their ilk—a little geology, a little oceanography, a little biology, a little ocean engineering. Not enough to make you an expert, you understand, but enough to make you at least turn over in your mind the possibility of becoming one.

Should you spend $29.95 for that reason? Probably not, but your town library should. And your Uncle Joe, knowing that you're somehow interested in the sea but not much more (his fixation is model railroading, you see), might find it to be a Christmas present with a purpose—a subtle wedge to get you to stop playing with boats and start thinking about a (ahem) career.

From The Rand McNally Atlas of the Oceans.

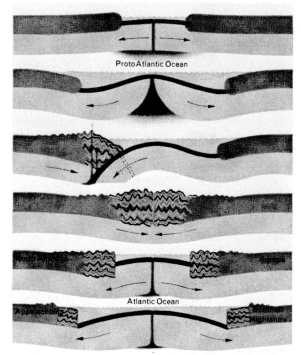

The Appalachians are a result of a complex history of converging and diverging crustal plates. In Precambrian times North America and Africa were split apart by a spreading ridge, forming an ocean called the ProtoAtlantic. This began to close in Cambrian times with a subduction zone beneath the North American continent. The closing continued until the Devonian, when all sediments between the two continents were crushed up into the Caledonian Mountains, remains of which are found in the northern Appalachians and the highlands of northern Europe. Later, in Carboniferous and Permian times, a further phase of compression produced the Hercynian Mountains, which form the remainder of the Appalachians. In the Jurassic the whole system split apart once more with the growth of the Atlantic Ocean complete with its central spreading ridge.

The Marine Paintings of Chris Mayger
introduced by David Larkin
Charles Scribner's Sons, New York
$12

Some of the most magnificent, and some of the worst, illustrative art appears on the covers of mass-market paperbacks. Chris Mayger has done some of the best marine covers—that for Ballantine's edition of *The Grey Seas Under* by Farley Mowat, for instance—and this book rounds them up. The text is short and sketchy, but that's okay. We're interested in the art, and it's reproduced in full and glorious color.

Below: The Flying Enterprise, *from* The Marine Paintings of Chris Mayger.
Bottom: A trilobite from Trilobites.

Trilobites
(A Photographic Atlas)
by Ricardo Levi-Setti
University of Chicago Press, Chicago, Ill.
1977, $9.95

I suspect that every classical musician has heard and passed on at least once the apocryphal story of the Italian cello player who walked out on his American debut audience because no one was crying.

"Aye, and we're a hard lot," Long John Silver would say. But even the hardest, nastiest, good-disavowing Luddite *has* to be moved at least a little by the alive presence of these creatures so very dead these past *hundreds of millions of years.* This must be one of the best books on a particular class of fossils available in print, for the average reader, certainly.

The earth belonged to trilobites longer than it can ever belong to us or anything near a kin of ours, and to see them in all their variety and poses where they died in these big, well-explained photographs is just plain moving! A copy of the book will have you and the kids on the road next weekend heading for the nearest known bed of them. Reading the book will give you a time perspective in spades.

Our Man Sam

Samuel Eliot Morison. Roll that name around on your tongue. It has a certain ring to it, no? It belongs to a man who was variously known as America's greatest maritime historian, Academia's most intimidating presence in the classroom, or one of our foremost intellectual tyrants. We never met Morison before he died, or sat in on his classes, but we have read a number of his books and heartily agree with the first assessment. He was, indeed, the finest writer of maritime history this country has ever produced.

Don't get us wrong. We don't necessarily subscribe to all of his theories—for instance, we can skip his at-the-drop-of-a-hat putdowns of every claim made that somebody other than Columbus discovered America. Yet we must admit that as he disputed, say, the achievements of St. Brendan, he expressed himself with charm and flair.

And that is really what we like about Morison. He was a writer with a distinctive style that makes reading the dullest of his subjects an exciting adventure. He had a command of the English language that few non-fiction writers have—he wrote his history in a scholarly way, yet it reads like a finely crafted novel.

Samuel Eliot Morison's career was dedicated toward scholarship, yet he was a real person, not a recluse. He sailed extensively and traveled around the world, visiting the sites of the events he was to write about. You could hardly call him a common man, however. He was a Boston Brahmin, sins and virtues intact.

Morison's books. He wrote scores of them. We don't list them all here, but will put down his maritime titles:

The Maritime History of Massachusetts (o.p.)

Portuguese Voyages to America in the 15th Century (Octagon, New York)

Admiral of the Ocean Sea: A Life of Christopher Columbus (Atlantic-Little, Brown, Boston)

History of U.S. Naval Operations in WW II (15 vols.) (Atlantic-Little, Brown, Boston)

Christopher Columbus, Mariner (Atlantic-Little, Brown, Boston)

John Paul Jones: A Sailor's Biography (Atlantic-Little, Brown, Boston)

The Two Ocean War (Atlantic-Little, Brown, Boston)

Spring Tides (o.p.)

Life of Commodore Matthew C. Perry (o.p.)

The European Discovery of America: The Northern Voyages (Oxford U. Press, New York)

The European Discovery of America: The Southern Voyages (Oxford U. Press, New York)

The Caribbean as Columbus Saw It (o.p.)

The Ropemakers of Plymouth (Arco Press, New York)

If you have never tried Morison, you might not know where to begin. You could start with a recently published anthology of his best writings, edited by his daughter:

Sailor Historian:
The Best of Samuel Eliot Morison
edited by Emily Morison Beck
Houghton Mifflin, Boston
431 pages, 1977, $15

This is a fine selection that has been taken from Morison's books, essays, and speeches. It's not enough, of course, but it's sufficient to give you a flavor of the man's writing and will point you in the direction of further readings. But if you read nothing else by Morison, read his essay, reprinted in its entirety, on historical writing—"History as a Literary Art." There you will find what we believe to be the purest statement ever made on the craft of writing history.

46 Bending a keel plate at Clydebank about 1900. This powerful hydraulic machine was designed by Hugh Smith and Company of Possil, Glasgow, to bend heavy plates for the largest type of ship. The open ends of the jaws permitted plates of any length to be worked.

From Clyde Shipbuilding From Old Photographs.

Clyde Shipbuilding From Old Photographs
by John Hume and Michael Moss
B.T. Batsford, 4 Fitzhardinge St.
London, England
143 pages, biblio., 1975, £3.95

Shipbuilding on the Clyde River in Scotland might seem like a pretty esoteric subject for us here, but you must remember that a huge number of ships, primarily of iron and steel, were built on the Clyde. And we may not seem that way, but we have a thing for metal ships. The photos published in this book cover the period from the 1850s to World War I, and the ships shown are primarily steam and motor ships.

An L. Francis Herreshoff Reader
by L. Francis Herreshoff
International Marine Publishing Company
324 pages, illus., 1978, $15

The nautical world in all its variety, seen through the eyes of a knowledgeable, albeit provocative, observer.

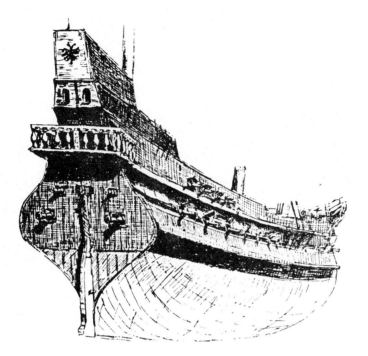

MODELS and MODELING

New News and Groups

The Floating Drydock has announced a newsletter, *The Journal of the Floating Drydock.* First issued in January of 1978, each issue features a "ship of the month" with history and photos of a particular U.S. Navy vessel. Correspondence on modeling, tips on shop practice, U.S. Navy ordnance, and camouflage, contests and builders' stories will round it out.

The Journal of the Floating Drydock
The Floating Drydock
Box 16066
Philadelphia, Penn. 19114
U. S., Canada $6.00/year
Overseas $7.00/year

For 20 years The Shipcraft Guild has been enjoying mutual company and hoarding the gold. It recently opened its membership to all comers, however. This association of ship modelers and marine artists meets once a month (3rd Tuesdays) to share and enjoy demonstrations, slides, trips, and so on. They keep a file of relevant publications, books, and plans for personal research, and offer their own interesting *The Binnacle,* a newsletter of events, sources, tips, and the like for the members. Active membership (voting), $10.00. Inactive (living too far from NYC to make the meetings), $8.00.

The Shipcraft Guild
11 College Drive
Jersey City, N.J. 07305

There are few things which can compare, in complete uselessness, with a ship model in a bottle... A ship in a bottle brings out the finer feelings, the benevolent humanity we all have somewhere in our characters.

—William McFee

Members are always ready to help others who are having trouble with their models, or are uncertain as to how a thing is done. For instance, one member came up with an excellent way to make billowing sails, that stay billowed. This is important to give a model the final touch of authenticity. Other demonstrations have been on rigging, painting, soldering fine parts, and even making the crew members for the models.

Members are encouraged to bring in their models while they are making them, as it is always interesting to watch progress of this kind. Usually they have incorporated new ways of doing things which will be a big help to other members in their model making.

From The Shipcraft Guild.

The organizational aspect of modeling is much more vast than we ever suspected and, once tapped, we don't know whether to let her gush or call out the Guard and sandbags. Several correspondents have written to say that, yes, we've listed these, them, and those, but what about all these and those over there? So, we write to all of those and they write back to say that's nothin', wait 'til you find out about *them*!

For example, one group that we have not listed is the North American Model Boat Association International. This organization has 1,500 members (!) and sponsors regional, national, and international class sail and power events annually. The intimidation comes when NAMBA's subsidiary groups are considered, local and regional, and each with their own newsletters and events. If you can handle it, write:

NAMBA - International
Route A, Box 19
Lower Lake, California 75457

We suppose that it is natural for an organization of artisans to call itself a "guild," for craftsmen have so organized themselves for some seven or eight hundred years. The original guilds, however, were organized not simply for internal mutual protection and interest, but also to protect the client or customer and to set standards of quality and training toward that end. Many contemporary "guilds" emphasize the former role and may more appropriately be called a "club" or "society."

Not so the American Ship Carver's Guild. Founded in 1976 in commemoration of the Bicentennial, this organization is a woodcarver's guild proper, with chapters being established throughout the country. Their bylaws provide for gradients of membership: Apprentice, Journeyman, Artisan, Craftsman, Artificer, and either Shipcarver or Master Carver. This enables the Guild to "set up suitable training programs and help in becoming more proficient," and also to establish a "Warranty of Marketability" for the prospective client. Membership is by application to:

American Ship Carver's Guild
Box 252
Huntington Station, N.Y. 11746

More Plans

In England we've found a new plans source for the modeler, especially plans in the justly famous Underhill series. List "S" illustrates details of 66 ship designs, 8 ship's boats, and 8 ship's guns. Price is 60p including postage. List "P" illustrates details of 35 powercraft designs, and 8 ship's guns. Price is 40p including postage.

Bassett - Lowke (S.M.) Ltd.
18/25 Kingwell Street
Northampton NN LLPS
England

The prospect of frame-and-plank construction is terrifying if *You Don't Know How.* If the truth be told, I still don't do it properly and prefer to cheat; carefully take the page out of the book, run down to the local newspaper, pay a few bucks to have them line-shot to the size I want, then take the plans home and trace with a black, soft editor's pencil (sharp). Trace over on the backside to the framestock and, *voilà,* station frames are perfect. It *is* possible to photograph lines and blow them up in one's own enlarger, but most enlarger lenses do have "edge-fall-off" and are not really "flat field" when doing big enlargements. Also, taping together all those sections accurately can drive you crazy.

But Robin Rielly really pulls it together for you. He offers plans for modelers in good, big scale on several pages—profile, deck, sail, and details sheets, plus a sheet *with every frame drawn full size!* Hot stuff. Each set is accompanied by a paper describing Rielly's research of the craft, building procedures, tips and suggestions, and a bibliography.

> **Robin L. Rielly - Yacht Designs**
> **Box 661**
> **Toms River, N.J. 08753**

Modeler's Plans from Robin Rielly

Prince de Neufchatel
Baltimore Clipper Privateer of 1814 — 5 large sheets on ¼" scale — lines — construction plan — frames — sail plan — deck view and detail drawings. Builds hull approximately 29" long
$25 postpaid

Elsie
Gloucester Fishing Schooner of 1910 — ¼" scale — hull about 30" long — 5 large sheets — lines — construction plan — frames — deck details — sail plan
$25 postpaid

Lucy M.
Typical Chesapeake Bay Skipjack — ¾" scale — 3 large sheets — sail plan — lines — construction plan — deck details — frames
$18 postpaid

HMS Triumph
British 3rd-rate 74-gun ship from 1764 — hull approximately 50" long — ¼" scale — Available in Fall 1978 — 10 sheets of drawings, construction notes, and ten 8 x 10 photographs showing details of the original Admiralty model from the Rogers Collection at Annapolis. Price to be determined as the drawings are not yet completed.

Meanwhile, modelers interested in warships would probably have to go to the Smithsonian or the Pentagon to find more detailed or better printed plans than those offered by Morrison. They are stunning.

> **Morrison Repla-Tech**
> **48500 McKenzie Hwy.**
> **Vida, Oregon 97488**

Mr. Morrison included an interesting note with his materials. It says, "We are deluged with requests for information on airplanes and ships. For ships, contact: The International Naval Research Organization, Inc., 1729 Lois Court, Toledo, Ohio 43613."

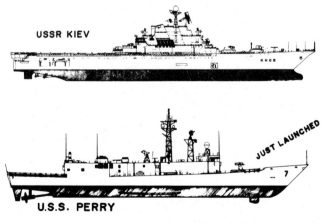

Above and right: Plans from Morrison Repla-Tech.

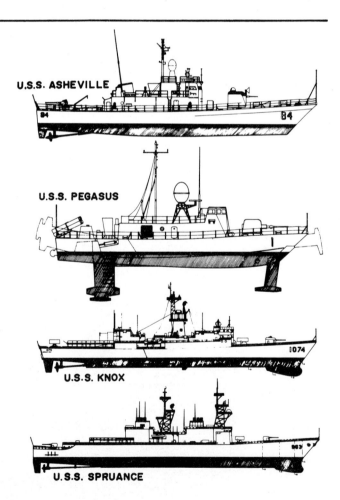

Some One-of-a-Kinders

Anyone, anyone interested in modeling must get the Ship Modelers Associates Catalog. It has everything and as more of everything comes along—lists, plans, tools, materials, or books—owners of the catalog receive regular additions and updates. Of all sources we have listed, this one has the most vitality. A business at its very best!

**Ship Modelers Associates
247 Washington Street
Hartford, Conn. 06106**

Another unusual outfit is Stawbitz of Buffalo. They offer big, husky, *fiberglass* model hulls in three scales: 1/16th (Coast Guard 44' rescue lifeboat and a landing craft), 1/32nd (torpedoboat and a seagoing tug) and 1/72nd (Fletcher-class destroyer, Coast Guard high-endurance cutter, and a tug). These are not kits—only hulls, decks, and related large structures are offered, together with a short brochure of suggestions on outfitting the craft. It's the bare-hull deal in miniature. Prices range from $50 for the small tug to $250 for the 63" destroyer.

**Stawbitz of Buffalo
105 Hollybrook Drive
Williamsville, N.Y. 14221**

*Right: Plank-bending machine from Ship Modelers Associates.
Below: A finished Stawbitz model. It is made up of basic units of hull, deck, cabin, and wind shelters, motor housing, and stern support plate. Three sheets of detailed plans plus creative craftsmanship finish her off.*

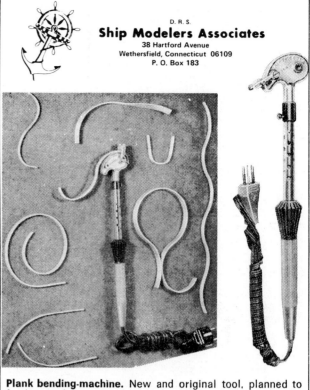

While there are some places offering fiberglass model *sailing* hulls for AMYA racing (12 meters and J-boats), only one offers traditional-craft hulls for RC-outfitting:

David Mainwaring
36 Hawthorne Ave.
Needham, Mass. 02192

Below, left: Sail plan of the Friendship sloop Florida, *a 25-footer popularized as the Pemaquid. Below: Sail plan of a Friendship sloop model at 1¼-inch scale, available from David Mainwaring.*

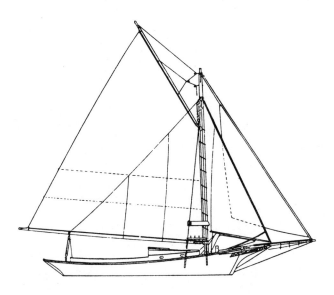

Another hole in the market has been model kits of Great Lakes vessels, a couple of schooners being about the beginning and end of it. Here's a place that offers Great Lakes bulk carriers in several configurations and from various periods. They are plastic waterline jobs, but they look quite good and are to HO scale, doing the two birds trick. They also have a 5-track rail-car ferry to give train modelers another fever.

VDCD Marine Model
1418 Mentor Ave.
Painesville, Ohio 44077

Modern Pilot House Close Up

Conventional Pilot House

Left and above: Great Lakes bulk freighter from VDCD Marine.

COMMODORE M.O.B.Y.C. (owner of leading boat): "Look 'ere, Bill Grant, if ye don't stop shuvvin' yer boat I'll disqualify yer!"

Modelers who enjoy working in plastic and looking for something different may want to explore some British and European vessels in wholesome sizes and at reasonable prices, from:

> Kingston Mouldings
> 113 Commercial Road
> Lower Parkstone
> Poole, Dorset
> England

And for the British model power racing connection, their answer to our Dumas is:

> S.H.G. Marine
> Unit C4, Stafford Park
> 2 Telford, Salop
> England

Sun XXI tug from Kingston Mouldings.

Sun XXI Tug

Near scale modern tug hull. Moulded rubbing strip, keel and bulwarks. Fully detailed constructional drawing supplied.

Length 36"
Beam   9"

Black only.

The Obvious and the Obscure

We love our mailbox, our little window on the world, but it can be a stormy relationship at times. For example, we continue to hear for the first time about sources we should have known about a long time ago—big places that "everyone" knows about, really obvious emporiums that have "everything" or nearly so, and that give good service. Ship Modeler's Associates, listed above, is a good example. And so is Polk's Model Craft Hobbies. Here and there in the literature and in letters we've seen phrases like ". . . and then of course there's Polk's. . ." Like good Quietists, we've always believed that, sooner or later, all would be revealed. Polk's is an obvious place, a well-established five stories of modeling supplies, with a huge ships' department, and it has been revealed later. It offers a host of different catalogs.

**Polk's Model Craft Hobbies
314 Fifth Avenue
New York, N.Y. 10001**

Another postal pique we often endure is one to the effect, "I've certainly enjoyed your catalogs very much and always look forward to the next one. It took me years to find some of the sources you list. I wish that these books existed years ago when I was starting out to build the massive files I now enjoy. Well, best of luck on your continuing venture. I am, Most Sincerely Yours, (signed) Hoarding SOB."

Dear Hoard, ol' friend: Always glad to be of help. Best Regards, Eds.

Model-Maker

Dear Editors:

As a curiosity, readers may be interested to learn about a Dutch-born ship model maker in Emden, Germany. It so happens that he used to work as a janitor for a shipping company, which went bankrupt some time ago, on account of the critical situation of that branch of European economy. But whereas there seems to be much excess tonnage worldwide, Hans Veldekamp has his own order books well filled for some time to come, and continues to turn out beautiful, authentic replicas of historic ships from the days of sail, even insisting on using the same kind of wood as in the original ships. His own secret dream is to build a model of Nelson's HMS *Victory* for himself, but with a growing reputation such as his, there may be no time for him to indulge in such fancies in the near future. (Hans Veldekamp, Ringstrasse 2, D-2970 Emden, Germany)

**Karl Freudenstein
Bonn, West Germany**

Hardware Notes

A new line of model steam engines has emerged, the Aster double- and triple-cylinder configurations. These are light displacement but very tight and powerful mills designed specifically for model boats, including RC. Aster has boilers for the engines, complete with pressure gauge, sight glass water level indicator, safety valves, regulator, and steam pipes. Polk's, listed above, is the distributor.

The new Aster steam engines, available from Polk's.

Aster's NEW line of marine steam engines feature a unique die-cast cylinder with a brass cylinder liner for exceptionally long wear. Stephenson's reversing gear is fitted as standard.

With a low center of gravity, these engines are ideally suited for model boats two to four feet long (60 cm to 100 cm). The open column design makes for a light weight engine that produces s lot of power. Use it in tug boats, steam yachts, fishing boats, perhaps a model of the African Queen.

The pistons and glands are sealed with graphited yarn to prevent steam leakage and make the most efficient use of the steam. The small displacement means that little steam is used and only a small boiler is required.

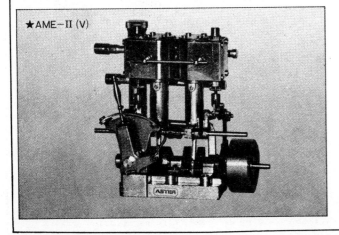

★AME-II (V)

★AME-III (V)

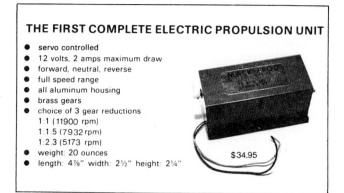

THE FIRST COMPLETE ELECTRIC PROPULSION UNIT

- servo controlled
- 12 volts, 2 amps maximum draw
- forward, neutral, reverse
- full speed range
- all aluminum housing
- brass gears
- choice of 3 gear reductions
  1:1 (11900 rpm)
  1:1.5 (7932 rpm)
  1:2.3 (5173 rpm)
- weight: 20 ounces
- length: 4⅞" width: 2½" height: 2¼"

$34.95

There is also a new *electric* drive unit now available for models, from:

M.A.C.K. Products
Model Marine Division
Box 33
Rahway, New Jersey 07065

From the Foredom Electric Company catalog.

Any modelmaker who does not have a colleted grinder and is wondering whether or not to get one should stop wondering. Get one. The Dremels are excellent, but the Foredoms should be considered. They are more expensive than the Dremels, but also more powerful and much handier in tight places. Dental students start out with them.

The Foredom Electric Company
Bethel, Conn. 06801

New solid state speed and torque control . . . costs less to operate . . . assures full torque at all speeds . . . available for foot or hand operation. Special "full feedback" circuit assures that no power is wasted. Full torque, smooth control allows precision

performance on the widest range of Hang-up or Bench type. Two interchangeable speed controls (manual or foot operated). Choice of 15 interchangeable handpieces for speeds up to 35,000 RPM (with No. 35 Handpiece).

HANG-UP STYLE

Model No.	Price*
R-5	$ 141.00
R-5D	149.00
R-8	146.00
R-8D	154.00
R-44A	151.50
R-7	179.00
R-7D	187.00
R-30	155.50
R-14	184.00
R-14D	192.00
R-25	194.50
R-35	211.00
R-55	186.00
R-56	178.00
R-57	200.00
(Without Handpiece) R-0	125.00

BENCH STYLE

Model No.	Price*
RB-5	$ 152.00
RB-5D	160.00
RB-8	157.00
RB-8D	165.00
RB-44A	162.50
RB-7	190.00
RB-7D	198.00
RB-30	166.50
RB-14	195.00
RB-14D	203.00
RB-25	205.50
RB-35	222.00
RB-55	197.00
RB-56	189.00
RB-57	211.00
(Without Handpiece) RB-0	136.00

*Price includes handpiece as illustrated and speed control of your choice. Specify which you want — foot (SR-1) or manual (SM-1).

Books

The outpouring of modeling books of a few years ago has gone back to its inevitable trickle. In fact, we notice that recent catalogs have a disconcerting "Discontinued" stamped across some venerable titles. It may be a word to the wise to get those books you've been meaning to before stocks at hand run out and you catch *outofprintitis procrastinacocus.*

The Shipmodeler's Guidebook to Ancient Ships
by N. Lee Lancaster
Louis Davidson
3531 Milford
Pensacola, Fla. 32506
24 pages, illus., 1977

Louis Davidson has announced *The Shipmodeler's Guidebook to Ancient Ships* by N. Lee Lancaster. While the profile drawings are no better than those available elsewhere, the detailed and explanatory drawings are great and reflect the findings of modern archaeology during recent years.

Illustration from Historische Schiffmodelle.

Historische Schiffmodelle
(Ein Handbuch Für Modellbauer)
by Wolfram zu Monfeld
Mosaik Verlag
8000 Munchen 80
Steinhauser Strasse 1
Germany
368 pages, illus., 1977, 58 DM

This book is the equivalent of any five that ever have or might ever be listed. It is simply overwhelming. That the text is in German is irrelevant. There are tens of thousands of details for the ship modeler in this beautiful book—get it if you can!

Half-Modeling Booklet

In MC-4 (page 16), we discussed the Apprenticeshop of the Maine Maritime Museum in Bath, Maine. They have been publishing a series of monographs, the latest one being *Half-Modelling*—a 24-page introduction to the history and use of the half-model and a guide to making them. The example used in the how-to section is a 22-foot Muscongus Bay sloop, the forerunner of the famed Friendship Sloop. Included in the booklet is a series of templates printed on heavy stock as an aid in your model building. $1.50 to the Apprenticeshop will get you a copy.

The Apprenticeshop
Maine Maritime Museum
Bath, Maine

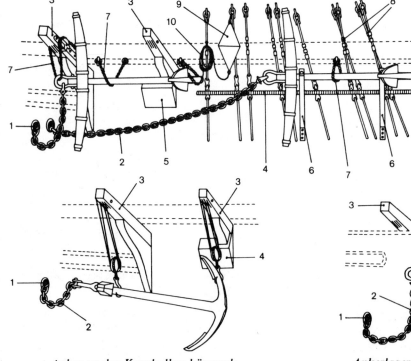

Ankerlager, 19. Jahrhundert:
1. Ankerklüse, 2. Ankerkette,
3. Kranbalken, 4. Rüste,
5. Schweinsrücken, 6. Anker-
lager, 7. Rüstketten,
8. Spannschrauben mit Püt-
tings, 9. Boje, 10. Reep

Anker an den Kranbalken hängend:
1. Ankerklüse, 2. Ankerkette,
3. Kranbalken, 4. Schweinsrücken

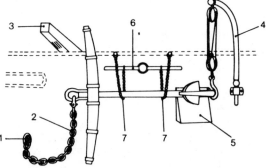

Ankerlager, 19. Jahrhundert: 1. Ankerklüse,
2. Ankerkette, 3. Kranbalken, 4. Krandavit,
5. Schweinsrücken, 6. Versenker, 7. Rüstketten

F I S H I N G

It will be a sweltering day in heaven before we ever cover this subject in true Catalog fashion. A field of interest so inherently bizarre doesn't need us. Unlike other subjects we like to discuss, it is the ordinary that is unusual in the sport of fishing, and somehow the ordinary just runs against our grain.

For example, we would like to talk about crazy stuff, such as the fact that cranberries work very effectively on freshwater trotlines for catfish and carp, or that any lure or bait works much better if rubbed or infused with anise-seed extract; but we can't, because it's nuts and all the fishermen know this stuff already and do it.

On the other hand, something really ordinary, such as Al's Goldfish lure, a little fish shaped out of metal and for decades a known killer of fish, is almost never mentioned and certainly not used among honorable gentlemen. No, a *real* fisherman uses gear because it is unlikely to work, and, if it does work, you have to set it aside. It's as if a good time is to go into a singles' bar with a big piece of spinach stuck between your front teeth. Any other way wouldn't be sporting.

Anyway, one day Colleague-Spectre got tired of posing for postcards, or what seemed like it, and hauled out Al's Goldfish so's he could catch his fish. Riding home in the trunk was just the beginning of things after that. Only the newest employee at the Credit Bureau talks to him now—and that makes Al's Our Kind of Lure. Get it at the sporting goods store. The factory is:

Al's Goldfish Lure Co.
Indian Orchard, Mass. 01151

A learned fool is one who has read everything and remembered it.

—Josh Billings

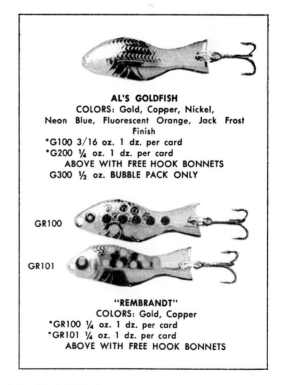

AL'S GOLDFISH
COLORS: Gold, Copper, Nickel,
Neon Blue, Fluorescent Orange, Jack Frost
Finish
*G100 3/16 oz. 1 dz. per card
*G200 ¼ oz. 1 dz. per card
ABOVE WITH FREE HOOK BONNETS
G300 ½ oz. BUBBLE PACK ONLY

GR100

GR101

"REMBRANDT"
COLORS: Gold, Copper
*GR100 ¼ oz. 1 dz. per card
*GR101 ¼ oz. 1 dz. per card
ABOVE WITH FREE HOOK BONNETS

That's it—Al's Goldfish Lure.

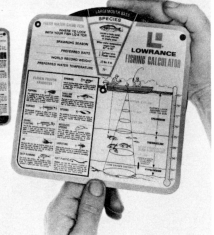

Another thing that seems unpopular is information; that makes Lowrance's Fishing Calculator a pretty good time, a species-specific dial showing where to go, how deep to fish, and with what. It's a buck from:

Lowrance Electronics Mfg. Co.
12000 East Skelly Drive
Tulsa, Okla. 78128

So, having brought your fish alongside, you'll be wanting a gaff. People don't talk about gaffs much and, except for dishing some out regularly, we're never told there's a choice. At Auto-Gaff we found all kinds of gaffs—short, long, with different kinds of hooks, handles—even a harpoon.

Auto-Gaff, Inc.
4 Reynolds St.
East Providence, R.I. 02914

Left, above: The Lowrance Fishing Calculator.
Below: Auto-Gaff's Flying Gaff.

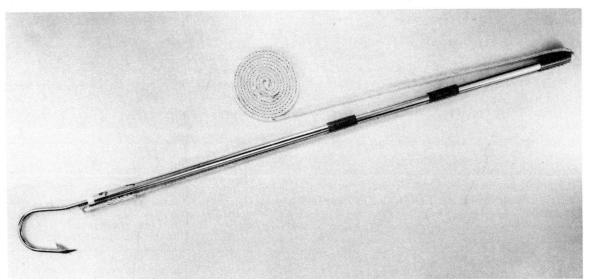

Rigging, Setting, and Fishing Trot Lines

by Warren Norville

You can fish with trot lines the year around, but why waste your time in the winter when good hunting can keep you busy and the larder full? The time to get ready (not the time to go) is when the first heavy roll of thunder in the spring shakes the earth and loosens the ground so the seeds can sprout. That's the time to break out your hooks and lines, and rig your trot lines.

The trot line itself should be made of a twine heavy enough not to cut your hands too badly and to hold at least a two-hundred-pound fish. It can be as long or as short as you like, but most sets begin with 20 hooks, with the sky the limit. Put the stages (the short line the hooks are on) two meters apart (gotta give figures in the new system). You don't need to rule this distance, but just take lengths on line that reach between your outstretched arms and this will be near enough. Do you fathom what I mean? At every fathom tie two overhand knots a couple of inches apart. The knots keep the short lines of the stages from slipping along the trot line.

(Continued on next page)

Clark Harris with two trotline anchors. They do look like truck rims, don't they?

Tying on the stages. Georgie March pulls the boat along the line while Clark Harris ties them on.

(Continued from previous page)

The stages should be of lighter line and about two feet long. Put an overhand loop in the end to rig your hook and swivel. You need a swivel. Hooks should never be larger than a five ought and often they should be much smaller. Do *not* knot the other end of the stage, but since you'll likely be using nylon, sear the other end to keep it from unraveling. The best way to do this is in the cabin of your houseboat by candlelight. Burn the ends, both of them, *with* the candle. Don't burn the candle at both ends.

Roll up the trot line with the knots in it, but *without* the stages attached. Lay the stages, hooks on, in a neat, but separate bundle, hooks all on the same end. You are ready to go.

When the pecan leaves get as big as squirrel ears, it's time to head for the river (planting be damned). Go up or down the river 'til you find a slough. Tie one end of the trot line to a sturdy root on the bank and lead the other end out into the river at an angle to cross the approach to the mouth of the slough. Fish bite best when the river is rising or falling; this is when they are coming in and out of the woods by way of the sloughs. Anchor the river end of the trot line with the special Alabama Patented Trot Line Anchors—they look exactly like truck rims and can be found in any auto wrecking yard.

When the line is set, go back to the bank and get the end of the line. Pull yourself in your boat along the line. Now is the time to tie on the stages. This way you don't end up with a tangle of hooks and stages. You can bait the hooks as you go or make two trips. If the river's running, you best make two trips. When it's time to take the line in, don't try to wind it up with the stages on, but cut them off at the knots with a sharp knife. You don't lose much and, again, no tangles. For bait use cut bait, cheese (a special kind for bait), chicken livers, or what have you. On the Alabama River they use very small pieces of bait. Seems to aggravate them catfish and they bites better.

With the line set, go back to the houseboat and drink . . . coffee? . . . until time to check the lines again in about two or three hours. Don't wear yourself out, though. You may need your energy to clean fish.

Snice

Those of us lucky enough to live where it's uninhabitable can go on pretending as well as they can anywhere. You still need gear for ice fishing, of course, and here are a few pieces.

You can buy hole drillers and skimmers from:

**Feldmann Engineering
633 Monroe Street
Sheboygan Falls, Wisconsin 53085**

If you would rather be popped-up rather than tipped-up, here is the Worth Pop-Up for $8.95, from:

**Worth Fishing Tackle
Box 88
Stevens Point, Wisconsin 54481**

Arnold is a very well-known supplier of ice fishing gear—drills, skimmers, creepers, tip-ups, spuds—the works:

**Arnold Tackle Corporation
100 Commercial Ave.
Paw Paw, Michigan 49079**

Tiger Claw Ice Creeper
No. TC-90. "Don't be a slipper—use a gripper." Be safe with Arnold's heavy 12 ga. steel ice creepers. Cleat 2⅛" x 2½" zinc plated. Web strap ⅝" x 20" with nickel plated buckle and tip. One pair per package, 12 per carton. Weight 5 lbs.

*Above: Ice creepers from Arnold Tackle.
Below: The Worth Pop-Up.*

Ice skimmers from Feldmann Engineering.

The best part of jug fishing is getting the jugs ready. Warren Norville and his son-in-law, Hardy Demeranville, proceed like true experts.

Jug Fishing

by Warren Norville

The best time for jug fishing is the middle of March on the river I grew up on. This is tidewater, and you can tell when the fish are coming in by seeing the first ripples of the minnows on the slick surface in the calm of the evening. The fish we seek are gafftopsail catfish. These saltwater beauties are the only catfish rated as gamefish, but we go after them for the skillet 'cause they are even better rated as food fish. As the Cajuns say, "Dem fish is some good! I'm gonna told you!"

You have to get ready long before March, however. I find being prepared is a year-round job that must be given special attention as early as September. You have to start early to get enough jugs together. I have my best luck with empty fifth bottles that held some kind of spirituous liquors. They have just the right amount of buoyancy to let the fish pull them under without yanking the hook from his mouth, and yet pull him back up when he gets tired.

I use about eight feet of seventy-pound-test nylon twine and a four- or five-ought hook. No sinker unless the current is swift. For bait I use cut mullet, as big as I can get on the hook. The fish seem to bite best when a warm rain is falling and the March winds are blowing.

It's best to set your jugs out on weekdays. You don't catch as many waterskiers (the beggars ski in wetsuits in March). It's against the law to fillet them, if you catch one, and they don't fry up near as well as catfish.

Set your jugs out at night, too, just like you do a trot line. Check them the next morning. In the daytime, check them every couple of hours or so, again like you do your trot lines. Trot lines and jug fishing go together like grits and gravy.

Don't put your name on the jugs. You are going to lose some anyhow, and this way nobody is going to come knocking on your door in the wee hours or the middle of the day complaining about a line in their screw or a hook in their stern. Just remember what you've been drinking.

Hauler

Since the development of the hydraulic hauler, few serious professional fishermen would consider a mechanical one unless capital was short or their "mixed" fishing required only occasional hauling. For the part-time or amateur fishermen with a few tubs or traps, though, a mechanical hauler is a great aid. Various places offer hauler packages but, in fact, they are not that difficult to make up one's self, using a lawnmower or motorbike engine. But for those going all the way, we found this set-up at a big fishing-gear supplier:

Atlantic and Gulf Fishing Supply Corp.
591 S.W. 8th Street
Miami, Fla. 33130

Good Magazine

Saltwater fishermen from anywhere will enjoy *Saltwater Conversation,* a bimonthly publication devoted to recreational fishing in South Carolina. Though the emphasis is on South Carolina activities, record catches from many places for dozens of species are recorded and discussed. A pleasant and friendly magazine, it could stand to be copied in other regions.

Saltwater Conversation
c/o Charles J. Moore, Section Leader
Box 12559
Charleston, S.C. 29412
subscriptions are free

About Cooking Fish

The Maine Sea Grant Program has put out a terrific little book about cooking species of sea-life most Americans are not in the habit of considering with anything but the shudders. We really are a bunch of spoiled brats! Here's octopus, squid, mussel, periwinkle, whelk, sea urchin, eel, various seaweeds, and raw fish preparations.

The Uncommon Cookbook
edited and illustrated by Phyllis Coggins
Maine Sea Grant Publications
Ira C. Darling Center
Walpole, Maine 04573

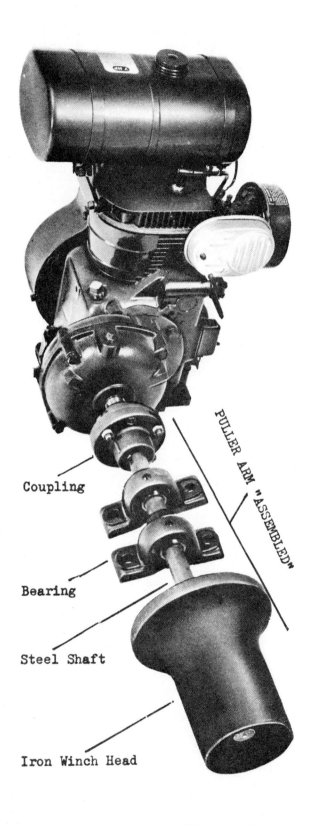

Coupling

PULLER ARM "ASSEMBLED"

Bearing

Steel Shaft

Iron Winch Head

The Power Puller from Atlantic and Gulf Fishing Supply

About Fishermen

Those Who Live From the Sea
edited by Estellie Smith
West Publishing Co., St. Paul, Minn.
$17.95, 1977

This is readable anthropology about the lives of fishermen and their communities all over the world. Any general reader will find it interesting and broadening, but fishermen will find in it a vast brotherhood.

Lack of government assistance is in part due to fishermen themselves. The government once made low-interest loans available to fishermen to buy motors, but the program ended in an economic disaster. The fishermen apparently felt little compulsion or responsibility to repay the loans, and the only provision for enforcement in the program was repossession of the equipment. This was difficult because first they had to locate the defaulter, and fishing people were disinclined to cooperate with the government in tracking down the culprit. If they did repossess the equipment, it often meant that the fisherman had had free use of a motor for an extended period, and all the government had to show for the investment was a burned-out motor. The fisherman's credit problem is further exacerbated by the impossibility of obtaining insurance on a canoe or other equipment, and banks are reluctant to give unsecured loans to a member of a group not reputed to be financially responsible.

Few fishermen have the capital required to obtain one of the three major pieces of equipment required (canoe, net, motor), and the high cost makes it difficult to obtain adequate funding from kinsmen. They frequently have to turn to a money lender, and to a fisherman this is usually synonymous with a market woman. To clarify why the fishmonger has capital to invest while the fisherman may have to borrow the money for petrol to go to sea, it is necessary to look at the economic role of women in the economy. Trading has long been the province of women (cf., Christensen 1961), and as Field has commented on the economic status of Akan women:

> They are—unless quite devoid of "drive"—economically independent. Few wives cannot say to defaulting husbands, 'If you want me to leave you, dismiss me at once: I knew how to buy my own headkerchiefs before I met you.' . . . By and large, men are improvident and open-handed, women both more reliable and close-fisted, for women have a very early training in the scrupulous handling of small sums. little girls of four may be seen in the market selling such wares as kenkey-dumplings, for each one of which they have to account to their mothers (Field 1960:30).

Above: From Those Who Live From the Sea.

Reading Maritime Anthropology

by Jim Acheson

Talk of ships and maritime affairs usually revolves around the large, mechanized vessels typical of present industrialized societies, or else the colorful steamers, sailboats, and fishing craft of our own maritime past. Yet there are literally dozens of cultures around the world whose people live by the sea, and many millions who eat the fish caught by people of such societies, or live off the trade goods that pass through their hands. The variation in such societies is enormous. They range all the way from small Alaskan Eskimo settlements, where the mainstay of life is salmon and whales caught from nothing bigger than a skin-covered boat powered by an outboard motor, to the large factory-ship operations of the Russians, Poles, etc., whose crews are at sea for months on end and whose families live in Leningrad and Gdansk. In between are the thousands of maritime communities of the Middle East, Africa, India, and East Asia whose trading and fishing fleets are only now in the process of switching from sail to engines.

Despite the obvious importance of maritime societies and products, anthropologists have largely ignored them in favor of studies of small hunting bands, agricultural peasant societies, and, recently, cities. While the study of maritime societies is still not one of the flashing, all-consuming interests of anthropologists, some very good studies of maritime communities have been published recently. Some focus on the organization, ideas, beliefs, and behavior of people manning boats, to the virtual exclusion of the communities they come from. Others center their interest on life in fishing communities themselves, and largely ignore technology, social organization, and other facets of life at sea.

My favorites are the following:

North Atlantic Fishermen: Anthropological Essays on Modern Fishing, edited by Raoul Andersen and Cato Wadel. Newfoundland Social and Economic Papers No. 5. Institute of Social and Economic Research, Memorial University of Newfoundland, St. John, Newfoundland, 1971.

A good book of essays about selected socio-cultural aspects of fishing in fisheries ranging from Newfoundland to Sweden. There is more in this book pertaining to current problems in modern, industrialized fishing communities ringing the north Atlantic than in any other single volume.

Cat Harbor: A Newfoundland Fishing Settlement, by James Faris. Newfoundland Social and Economic Studies No. 3. Institute of Social and Economic Research,

(Continued on next page)

(Continued from previous page)
Memorial University of Newfoundland, St. John, Newfoundland, 1972.

People familiar with the coastal regions of New England will find much that is familiar in the anthropological account of this small Newfoundland outport, and enough that is different to remind them that English-speaking Newfoundland has a very different culture.

Malay Fishermen: Their Peasant Economy, by Raymond Firth. London: Routledge and Kegan Paul, 1946.

A classic anthropological account of the fishing economies of two villages by one of the best known, living social anthropologists.

The Raft Fishermen: Tradition and Change in Brazilian Peasant Economy, by Shepard Forman. Bloomington: Indiana University Press, 1970.

A short, readable, and technically excellent monograph about the fishermen of the northeastern part of Brazil who fish far from shore on light, wooden rafts with the sea washing over their feet.

East is a Big Bird: Navigation and Logic on Puluwat Atoll, by Thomas Gladwin. Harvard University Press, Cambridge, Mass., 1970.

An excellent and well-written account by an anthropologist who made himself an apprentice to a local navigator on a Micronesian atoll near Truk. The result is a rich description of navigating principles, canoe design, and the mental processes that underlie such activities.

Between Land and Water: The Subsistence Ecology of the Miskito Indians, Eastern Nicaragua, by Bernard Nietschmann. New York: Seminar Press, 1973.

Technical but easily read analysis of changes taking place in this Central American group who are shifting from a subsistence economy to one based on commercial exploitation of sea-turtles. Emphasizes an ecological approach, while providing a good overall view of the people and the area.

Takashima: A Japanese Fishing Community, by Edward Norbeck. Salt Lake City: University of Utah Press, 1954.

Norbeck, a professional anthropologist, completed this study of Takashima, a small island whose inhabitants lived by fishing and farming, in the late 1940s. The book contains little on the technology and life aboard fishing vessels, but rather focuses on the total culture—the economy of the island, social organization, family life, religion, etc. Still one of the best monographs on rural Japan.

The Marsh Arabs, by Wilfred Thesiger. New York, E.P. Dutton & Co., 1964.

This book contains a well-written but non-technical account of a group of Arabs who have lived for centuries in the vast swamps of Southern Iraq. Thesiger, a well-known traveler and explorer of the Middle East, lived for seven years with these people whose maritime orientation causes them to be looked down on by other Arab tribes in the area.

The Fishermen: The Sociology of an Extreme Occupation, by Jeremy Tunstall. MacGibbon and Kee, London, 1962.

A good analysis of the behavior, beliefs, and social structure of the men of the British offshore trawler fleet, both on the ships and ashore.

Point Hope: An Eskimo Village in Transition, by James W. Van Stone. Seattle: University of Washington Press, 1962.

A clear and straightforward account of a modern Alaskan Eskimo group where sea mammal hunting is still the major orientation of the village.

The Quest of the Schooner Argus, by Alan Villiers. New York: Chas. Scribner and Sons, 1951.

Villiers, a professional seaman and writer, describes life on boats of the Portuguese White Fleet fishing off the coast of Newfoundland and Greenland in 1950. Villiers gives us a fascinating description of the ships, fishing technology, and day to day life aboard such vessels. Less adequate on the structure of Portuguese society, and the biology of the Grand Banks. The same kinds of vessels and technology were used by New England fishermen in the latter part of the 19th century. Gives a good idea what life aboard such vessels must have been like.

Planting adult quahogs with the tide up. They need only be dropped onto the grant. They will bury themselves where they land.

Practical Shellfish Farming, by Phil Schwind
International Marine Publishing Company
Camden, Maine
102 pages, illus., 1977, $8.95

Cap'n Phil reveals how to farm for shellfish and make a realistic go of it.

Common Seaweeds of the Pacific Coast
by Robert Waaland
Pacific Search Press, Seattle
1977, $5.95

Exactly. Just the sort required, with all the relevant species you are likely to encounter, including a good mix of the scientific and anecdotal information needed for identification and whatever else is known about the plant. Coverage is by family and zone. Only gripe is the width of the book for field purposes—you'll want a pocket almost six inches wide.

The Sea Vegetable Book
(Foraging and Cooking Seaweed)
by Judith Cooper Madlener
Clarkson N. Potter, N.Y.
1977, paperbound, $6.95

Everyone knows that you can eat seaweeds, at least many types of them, and our demure palates will leap at the chance to have seaweed soup or pudding at least once so that we can say we've had it. Yes, sir. You have to get up pretty early in the morning to stay ahead of us!

This book is so thorough on the subject that it is extremely unlikely that another publisher would underwrite a rival. Fifty-two seaweeds are given complete field coverage and then 145 (!) recipes for their preparation and serving are provided. The full-page line drawings are so sensitively done that I doubt photography could touch them for identification purposes. What a good book!

Above: From Practical Shellfish Farming.
Below: From Common Seaweeds of the Pacific Coast.

For many years it has been a favorite pastime of seaweed fanciers to prepare pressed and dried seaweed specimens. Such collections serve several purposes: they provide a permanent record of a collection or observation; they are a useful reference for later comparison or identification; and they are often quite beautiful and aesthetically pleasing. Such dried specimens are prepared by spreading a wet seaweed specimen of appropriate size on a damp piece of sturdy high quality "botany" or "biology" drawing paper or high rag content "herbarium" paper. The seaweed is then covered by waxed paper, cheesecloth, or muslin. This combination is then sandwiched between large blotters or newspapers which absorb moisture. Finally, a piece of corrugated cardboard is placed external to each blotter to provide ventilation and hasten drying. A number of these sandwiches are then piled up, and the bundle secured by means of a board and heavy weight or a standard plant press frame and straps to keep the specimens flat. The cloth overlay, blotters, and corrugates must be changed daily until the specimens are dry. If drying is hastened by excess heat, the specimens may become too crisp and brittle. Most seaweeds will adhere to the paper by means of their own gums or mucilages. To be scientifically valuable, there should be only one species per sheet (unless you have collected an epiphyte or parasite), and the sheet should be labelled with the name of the seaweed, the date and place of collection, the name of the collector and any pertinent field notes. A serious collector should also maintain a notebook and number each specimen so that it can be cross-referenced in the notebook. The notebook entry should contain the same sort of information as the label on the specimen sheet. If a number of specimens are collected at one site, the notebook is the best place to record extensive additional information about the particular habitat or site. If you feel a compulsion to collect seaweeds, be prudent and collect only what you will use. Be sure to comply with all applicable regulations.

Commercial Fishing Boat Books

We received a note from a model-maker recently asking for sources of plans for modern commercial fishing boats. It was then we discovered that 5 volumes of the *Mariner's Catalog* had passed without more than a passing mention of the three *Fishing Boats of the World* books. We're embarrassed, to say the least. These books, while expensive, are well-nigh indispensable for those who take fishing-vessel design seriously. Each volume is a compendium of the papers presented at one of the Fishing Boat Congresses sponsored by the Food and Agriculture Organization of the UN. Besides some pretty heavy text, there are hundreds of boat plans and details, and hundreds of photographs. *Fishing Boats of the World* (£13) reports the 1953 Congress; *Fishing Boats of the World:2* (£15) reports the 1959 Congress; and *Fishing Boats of the World:3* (£9.50) reports the 1965 Congress. All three are published by:

Fishing News (Books) Ltd.
1 Long Garden Walk
Farnham, Surrey, England

And while we're on the subject, Fishing News (Books) publishes the widest variety of serious commercial fishing books in the world. The prices of their books are uniformly high, but so is their content. Besides books on gear and methods, Fishing News (Books) has a number of publications on fish farming.

A Master's Guide to Building a Bamboo Fly Rod
by Everett Garrison with Hoagy B. Carmichael
Dist. by Stackpole Books
Harrisburg, Penn. 17105
296 pages, illus., index, 1977, $20

The late Everett Garrison was a legendary rodmaker, a man who designed and built fly rods like N. G. Herreshoff designed and built boats. His book, which for a how-to book is as beautiful as his rods, tells all about his theories and methods. We are not aficionados—the fishing rod that catches fish is our schtick—and never could understand the Garrison cult, but this book set us straight. This guy built fishing rods.

George W. Barnes, however, also builds fishing rods, but somehow it's not the same. He's an amateur like us, and his work bears no comparison to Garrison's; it's only creditable, as is his book. Barnes must have been born under an unlucky star, or perhaps last year he thoughtlessly crushed a snail as he walked under a ladder. Think about it—there hasn't been a book published for years on bamboo fly rod making, and the year Barnes published his book out comes the Bible, by one of the greatest rod builders of all time. Whatareyagonnado?

How to Make Bamboo Fly Rods
by George W. Barnes
Winchester Press, New York
110 pages, illus., index, 1977, $10.95

From A Master's Guide to Building a Bamboo Fly Rod.

SEAMAN

LIGHTHOUSES

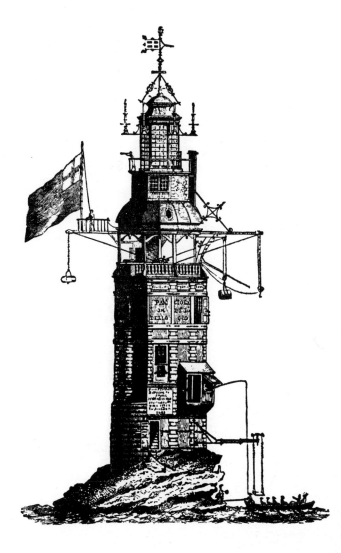

The totem of the mariner is the lighthouse. At once the symbol of hope and of fear—if you can see and identify one, you know where you are; if you're too close to one, you could be in trouble—lighthouses fascinate us all. They are benchmarks of progress: they signal harbor entrances, they point the direction of channels, they mark obstacles to navigation, they tell of departures and landfalls. Everywhere you turn there are lighthouses: along rivers, in cities, on islands, at the ends of country roads. They come in all shapes, sizes, and colors. Some are tourist attractions; others are virtually unknown. They are living objects: flashing, booming, ringing, honking, and shrieking.

We can't get away from lighthouses; even if we can't always see the real thing, endless images of them pass before us. Think of it. They appear in television ads, they are the symbols of many companies, they appear on books, maps, restaurant placemats, bank checks, and roadside signs. Businesses and organizations are named after them (the title Lighthouse for the Blind says a lot about both the function of the organization and our feelings for lighthouses).

As if you didn't already know, lighthouses figure prominently in literature. We haven't the time or the inclination to discuss all the references to them in *literature* literature, but over the past winter we read a few books about lighthouses themselves and the people who run them. Here are some we found enjoyable:

Lighthouse, by Tony Parker
Taplinger, New York
288 pages, 1975, $8.95

It took mankind a while to figure out what to do with the portable tape recorder once it had been invented—aside from recording favorite hit tunes and playing them back in odd places—but once academics and journalists discovered you could use the machine as a substitute for writing, the rush was on. Electronic oral history is Big Stuff these days, and some terrible pieces have seen print as a result. Tony Parker's *Lighthouse,* produced in the oral history tradition, is not one of them.

(Continued on next page)

(Continued from previous page)

Parker's thesis, unstated but implied, is that the lighthouse as an object is not what is interesting; rather it's the people who build, operate, and maintain them. Why do people voluntarily choose to become lightkeepers? How come they are satisfied with isolation and how do they deal with it? Who minds the store while the keepers are off on a rock tending flashing lights for months at a time? Is this a satisfying life or merely an institutionalized form of escapism? You'll find answers in Parker's book, based on his interviews with the lightkeepers and supporting staff of Trinity House, the administrator of the British lighthouse establishment.

The Lighthouse, by Dudley Witney
New York Graphic Society, New York
256 pages, illus., biblio., 1975, $29.95

A coffee-table book this is, surely, but for the lighthouse aficionado it's the finestkind. Excellent color photography, a little history, lots of romance, the strange absence of people. And our favorite light, Head Harbor in New Brunswick, is on the cover. Witney's subjects range the North American Atlantic coast from Newfoundland to Florida and encompass primarily the major ones. (We've seen this book lately on the bookstore bargain tables at a reduced price; check around before you buy.)

Charleston Light, from The Lighthouse.

THE MARINER'S CATALOG / 179

West Coast Lighthouses
A Pictorial History of the Guiding Lights of the Sea
by Jim Gibbs
Superior Publishing Company, Seattle, Wash.
206 pages, illus., index, 1974, $13.95

This is the west coast's answer to Dudley Witney's *The Lighthouse,* though with a much-less-than-slick presentation. The photographs, in black and white, are both historical and contemporary and the text is both straightforward and anecdotal. An excellent book for browsing.

The Lighthouses of the Chesapeake
by Robert de Gast
Johns Hopkins University Press
Baltimore, Maryland
174 pages, illus., bibliography, 1973, $12.50

The centerpiece of this book is the black and white photographs of lighthouses still standing in the Chesapeake. There's an introduction with a short history of lighthouses, and a follow-up section on the Chesapeake lights no longer standing, but it's the photographs that count. De Gast has produced some haunting images (he's from the closeups-of-the-peeling-paint school) notable for their absence of people, which is hardly his fault—all the Chesapeake lights are now automated. One thing that makes this book different from others in the genre is that there are a number of photographs taken from the inside looking out. You see what the keeper saw during all those years on watch alone.

Right: From The Lighthouses of the Chesapeake.
Below: From West Coast Lighthouses.

Recent view of **YAQUINA HEAD LIGHT STATION** showing the radiobeacon. Now automated, the majestic 93 foot masonry tower, one of Uncle Sam's finest lighthouses, was found to be in near perfect condition when inspected in recent years by a Coast Guard repair crew despite the fact the structure was commissioned in 1873. The tower has a marble rotunda.

Left: From Lighthouses of England and Wales.
Bottom: From Lighthouses: Their Architecture,
History and Archaeology.

*Needles: this tower was built to replace a clifftop light that was frequently
obscured by fog*

Lighthouses: Their Architecture, History and Archaeology
by Douglas B. Hague and Rosemary Christie
Gomer Press, Llandysul, Dyfed, Wales
307 pages, illus., bibliography, index, 1975, £4

A detailed, scholarly, yet readable treatment of British
lighthouses. We found two things of interest in this book—
the information on lighthouse construction, and the
bibliography, which includes references to primary source
material. These two points remind us of another book,
reviewed in the 3rd *Mariner's Catalog* (page 112), that
could be termed comparable in quality but covering lights
on the other side of the Atlantic:

America's Lighthouses: Their Illustrated History Since 1716
by Francis Ross Holland, Jr.
Stephen Greene Press, Brattleboro, Vermont
230 pages, illus., biblio., index, 1972, $15

SWAPE or LEVER-LIGHT

Lighthouses of England and Wales
by Derrick Jackson
David & Charles, North Pomfret, Vt.
176 pages, illus., biblio., 1975, $9.95

This book caught our attention because of its nice
sketches of lighthouses. It covers more than 90 lights, with
thumbnail descriptions of their history, location, and
access. The perfect guidebook for the tourist with a fixa-
tion on lighthouses.

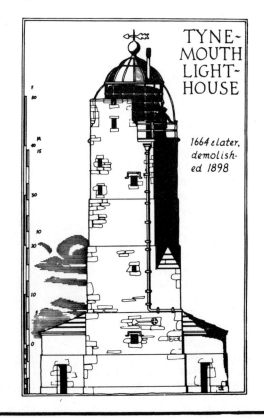

TYNE-
MOUTH
LIGHT-
HOUSE

1664 & later, demolished 1898

A History of Lighthouses
by Patrick Beaver
Citadel Press, Secaucus, N.J.
158 pages, illus., biblio., index, paperbound
1971, $4.95

A very readable book that emphasizes the development of lighthouse-building technology. The scope is worldwide, though the bulk of the text deals with Europe and America.

The Lighthouse Keeper

The government, being a multiheaded beast, does a lot of things that can only be termed paradoxical. On the one hand, the Coast Guard, in an effort to cut down manpower costs, is automating most of the light stations and lightships in the country. On the other hand, the Department of Health, Education, and Welfare, in conjunction with many state agencies, is paying money and other benefits to people who are unemployed. Can't these two endeavors be somehow coordinated?

After reading *Lighthouse* by Tony Parker (see review) and talking to many people, it becomes clear that there are those who would prefer living at an isolated light post than doing what they are doing. Perhaps Joe down at the Sunoco station feels that way. He could take a Coast Guard job at a lighthouse, and somebody on unemployment could take his old job. The Coast Guard could save the expense of automating a light, Joe could be doing what he wants to do, and HEW could have one individual off unemployment. And an added benefit is that a *person* will be on watch at a light station. Remember, automated lighthouses can neither see nor speak. If a lobsterman goes aground in sight of an unmanned lighthouse, he is most likely left to his own devices. If that lighthouse were manned, the keeper could quickly call in assistance.

Obviously, this is a simpleminded proposal. We would be happy to hear from a government official who can tell us why.

Books about lighthouses have one thing in common: they honor the quotation. Here are a few we found:

Nothing moves the imagination like a lighthouse.
—Samuel Drake
Never, in the history of architecture, has a secular building been thus worshipped and taken on a spiritual life of its own.
—E.M. Forster on the Pharos of Alexandria
Anythin' for a quiet life, as the man said when he took the sitivation at the lighthouse.
—Sam Weller
... lighthouses are marks and signs ... being a matter of an high and precious nature, in respect of salvation of ships and lives, and a kind of starlight in that element.
—Francis Bacon
"Sail on!" it says, "sail on, ye stately ships! and with your floating bridge the ocean span;
Be mine to guard this life from all eclipse,
Be yours to bring man nearer unto man!"
—Henry Wadsworth Longfellow
Dear Sir,
Thank you for your letter. I regret it is not permitted for visits to be made to off-shore lighthouses owing to difficulties of access.
Yours Faithfully,
The Corporation of Trinity House
—letter received by Tony Parker, author of *Lighthouse*

INDEX